Colección Támesis

SERIE A: MONOGRAFÍAS, 185

THE TRICKSTER-FUNCTION IN THE THEATRE OF GARCÍA LORCA

Drawing on anthropology, psychoanalysis, and literary theory, this book uses the image of the trickster to argue for a fresh and original reading of García Lorca's plays, highlighting androgyny, male fantasy, masochism, masquerade and the carnivalesque. The study includes detailed textual analyses of *Amor de Don Perlimplín con Belisa en su jardín*, *Así que pasen cinco años* and *El público*, as well as extensive examination of *La zapatera prodigiosa* and *Bodas de sangre*; in addition it makes reference to the lesser known *El sueño de la vida*, *Retablillo de Don Cristóbal*, *Dragón* and *El loco y la loca*, together with a relevant selection of García Lorca's drawings and prose.

Dr SARAH WRIGHT is Lecturer in Hispanic Studies at the University of Hull.

SARAH WRIGHT

THE TRICKSTER-FUNCTION IN
THE THEATRE OF GARCÍA LORCA

TAMESIS

First published 2000 by Tamesis, London

ISBN 1 85566 074 1

Tamesis is an imprint of Boydell & Brewer Ltd
PO Box 9, Woodbridge, Suffolk IP12 3DF, UK
and of Boydell & Brewer Inc.
PO Box 41026, Rochester, NY 14604–4126, USA
website: http://www.boydell.co.uk

A catalogue record for this book is available
from the British Library

Library of Congress Cataloging-in-Publication Data
Wright, Sarah, 1969–
    The trickster-function in the theatre of García Lorca / Sarah Wright.
        p. cm. – (Colección Támesis. Serie A, Monografías ; 185)
    Includes bibliographical references and index.
    ISBN 1–85566–074–1 (hardback : alk. paper)
    1. García Lorca, Federico, 1898–1936 – Dramatic works.
    2. Tricksters in literature.   I. Title.
PQ6613.A763 Z95 2001
862'.62 – dc21   00–030225

This publication is printed on acid-free paper

Printed in Great Britain by
Antony Rowe Ltd, Chippenham, Wiltshire

CONTENTS

For Stella and Isabel

ACKNOWLEDGEMENTS

I am especially grateful to Dr Alison Sinclair, of Clare College, Cambridge, who supervised the doctoral dissertation out of which this book grew, and who taught me to be bold and to have strength of purpose. Professor Paul Julian Smith and Dr Patricia McDermott have provided valuable insights and clarity – I thank them for their continued interest in my work. I am also particularly grateful to Juliet Mitchell, for whom I worked as research assistant in 1997, who offered inspiration and friendship.

The following offered perceptive academic advice, practical help, or encouragement: Andrew Anderson, Gillian Beer, Richard Cardwell, Catherine Davies, Christian de Paepe, Maria Delgado, Luis Fernández Cifuentes, David George, Jack Goody, Derek Harris, Estelle Irizarry, Temma Kaplan, Andrew Kennedy, John London, Antonio Monegal, C. Brian Morris, Helen Oppenheimer, Jacqueline Rattray, Naomi Segal, Eric Southworth, Henry Sullivan, Margaret Walters and Howard Young.

The Scottish Office Education Department, Clare Hall, Cambridge, who awarded me a Pippard Bursary, the British Federation of Women Graduates, the J. B. Trend Fund and the Gibson Fund at the University of Cambridge and FARE at the University of Hull made my research possible at different stages with various scholarships and grants. I am grateful to Carmen Ramiro, Pablo Vila and Ana Isabel Martínez for their generous hospitality during a trip to Madrid.

I thank the many friends I made in Cambridge; the staff, students, fellows and Paula Herbert at Clare Hall, Cambridge; the staff, students and Coral Neale of the Department of Spanish and Portuguese at the University of Cambridge; Cambridge University Library; the Modern and Medieval Languages Library at the University of Cambridge; the BFI; the Brynmor Jones Library at the University of Hull and the British Library; the Biblioteca Nacional, Madrid; the Centro de Documentación Teatral, Madrid, the Teatro Bellas Artes, Madrid, the Real Academia de la Lengua Española, Madrid, for performing a search on the word 'trickster'; and Isabel García Lorca, Manuel Fernández Montesinos, Araceli Gassó Gregori, Sonia González García and Rosa Yllán de Haro at the Fundación Federico García Lorca, Madrid, for their kind assistance.

I am grateful to William Kosmas and the Fundación Federico García

Lorca for permission to reproduce the drawing "Payaso con guitarra" on the cover of this book.

My colleagues in the Department of Hispanic Studies at the University of Hull have provided enormous support during the final stages of the writing of the book.

Ruth Van Velsen, Carmen Gutierrez Olondriz, Rosario Olondriz Navarro, Valerie Lobban and Tulah Tuke also deserve special thanks.

I would also like to thank Stephen Hart and the late Professor John Varey of Tamesis, and Caroline Palmer, Helen Barber and the editorial team at Boydell & Brewer.

Lastly, I thank Alejandro Escobar for his patience and support throughout.

ABBREVIATIONS

ALEC	*Anales de la literatura española*
BHS	*Bulletin of Hispanic Studies*
CW	*The Collected Works of Carl Gustav Jung*, trans. R. F. C. Hull, London: Routledge and Kegan Paul (1959), 1980.
MLN	*Modern Language Notes*
OC	*Federico García Lorca, Obras completas*, Arturo del Hoyo, ed. prólogo, de Vicente Aleixandre, Madrid: Aguilar, 1986.
RQ	*Romance Quarterly*
SE	*The Standard Edition to the Complete Psychological Works of Sigmund Freud*, trans. J. Strachey, vols I–XXIII, London: The Hogarth Press and the Institute of Psychoanalysis, 1974.

INTRODUCTION

THE TRICKSTER-FUNCTION IN THE THEATRE OF GARCÍA LORCA

Recent years have witnessed an explosion of interest in the life and works of Spanish poet and playwright Federico García Lorca (1898–1936). The 1998 centenary commemorations in particular, both within Spain and internationally, gave rise to a rich seam of intersections and connections regarding García Lorca's work. Lorca featured in numerous stagings and devised productions, related to both high and low culture, from ballet, to opera, dance and song to theatre and film. International conferences discussed Lorca in relation to tradition and modernity, presented the American Lorca and Lorca the Andalusian,[1] and produced a plethora of (often contradictory) readings of biography and texts. Over one hundred years after his birth, García Lorca remains a 'site of struggle' (Smith 1998b: 139), a locus of contested meanings and significations.

It is in part due to the mystery surrounding the circumstances of the death of García Lorca that he has become such a 'seductive' icon.[2] Gibson's fascinating and important biographical work in the mid-1970s substituted detail for enigma, a voice where there had been only silence.[3] Excellent historical and textual research by Anderson and Maurer has since gone a long way to complete the picture we have of the trajectory and detail of Lorca's life and work. Their jointly edited *Epistolario completo* emerged in 1997. But gaps,

---

[1] *Lorca-América: Contactos y Repercusión* took place in Seville in October 1998; organised by Andrew Anderson it featured connections between Lorca and Cuba, New York, Argentina among other papers (my thanks to Howard Young for supplying me with documentary information). *Lorca: Un clásico moderno*, took place in Granada in May 1998 (both of these conferences received extensive newspaper coverage in the Spanish press). See Paul Julian Smith, 'A Long Way from Andalusia', *Times Literary Supplement* (7 August 1998), for a comparison of the Granada commemoration with events in Newcastle, UK in May–June 1998.

[2] Smith (1998b), drawing on Fernández Cifuentes (1986), writes persuasively of García Lorca's capacity for seduction.

[3] Gibson's first work, *The Death of Lorca* (St Albans: Paladin) appeared in 1974. Marcos Zurinaga's 1996 film *Muerte en Granada* uses the thriller detective genre to re-create the labours of a critic (the film acknowledges a debt to Gibson) at work to discover the circumstances surrounding Lorca's death. With Esaí Morales in the role of researcher/detective and Andy García as the poet.

absences and omissions (the patchy trail of homosexual liaisons partially glimpsed,[4] the pursuit of texts which had been lost, censored or suppressed) create the desire to know more. An extended monograph study of *El público* (The Public) appeared before permission for its publication was finally given in the 1970s,[5] and the work was not to be performed until 1987. Recent years have seen the appearance in published form of a variety of works. Texts which were regarded as incomplete or marginal were published for the first time: the surrealist film script *Viaje a la luna* (Trip to the Moon);[6] the *Sonetos del amor oscuro* (Sonnets of Dark Love), homosexual in theme;[7] juvenilia (the prose, poetry and playlets of Lorca's youth [Maurer 1994; Soria Olmedo 1994; De Paepe 1994]).[8] The recuperation of works which were previously considered marginal or minor (for example, Llafranque's *Teatro inconcluso* in 1987), has in turn meant a shift in emphasis in the way Lorca's work is viewed: no longer merely the author of gypsy ballads and the rural trilogy, Lorca delivers startling surrealist undercurrents, or presents love between men as thematic alongside an interest in strong female characters. The recuperation of fragmentary, minor or incomplete works contributes to the picture we now have of García Lorca's *oeuvre*. The careful cataloguing of texts and critical works has also constituted a welcome addition to the growing field.[9] Space does not allow for commentary on the panoply of critical works that have been published in recent years. But C. Brian Morris's excellent *Son of Andalusia* deserves mention as the most comprehensive study of the Andalusian heritage in Lorca's work (Morris 1997), while Paul Julian Smith's (1998) *The Theatre of García Lorca: Text, Performance,*

---

4   A recent contribution by Gibson to the theme is an article, 'Federico García Lorca y el amor imposible' (Gibson 1999: 135–60).

5   Rafael Martínez Nadal's *El Público. amor, teatro y caballos en la obra de Federico García Lorca*, Madrid: Ediciones Hiperión, 1970, printed in English as *Lorca's "The Public": A Study of His Unfinished Play ("El Público") and of Love and Death in the Work of Federico García Lorca*, London: Calder and Boyars, 1974. A facsimile edition of the play finally appeared in 1976 (Oxford: Dolphin Book Co.). See Fernández Cifuentes, '*El Público* de García Lorca versus *El Público* de Martínez Nadal' (1986: 275–93).

6   Antonio Monegal (ed.) *Viaje a la luna*, Valencia: Pretextos, 1994. Frederic Amat composed the 72 sequences of Lorca's script into a 20-minute film version in 1998. Sponsored by Ovideo TV, Canal Sur and the Fundación Federico García Lorca.

7   Javier Ruiz Portella (ed.) *Federico García Lorca: Sonetos del amor oscuro: Poemas de amor y erotismo: Inéditos de madurez*, Barcelona: Altera, 1995, having only very shortly earlier been published in the revised edition of the *Obras completas*.

8   C. Maurer (ed.) *Federico García Lorca: prosa inédita de juventud*, Madrid: Cátedra, 1994; A. Soria Olmedo (ed.) *Federico García Lorca: teatro inédito de juventud*, Madrid: Cátedra, 1994; C. de Paepe, *Federico García Lorca: poesía inédita de juventud*, Madrid: Cátedra, 1994.

9   A CD Rom presents an excellent introduction to Lorca's life and work, collects musical pieces (including those Lorca wrote for piano) and includes fascinating glimpses of the poet on film. Published by Christopher Maurer, *Federico García Lorca 1898–1936*, Vanderbilt: Vanderbilt University Press with the Fundación Federico García Lorca, 1998.

Psychoanalysis, presents a thorough and often exhilarating reappraisal of García Lorca's life and work through an examination of what he terms the 'cult' surrounding García Lorca and of certain texts with the application of intelligent cultural studies. Lorca studies proliferate in all directions: alongside the historical and textual, the folkloric and testimonial, we now find gay studies, feminist readings and cultural studies.[10] There is an opening out and onto new fields, an exploration of new territories in connection with Lorca scholarship, to find interpretations which, although often contradictory, constitute enriching additions to the field, readings which mean that Lorca 'refuses to be confined to any one side of the paradigm – tradition and modernity, centre and periphery, gay and straight' (Smith 1998b: 143).

It is in the spirit of this opening out of Lorca scholarship, that in this book I attempt textual readings of a series of Lorca's plays. In the first place, continuing the important recent trend, I choose to examine those challenging and complex pieces which have in the past been dismissed as minor or uncompleted works. This is a focus which works constantly to change the way we view Lorca's work as a whole, recuperating those texts which are marginal to the Lorca canon. In the second place, I have chosen to combine close analysis of one motif with wider, more general questions of theatre, sexuality and subjectivity at the margins. In keeping with the notion of a refusal to be confined or pinned down to any one meaning, I choose the image of the trickster as central motif.

The trickster can be found wherever there is a literary or an oral folk tradition and characteristically is the protagonist in a plot involving switches in gender, shape-shifting or the mischievous intermingling of the sacred and the profane, performing miracles or violating taboos. The trickster mocks order and takes pleasure in the confusion of boundaries, standing at the cross roads of paradox and ambiguity. An unpredictable master of deception and artifice, the trickster is the simpleton who is fooled and yet at the same time engineers malicious pranks: trickster tales cause laughter in their transgression of

Christian de Paepe's *Catálogo general de los fondos documentales de la Fundación Federico García Lorca*, Madrid: Ministerio de Cultura, 1995, collects manuscript archive information. The Centre for the Study of the Hispanic Avant-Garde at the University of Aberdeen is compiling an annotated critical bibliographical database of Federico García Lorca compiled by Andrew A. Anderson, Derek Harris and Jacqueline Rattray.

10 An early gay-reading of Lorca's work was Paul Binding's *Lorca: The Gay Imagination*, London: GMP Publishers, 1985. Later readings are presented by Paul Julian Smith (1998b) and David Johnston's *Outlines: Federico García Lorca*, Bath: Absolute Press, 1998. Feminist studies include Julianne Burton's 'The Greatest Punishment: Female and Male in Lorca's Tragedies', in *Women in Hispanic Literature*, ed. B. Miller, Berkeley: University of California Press, pp. 259–79. Luís Fernández Cifuentes's excellent *García Lorca en el teatro: La norma y la diferencia*, Zaragoza: Prensas Universitarias de Zaragoza, 1986, deconstructs texts by and about Lorca by opening them out on their historical context: an early example of cultural studies. Smith's (1998b) work presents an example of cultural studies applied to Lorca.

sacred beliefs, yet at the same time they focus attention on the nature of those beliefs, highlighting the threshold between order and disorder, sacred and profane, centre and periphery.

Trickster tales were documented by anthropologists and historians of folk-lore at the end of the nineteenth and early twentieth centuries (Boas 1898; Lowie 1909). In early studies, the term was capitalised, and 'Trickster' was a nameable type.[11] The label subsequently became attached to other mythical characters, such as Hermes,[12] and became associated with the figures of the *Commedia dell'arte*: the Clown and the Fool, and with the 'carnivalesque' roguish characters of the literature of the picaresque. Jung (1954: 260) writes, that, 'this phantom of the trickster haunts the mythology of all ages [. . .] sometimes in strangely modulated guise'. Over time, the capitalised Trickster 'has become a lower cased label (trickster) for a category' (Basso 1987: 5), a classification which encompasses a series of related themes.

For Jung (1954), the trickster is an archetype.[13] Deriving his inspiration from the festive aspects of literature (also celebrated by Bakhtin [1965]), he finds the trickster in the Feasts of Fools and customs based on the ancient Saturnalia. The trickster presents evidence of some primitive aspect of the human psyche, reminding Western civilisation of the primitive, bestial and chaotic sides of himself that he would rather forget, erupting destructively, 'like a personal "gaffe" ', 'slip', 'faux pas' (Jung 1954: 262). The trickster is the embodiment of the collective shadow – those contents of experience which, coming up from below the threshold of consciousness and civilised acceptability are dark, chaotic and threatening. These dark aspects of culture are rather like Nietzsche's Dionysiac in the face of the Apolline.[14] The Apolline relates conceptually to masks, the glittering artifice which is cultural construction, while the Dionysiac represents what lies out of the grasp of culture. The Dionysiac can relate to the limits of the physical body, to death,

---

11 The Trickster was a type alongside, for instance, the Raven and Coyote figures.

12 Norman Brown's *Hermes the Thief*, published in 1947, made reference to the trickster.

13 Jung's essay, 'On the Psychology of the Trickster Figure', was published in 1954 as part of Radin's *The Trickster*, a volume which consisted of three essays on the trickster (from Radin, Jung and Kerènyi) and offered the first comprehensive portrait of the trickster type. For Jung, the trickster archetype was a progression of theories on types (1921a, 1921b, 1921c, 1934, 1943–48, 1954).

14 In *The Birth of Tragedy*, Nietzsche distinguishes between the Apolline, repre-senting, 'the beautiful illusion of the dream world's': artifice, fantasy, imitation and construct (and hence civilisation) and the Dionysiac – the ecstatic chaos which 'rises up from man's innermost core' (1871: 15, 17). See Sinclair (1990: 246–64), 'Avant-garde Theatre and the Return to Dionysos', for a discussion of the Dionysiac in relation to Nietzsche, Jung and Lorca. Nietzsche's text was translated into Spanish as *El origen de la tragedia*, published in Spain in 1900 or 1901. Sobejano (1967: 77) has conducted a study of Nietzsche's ideas in Spain. Soria Olmedo (1999: 205–23) studies Lorca's relationship to Nietzsche.

and also through the binding nature of these, to the collective experience. The trickster negotiates the relationship between artifice and what lies in obscurity beyond. The desire to grapple with those dark elements means that culture is in a state of constant renewal and this lends the trickster a rejuvenatory quality (and consequently can be a symbol of hope). The trickster represents, 'everything that a man can never get the better of and never finishes coping with' (Jung 1954: 271). Following on from Lévi-Strauss (1967: 223), for whom the trickster is a mediator between two worlds, I suggest that the trickster is a symbol of the point of intersection or paradox between cultural spheres. The trickster hovers at the borders and boundaries – and in this way becomes symbolic of the constructed nature of most social rules and ideologies. He/she 'reminds us that the cultural boundaries are arbitrary, and he releases the desire, at least vicariously, to challenge the boundaries' (Spinks 1991: 178). The trickster has become a sign for semioticians, or rather, a '*mise en abyme* or metasemiotic figure' (Bal 1988: 137).[15] He/she is a revealer of the play of signifiers, leading a textual dance through worlds and constructions: the trickster symbolises the constructed nature (the masks) of our cultural symbols and boundaries.[16]

From the starting point of his definition of the trickster as a symbol of duality, Lévi-Strauss (1966) goes on to posit that the function of the trickster is related to the relationship between life and death. The trickster's position on the boundaries is by design rather than accident: 'the boundaries themselves are symbols – social symbols of deep structural rules governing the processes by which continuity and order are maintained in the face of historical pressure'. Moreover, the 'life/death dichotomy' is the 'most evident result of that pressure' (Lévi-Strauss 1966: 234). After all, death represents the ultimate threshold, the other (unknowable) side of the limit of culture. Thus the function of the trickster, at base, is to negotiate the life/death dichotomy. Death is the final taboo, and it is infused with power and danger. Death is, 'always only represented', it is an absence for, 'there is no knowing death, no experiencing and then returning to write about it' (Goodwin and Bronfen 1993: 3). Furthermore, 'if any given cultural construct [. . .] may be construed as a response to the disordering face of death' (Goodwin and Bronfen 1993: 4), then the trickster is a means of straddling the divide between culture and death. The laughter accompanying the trickster's exploits is merely a release of tensions in the face of death: the trickster shows that

15 Pelton (1980), Spinks (1991), Hynes and Doty (1993), Bal (1988) and Doueihi (1993) all treat this aspect of the trickster.

16 I therefore question Bordo's (1990: 144–5) warning that 'readings that enact this protean fantasy are continually slip slidin' away through paradox, inversion, self-subversion, facile and intricate textual dance [. . .] They refuse to assume a shape for which they must take responsibility'. I contend that it is precisely 'textual dance' which constitutes the constructed world, which is the responsibility the trickster must bear.

cultural constructions are illusions created in order to diffuse, fix or delay the disordering chaos which death represents. The trickster, then, highlights the glittering artifice of the masks which disguise the absence which is death.

Above all, the trickster is the guardian of the liminal realm, on the threshold between two worlds, at the limits of culture, a space where boundaries are broken down and categories intermingle.[17] Theatre, I suggest, can be seen as just such a liminal space, in this case a space for play. As far back as Plato's *The Republic* (c.375 BCE), the distinction has been drawn between the real on one hand, and play, mimesis and theatre on the other. Goody (1997) has traced the relationship between theatre and play since Plato, and describes how from early times theatre aroused antipathy and was relegated to low status. As a consequence, over time theatre became associated with the margins of culture, transformed into the space for licentiousness,[18] the projected 'other' of ordered civilisation.[19] As a result, theatre as play becomes the space for the playing out of (feared or simply playful) liminal concerns: the breaking down of once sacred boundaries and the blending of categories. Theatre can be seen as the 'safe' arena for the playing out of dangerous pursuits. It provides the safe distance from which to explore fears surrounding loss of control in the face of disorder, while the playful combination of categories presents the thrill of risking new possibilities and suggestive freedoms.

My interest in the trickster first grew from a fascination with the profusion of figures derived from the *Commedia dell'arte* in Lorca's work. Harlequins and clowns often appear in drawings, a phenomenon which in part derives from a revival in the form across Europe in the early twentieth century, connected to a desire for a rediscovery of folkloric roots.[20] *Arlequín y fuente*

---

[17] Liminal, from the Latin *limen*, means threshold or limit. Victor Turner (1969: 95), relying on Van Gennep's *The Rite of Passage* (1960) defines the 'liminal phase' of ritual as the temporal moment and spatial site at the heart of ritual. This is the space where boundaries are confused and *communitas*, or the shared, communal experience can take place. For Turner, the clown, court jester and liminal trickster figures are related to his definition of liminal.

[18] Perhaps the most extreme example of Plato's symbolic banishment of theatre from the *Republic* is the Elizabethan stage as depicted by Stephen Mullaney in *The Place of the Stage: License, Play and Power in Renaissance England*. Mullaney (1988) shows how the cultural and ideological marginalisation of theatre was twinned with its physical and topological separation: it was confined to the area outside the city-walls, a space hitherto reserved for brothels, bear-pits and leper colonies.

[19] We could argue that 'reality' banishes theatre to the realm of the playful in order to be distinguished from the fictitious, to endorse its own authority.

[20] George (1995: 40) writes that Gual, Benavente, Picasso, Pérez de Ayala, Rivas Cherif and Valle-Inclán shared a *modernista* belief that in the revival of *commedia dell'arte* could 'typify the essence of popular theatre and street spectacle [. . .] linked to a rediscovery of man's primitive roots, which had been sullied by centuries of Western civilization'. Outside of Spain, Serge Diaghilev's *Ballet Russes*, the work of *Jean Cocteau* and

from 1927 (336.3),[21] depicts a harlequin figure in a black and white suit, split down the middle, and is therefore fully compatible with the traditional description of the harlequin's asymmetrical, bi-coloured tunic (Gifford 1979: 18–19). The *Arlequín ahogado*, c.1927 (137) portrays a harlequin face splintered along the lines of a spider's web, in a coalition of the dismemberment of facial features and the seductiveness of the mask which threatens to drown the figure. *Arlequín veneciano* (122), a skeletal figure in a Venetian mask; *Arlequín* (127) and *Arlequín Poema* (126) all date from 1927, the latter being accompanied by a poem dedicated to the harlequin. The *Arlequín desdoblado*, 1927 (117), *Cabeza de payaso desdoblado*, 1926 (332); *Payaso de rostro que se dobla* (198); *Payaso de rostro desdoblado y cáliz* (135); *Máscara y rostro* (276.1) and the *Cabeza desdoblada de payaso y lágrimas* (282), which all date from 1936, show an experimentation over a sustained period with form and style. Harlequins were also often used as self portraits (for Lorca), such as the illustration *Querido Melchorito*.[22] The general theme of all of these depictions of harlequin is the juxtaposition between playfulness and restrictiveness in relation to the mask. The harlequin can be seen as a costume or mask in itself (such as is the case in the film script *Viaje a la luna* where the Traje de Arlequín is put on, taken off, and carried around). The mask can suggest the freedoms of disguise, yet repeatedly in the drawings it is associated with restrictiveness and entrapment. The figures of the *Commedia dell'arte* may suggest playful freedoms, but their glittering masks hide sadness and imprisonment. Lorca's drawing *Arlequín* (1927) draws out the theme of duality represented by the costume of the harlequin figure, related to the binary opposition of the sun and moon, and linked by Hernández to death. Duality, disguise and death are all concepts which relate Lorca's harlequins and clowns to the trickster.

My interest in Lorca's work focuses mainly on the theatre. However, increasingly, I noticed characters in Lorca's plays who in some way stand apart from the main action of the play, or maintain a peripheral relationship to it. In *Así que pasen cinco años*, for example, a harlequin and clown appear from a circus which has sprung up in the middle of a wood. These non-naturalistic characters are pure fictions who represent a hiatus in the action of the play. Likewise the sprite-like Duendes of *Amor de Don Perlimplín con Belisa en su jardín* (The Love of Don Perlimplín for Belisa in His Garden)

---

the strains of Symbolism and Expressionism revealed a similar preoccupation with the form.

21 All references to drawings and paintings are taken from Hernández (1990), unless otherwise stated. The numbers in brackets refer to catalogue numbers rather than page numbers.

22 Hernández (1990: 66) writes that 'cuando en enero de 1933 [García Lorca] regala a un joven amigo un dibujo de un rostro desdoblado de pierrot, le dice expresamente: "te voy a dar mi autorretrato" '.

emerge out of the twilight, a liminal time between night and day, and their function is to produce a commentary on the action. Many of Lorca's plays, meanwhile, feature prologues, in which *prologuistas* in a variety of guises mediate the space of the prologue between the world of the spectators and the main action of the play. These *prologuistas* retain, therefore, the sense of the trickster as *farandulero*: at once a 'persona que recitaba comedias' but at the same time, someone who is 'hablador, trapacero, uno que tira a engañar' (*Diccionario de la Real Academia Española*).[23] Yet these tricksters simultaneously reveal the power of deception, the tricks of their trade. Repeatedly, trickster-figures beckon the audience into the liminal realm of the theatrical space, acting as mediators between reality and fiction. The 'trickster-function', then, is the metaphorical entry of the audience into the liminal space which is theatre, a space for the audience to try on or try out the imaginary worlds presented by theatre, to face the limits of culture through theatre, and to revel in its playful confusion of once sacred boundaries. The trickster-function is thus related, in this study, both to specific characters and to general thematics in connection with liminality.

Certain critics have treated the theme of clowns and harlequins in Lorca's work. For example, George (1992; 1995) explores connections between the figures of the *Commedia dell'arte* and Lorca; De Ros (1996) examines carnival elements in *El público*, and Cardwell (1995) draws on a study of *Así que pasen cinco años* to make perceptive analyses of the 'poeta-payaso' in that play. For Cardwell, 'las consideraciones estéticas del *clown*-artista glorifican y cuestionan simultáneamente la naturaleza y la función de su arte', as this figure explores 'la relación entre la vida y el arte, entre la ilusión y la realidad y lo ontológico en su tentativa para comprender la relación entre el "ser" y el "otro"'. For Cardwell, the 'poeta-payaso' is symbolic, 'no sólo del juego grotesco que es nuestra vida sino también del sentido lúdico del arte' (Cardwell 1995: 122). While my study will overlap with thematics raised elsewhere by critics of Lorca's work, and draws on the extensive corpus of

---

23 *Farandulero* is the closest translation of 'trickster' in Spanish. A search conducted by the *Real Academia de la Lengua Española* revealed that there is no exact equivalent in Spanish, but that, 'el trickster' may stand. Rodríguez and Lanning (1995: 37) recognise 'el *trickster*', italicised, as a category: 'el arquetipo del *trickster*, elaborado por antropólogos y sicólogos [. . .] tiene, desde tiempo immemorial, su representación en la cultura hispánica a través de la figura folklórica del "tretero" Pedro de Urdemals'. Spanish folktales (from the picaresque to Don Juan) offer a tradition dominated by trickster-figures. Espinosa (1946) collects such tales from Spain and Latin America. The trickster tradition is also very strong in the Arab world. Radin's (1954) text links the German trickster (the *Schelm*) to the Spanish *pícaro*, which first appeared in Spain in 1525 meaning, 'kitchen boy', and later was defined in 1726 (Diccionario de la Real Academia Española) as 'low, deceitful, shameless'. *Lazarillo* (1554) and Quevedo's *El buscón* (1626) can both be seen as examples of marginal trickster-figures.

existing literature on the trickster,[24] the present analysis of the trickster-function in García Lorca's work, in terms of critical approach (moving between anthropology and psychoanalysis) and the selection of texts addressed is, to my knowledge, completely new.

The initial section of this study extends an invitation to the play. The first chapter focuses on those *prologuistas* and other trickster-figures who lead the audience into the liminal, theatrical space. The role of the *prologuista* is to display the art of obfuscation in the delaying of the narrative secret, while simultaneously delighting in the sacred delight of poetic creation. The *prologuista* (often named the Autor) is defined as an *agent provocateur* who draws the audience and characters into a dialectical relationship with one another. Progressively, the plays under discussion can be seen as a liminal space for the staging of a dialogue between audience and characters. Through the trickster-function, the audience is encouraged by trickster-figures to enter the liminal space which is theatre, ready to address the liminal concerns which theatre affords.

A variety of trickster-figures will perform this function in the readings which follow in this book, from the *prologuistas* (often Autor or Director) of the first chapter, to the Duendes (sprite-figures) of *Amor de Don Perlimplín con Belisa en su jardín* (The Love of Don Perlimplín for Belisa in His Garden) in chapter two, the Arlequín and Payaso (Harlequin and Clown) of *Así que pasen cinco años* (Once Five Years Pass) in chapter three, the Moon of *Bodas de sangre* (Blood Wedding) in chapter four, to *El público*'s (The Public) profusion of characters derived from carnival in chapter V.

A series of themes will be addressed in sections two and three: the visual, time, the body and theatre, all at the margins. Section two is divided into three chapters which address the limits of gender: focussing on femininity, masculinity and androgyny respectively. The presence of androgynous characters (which, interestingly, are often the ones which are borrowed from the world of *Commedia dell'arte* or carnival and are therefore most closely related to the trickster), make masculinity and femininity into constructs. Chapter II addresses Lorca's short farce, *Amor de Don Perlimplín con Belisa en su jardín*. Interpretations of the play have in the past produced incompatible accounts of the possible motives of the play's male protagonist for his subsequent actions. This chapter argues rather for the play as a whole (and therefore its truth) to be seen as an effect of the veil. The motif of the *femme fatale* is used in order to address both femininity, and the instability of the visual medium in this play.

Chapter III focuses on the complex piece *Así que pasen cinco años*. The

24 Pérez Firmat (1986) *Literature and Liminality: Festive Readings in the Hispanic Tradition*, presents an analysis of the trickster in the tradition of Hispanic literature, particularly with reference to the figure of Don Juan. Other readings which link the trickster to Hispanism are Irizarry (1987) and Pielmuter Pérez (1976).

play is subtitled 'leyenda del tiempo'. The articulation of time in this play features deferral, circularity and suspension, which are all characteristics of masochism in psychoanalysis. In using the dynamic of male masochism for this reading, my aim is not to offer a diagnosis of the play's protagonist, but rather to draw in all of the characters and the entire action of the play, in order to stage a dialogue between contradictory accounts of masculinity (masculinity taken to the limits), moving through a peculiar relationship to time (time at the margins). Lastly, as the structure of the text mimics the aesthetics of masochism, I reflect briefly on the 'pleasures' of this text in performance.

Where earlier chapters recuperate those plays which are marginal in García Lorca's *oeuvre*, chapter IV 'liminalizes' a play which is firmly entrenched in the Lorca canon, by concentrating on the androgynous figure of the Moon. The Moon lends an uncanny, anti-naturalistic aspect to this lyrical, rural drama. The Moon is introduced here as an articulation of the death drive, a reading which has consequences for the presentation of heterosexual love as traditionally understood in this play.

The final section deals with theatre and the body at the margins. Chapter V produces a new reading of the notoriously difficult play, *El público*: the limits of the body are explored through a focus on scatology, while the margins of the theatrical experience are addressed through a discussion of collectivity. The collective experience is explored in terms of pain, provocation, taboo and death. Repeatedly in these readings, and in the conclusion, art is seen as a means to engage with the life/death divide, while artifice is seen to mask the absence which is death, and the remains of a collective solipsism.

The introduction of the concept of the trickster-function, a model which draws on anthropology, psychoanalysis and literary theories, is a new approach which provides the opportunity for fresh interpretations of the chosen playtexts, viewed as theatre engaging an audience. *The Trickster-Function in the Theatre of García Lorca* affords critical attention on a selection of Lorca's most challenging, complex and least studied works. Using the image of the *trickster* as leitmotif, it argues for a new reading of García Lorca's plays which highlights androgyny, male fantasy, masochism, masquerade and the carnivalesque.

SECTION I

AN INVITATION TO THE PLAY

I

AUTHOR(ITY) AND THE LAUGHTER OF SIGNS: THE AUTOR/DIRECTOR/POETA AND OTHER TRICKSTER-FIGURES IN THE THEATRE OF FEDERICO GARCÍA LORCA

> Respetable público; mejor dicho. . .
> Federico García Lorca.

> . . . objections, digressions, gay mistrust, the delight in mockery are signs of health: everything unconditional belongs to pathology. . .
> Friedrich Nietzsche, *Beyond Good and Evil.*

In a number of García Lorca's plays, the figure of the Autor/Director/ Poeta appears as an *agent provocateur* who dazzles with his display of verbal wit and light and show. Lorca himself played the part of the Autor in the 1930 and 1933 productions of *La zapatera prodigiosa* (as has been documented by Vilches de Frutos and Dougherty 1992: 47, 65),[1] yet in this chapter I argue that there is no simple equation to be made between the Autor and his creator. Rather, the Autor/Director/Poeta is a trickster-figure whose function is to open a dramatic dialogue with the audience, and, in what I have chosen to call the trickster-function, to lead them into the liminal space which is theatre. The motif of dialogue will be seen to extend to the words used, and to the theatrical space, which becomes a site where multiple signs collide.

Certain plays under examination feature a *prólogo/advertencia* delivered by an author-figure while others involve interaction within the plot of the characters of Autor, Poeta or Director. *El maleficio de la mariposa* (The Butterfly's Evil Spell, 1920), *Tragicomedia de Don Cristóbal y la señá*

---

1 The 1930 production took place in the Teatro Español de Madrid on 24 December with the *Compañía Dramática Española Margarita Xirgu* and the *Grupo Caracol*, directed by Cipriano Rivas Cherif, and the 1933 production formed part of a *función de gala* with *Amor de Don Perlimplín con Belisa en su jardín* at the *Club Anfistora*, Teatro Español de Madrid, on 3 April 1933. 'Margarita Xirgu asumió el papel principal y el propio Federico desempeñó el papel del Autor' (Vilches de Frutos and Dougherty 1992: 47).

Rosita (The Tragicomedy of Don Cristóbal and Mam'selle Rosita, 1928), the unfinished *Dragón* (Dragon, 1928) and *La zapatera prodigiosa* (The Prodigious Shoemaker's Wife, 1930, revised 1933) all feature prologues while the *Retablillo de Don Cristóbal* (Don Cristóbal's Puppet Play, 1928) and *El sueño de la vida* (The Dream of Life, 1936) open with a prologue delivered by a Poeta and an Autor respectively, and also feature interaction within the plot between these figures and other characters.[2] *El público* (The Public, 1930), on the other hand, has no prologue, but comprises a dialogue within the plot between the Director and the other characters, thereby rendering the whole play a form of prologue or liminal space.

The movement from this inclusion of the *prólogo* as a discrete section to an opening up of the theatrical space can be seen as a type of progression. While an awareness of the dates of composition of the plays is important to this discussion (always bearing in mind that Lorca tended to work on several pieces of work at once, often with long gestation periods),[3] as is apparent from the above list of works under discussion, my intention is not to examine the plays in chronological order. In an excellent article entitled, 'The Strategy of García Lorca's Dramatic Composition 1930–1936', Anderson (1986a: 211–30) has drawn attention to the importance of considering other types of progression in Lorca's *oeuvre* besides chronological sequence. Thus Anderson queries the notion of a rural trilogy[4] on the basis that while critics have tended to view Lorca's work as a journey towards *Bodas de sangre* (Blood Wedding), *Yerma* (Yerma) and *La casa de Bernarda Alba* (The House

---

[2] See also the 'Diálogo del Poeta y Don Cristóbal' (*OC* III: 455–6) which takes the form of a prologue addressed to an audience: 'al iniciarse la representación de los *Títeres de Cachiporra*, que ayer, para regalo del espíritu, nos ofrecieron en el Avenida Federico García Lorca y Manuel Fontanals, el fantoche llamado Don Cristóbal y el poeta sostuvieron este diálogo de presentación'; dated 26 March 1934. The 'prólogo' to *Mariana Pineda* is not included in this list as it does not take the form of a monologue addressed to an audience, but instead forms part of the first scene of the play.

[3] Thus while Lorca mentioned *El sueño de la vida* just twice in two interviews given in 1936, it is conceivable that it was begun sometime earlier.

[4] In the 1930s, Lorca made the following statements: 'Hay que volver a la tragedia. Nos obliga a ello la tradición de nuestro teatro dramático [. . .] yo quiero dar al teatro tragedias', Chabás (1934), 'Federico García Lorca y la tragedia' (*OC* III: 604–6; 605); 'Mi trayectoria en el teatro [. . .] yo la veo perfectamente clara. Quisiera terminar la trilogía de *Bodas de sangre*, *Yerma* y *El drama de las hijas de Loth*. Me falta esta última', Prats (1934), 'Los artistas en el ambiente de nuestro tiempo' (*OC* III: 610–15; 614); 'la trilogía acabará con *La destrucción de Sodoma* [. . .] Sí, ya sé que el título es grave y comprometedor, pero sigo mi ruta. Yo soy un poeta y no he de apartarme de la misión que he emprendido', Anon. (1935) 'Después del estreno de *Yerma*' (*OC* III: 619). Anderson (1986a) tells us that we know that the last play in the trilogy, a biblical work entitled either [*El drama de*] *Las hijas de Loth*, or *La destrucción de Sodoma*, existed, 'at least in a rudimentary form, for during the summer of 1935, Lorca gave a reading of it to two friends who were members of La Barraca, Rodríguez Rapún and Sáenz de la Calzada, and the latter has in fact given a two-page résumé of the plot', Anderson (1986a: 218).

of Bernarda Alba), with the avant-garde texts as mere stepping stones to the later works, García Lorca himself conceived of his dramatic output very differently. In a series of statements uttered throughout the 1930s,[5] Lorca consistently names *El público*, *Así que pasen cinco años* and *El sueño de la vida* as '*mi obra*', culminating in a statement in April 1936 to the effect that, 'yo en el teatro he seguido una trayectoria definida. Mis primeras comedias son irrepresentables [. . .] En estas comedias está mi verdadero propósito. Pero para demostrar una personalidad y tener derecho al respeto he dado otras cosas' (*OC* III: 674).[6]

My motivation for the contrivance which places the 'comedias irrepresentables' as the culmination of a progression is therefore two-fold. At first sight, it would appear that authorial intent seems to provide a justification for this choice, but paradoxically, these are also the plays where the role of the author is evacuated of authority, and where the theatrical space is opened out into a dialogue of signs and signifiers. The author-function is thus replaced by the trickster-function (a conception of theatre as a liminal space) in the plays examined. Viewing the plays as forming such a progression will give room for further speculation regarding both Lorca's dramatic conception and his achievements as a theatre practitioner.

The practice of opening a play with a dramatic prologue is far from new, and can be traced back to the beginnings of drama in Greek theatre. The prologue is a comment on the action, an extra-diegetic narrative designed to introduce the audience to the major themes of the play. In Lorca's theatre, the prologue articulates themes relating to the rôle of theatre itself – it thus becomes a meta-discourse, opening a liminal space between the framed performance of the text and the external world of the spectators. The *prologuista* of Lorca's earlier plays introduces the performance, sheds light

---

5   In a reading of *El público* at the house of the Chilean ambassador to Spain, Carlos Morla Lynch, Lorca remarked to Rafael Martínez Nadal apropos of this play: 'Ya verás qué obra. Atrevedísima y con una técnica totalmente nueva. Es lo mejor que he escrito para el teatro [. . .] La obra es muy difícil y por el momento irrepresentable, tienen razón. Pero dentro de diez o veinte años será un exitazo; ya lo verás' (Nadal 1970: 17). Speaking of the première of *La zapatera prodigiosa* in 1930, Lorca asserted: 'No; no es *mi obra*. Mi obra vendrá [. . .] ya tengo algo [. . .] algo. Lo que vendrá será *mi obra*. ¿Sabes cómo titulo mi obra? *El público*. Esa sí [. . .] ésa sí [. . .] Dramatismo profundo, profundísimo', 'Antes del estreno. Hablando con Federico García Lorca' (Maurer 1979: 102–3). In 1931 Lorca stated: 'El teatro nuevo, avanzado de formas y teorías, es mi mayor preocupación', Gil Benumeya (1931), 'Estampa de Federico García Lorca' (*OC* II: 502–5; 503). In the autumn of 1933, a friend and critic noted: 'Si le habláis de *Bodas de sangre* [Lorca] habla con entusiasmo de dos obras que no ha podido representar y que son, según él, el teatro que quiere hacer. Estas obras se titulan *Así que pasen cinco años* y *El público*', Suero (1933), 'Crónica de un día de barco con Federico García Lorca' (*OC* III: 539–53; 544).

6   Morales (1936), 'Conversaciones literarias: Al habla con Federico García Lorca' (*OC* III: 671–6).

on its themes, warns, beckons or challenges and then disappears behind the curtain, never to appear again. A persistent theme introduced by these *prologuistas* is that of the deceptiveness of appearances. Reed Anderson (1988: 209) writes that, 'theater's most distinctive quality is that, in the process of creating a fiction for an audience, it must show rather than narrate [. . .]. The illusion of presence and actuality is a construct, then, and there are many conventions in the theater by which that construct may either be hidden from the audience or in varying degrees made obvious'. The *prologuista* is a trickster-figure, no more than a digression, a showy distraction, symbolic of the ambiguous space on the threshold between presence and absence, creating and then blurring the delineation of a gap between the world of appearance and illusion and the external reality. At the same time, the prologue creates a distinction between show and display on the one hand, and narration on the other. These distinctions are already beginning to complicate the traditional use of the prologue as a statement of authority as to the meaning of the piece. In this chapter, I argue that the function of the prologue is not to attribute meaning from the 'Author-God' (Barthes 1977: 146), but rather to stage a dialogue between author-characters and audience, and to turn the play into what Barthes terms a 'multi-dimensional space in which a variety of meanings, none of them original, blend and clash' (1977: 146).

METAPHORS OF AUTHORITY, TRICKERY AND ILLUSION

> 'Such tricks hath strong imagination'.
> William Shakespeare, *A Midsummer Night's Dream*, iv, i.

In *La zapatera prodigiosa*, a shoemaker is married to a coquettish woman much younger than himself. After hearing the local gossips' tales of his wife's alleged loose conduct, the shoemaker leaves town, to return later in disguise as a puppet-master. In his absence, the shoemaker's wife has grown to love the fantasy image she now holds of her husband. When the shoemaker/puppet-master tests her with his puppet play (a scene which has resonances of Hamlet's testing of Gertrude through the troupe of travelling players), the little shoemaker's wife declares her faithfulness and love for the absent husband. The puppeteer tears off his disguise and the pair are reunited. The play opens with a prologue delivered by the Autor.

At the beginning of the Prologue to *La zapatera prodigiosa*, the Autor rushes on stage, before the play has begun, almost as an afterthought, and addresses the audience: 'Respetable público'. The prologue traditionally is an exposition of the themes of the play and its characters, that is it maps out the linear narrative to follow, or else grabs the audience's attention. The prologue provides a frame for the action, and the presence of the Autor on stage places a signature on the text. 'Autor' seems to be cognate with 'authority'. The

Autor is the creator of the fictional, theatrical world and he requests a hearing. This figure appears to hold the key as to the meaning of the piece, a suggestion enhanced by the letter he carries on stage which is mysteriously never referred to, merely wafted authoritatively (*'Sobre cortina gris aparece el Autor. Sale rápidamente y lleva una carta en la mano'* [*OC* II: 375]).

Certain factors soon begin to complicate the equation of Autor with authority, however. In the first place, his dress – top hat and tails – suggestive of the upper class professional or intellectual man, is revealed at the end of the prologue to be nothing more than the garb of a vaudeville magician.[7] The Autor wears 'una gran capa llena de estrellas [. . .] maravillosa capa' and at the end of the prologue we learn that the *Autor* indulges in cheap tricks:

> (. . . *se quita el sombrero de copa y éste se ilumina por dentro con una luz verde: el autor lo inclina y sale de él un chorro de agua. El autor mira un poco cohibido al público y se retira de espaldas, lleno de ironía*) Ustedes perdonen (*Sale*).   (*OC* II: 377)[8]

The magician is a trickster-figure who retains the duality of, on the one hand, the master of illusion and *legerdemain*, the *prestidigitador*,[9] and on the other the shaman or wizard. This image provides us with a way of viewing the ambiguity of the Autor figure: at once powerful creator of images and mere showman. (The dichotomy between false illusion and magical power extends to the role of theatre itself and to a distinction between the showy, elaborate scenario of the spectacle and its function as a space for the playing out of ritual scenes.)

The magician is first and foremost a metaphor for the creative imagination and for the artistic mastery involved in the creation of the magical theatrical

---

7   Traister (1984: 3) writes that 'physician, alchemist, professor all wore the same long robe, which might mark either the scholar or the magician' of the Renaissance, and MacRitchie (1996: 69) maintains that 'the standard repertoire of illusions was mostly invented in the nineteenth century. Then Horace Golding first sawed a lady in half, and Maskelyne lectured in a semi-scientific vein to audiences at London's Egyptian Hall. The dinner suit or tail coat still work as a stage outfit dates from those early, quasi-scientific appearances'. The magical theme was continued during the 1930 production of *La zapatera prodigiosa* as the support play was changed from the dramatisation of the Chinese legend, *El príncipe, la princesa y su destino*, to Calderón's *auto sacramental*, *El gran teatro del mundo* (see Anderson 1991b: 64). Calderon's play dates from 1645 (Frutos Cortés 1983: 21) and opens with the figure of the *Autor* who is described thus: '*Sale el Autor con manto de estrellas y potencias en el sombrero*'.

8   All references to the text are from the revised 1933 version. In an article of 1933, Lorca states that he had finished the first version in 1926: 'era el verano de 1926. Yo estaba en la ciudad de Granada rodeado de negras higueras, de espigas, de pequeñas coronitas de agua; era dueño de una caja de alegría, íntimo amigo de las rosas, y quise poner el ejemplo dramático de un modo sencillo, iluminando con frescos tonos lo que podía tener fantasmas desilusionados'; Hernández (1982).

9   The *prestidigitador* will appear as a character in *El público*.

world. We no longer have documentation of the long history of magicians who appeared on the international stage as performers, but their influence remains in such characters as Prospero, Faust and Friar Bacon.[10] The magician was often included in plays, regardless of the requirements of the plot, in order to appease the popular appetite for shows and spectacles. For example, Louis B. Wright, in his article 'Juggling Tricks and Conjury on the English Stage Before 1642', states that:

> ... the art of jugglery or legerdemain early reached a high degree of perfection; the tricks included sword-playing, juggling with coins and balls, illusions of various sorts, mind-reading, and other exhibitions so marvellous that the suspicion of black art often fell upon jugglers and conjurers.
>
> (Wright 1927: 269)[11]

Delgado's (1998: 67–91) excellent article on the theatre of Rambal shows how Spanish audiences, contemporaneous with the writing of García Lorca's plays, were equally fascinated with the theatrical possibilities for magic tricks and illusion.[12] At the same time, the newly emerging field of cinema was peering into the possibilities which science and mechanics could afford magical illusion. Optical trickery gave rise to uncanniness and disorientation in the spectator.[13] At the turn of the nineteenth and twentieth centuries, the films of Georges Méliès and his Spanish counterpart Segundo de Chomón capitalised on this relationship between early cinema and magic by creating

[10] For a discussion of these characters as magicians, see for example Traister (1984); Mortenson (1972: 194–207); and the seminal work by Curry (1935: 25–36; 185–96).

[11] The discussion of antecedents on the English stage is relevant here as Lorca was influenced by Shakespeare's theatre. See, for example, Anderson (1985: 187–210). Prologues often involved magic tricks to grab attention, such as *Wily Beguiled* (1600) in which a juggler (magician) will not be sent away, but stays to entertain the audience before the play opens: 'As the Prologue is about to speak his part, the juggler asks: "Will you see any tricks of legerdemain, sleight of hand, cleanly conveyance or *deceptio visus*? [. . .] The Prologue bids the juggler be gone, but the latter stays, recites his accomplishments, and performs the trick" ' (Wright 1927: 276).

[12] Delgado's article, 'Enrique Rambal: The Forgotten *Auteur* of Spanish Popular Theatre', includes photographic documentation of a huge queue at the box office of the Teatro Arriaga in Bilbao in April 1936 for one of Rambal's productions. Rambal's 'grandiloquent and marvellous theatre where anything could happen' (Delgado citing Saura) featured rotating stagedrops and even a parade of constructed elephants for one production. I am grateful to María Delgado for allowing me a copy of this article prior to publication.

[13] Where the interest in the power of the magician grew out of the Renaissance's explosion of scientific rationalism – as science and rationalism progressed, so did the interest in unexplained phenomena and a fascination for magic – so a similar process occurred at the turn of the twentieth century. The discovery of new technologies and new scientific methods existed side by side with a fascination for magical tricks. The cinema was born out of this ambivalence. Early pictures were shown as fairground attractions, and the Egyptian Hall in 1897 was presenting 'Improved Animated Photographs' (Hammond 1974: 8). Urrutia (1992: 45–53) explains that in the Spain of the early 1920s,

films such as *Extraordinary Illusion* (1903); *L'Enchanter Alcofrisbas* (1899) and *La Page Mystérieuse* (1889) in the case of Méliès[14] and *El hotel eléctrico* (1905) in that of Chomón. Several films, such as Méliès's *The Brahmin and the Butterfly* featured butterfly women, and may have been influenced by a conjuring trick which took place at Maskelyne and Cooke's Egyptian Hall in 1887. Buatier de Kolta's show *The Cocoon* featured a butterfly woman who emerged from a chrysalis, which reminds us of Lorca's *El maleficio de la mariposa* in which all of the characters are insects. Méliès's films oscillate between the magical aura of the photograph as wizardry, and the exposure of the sleight of hand techniques involved in the production of the illusion. The magician's history emphasised the subtle distinction between trickster and illusionist on the one hand, and powerful creator of images on the other.

Lorca's depiction of the Autor as a magician seems to refer metaphorically to the audience's fear of opening their minds to anything new – the audience should approach the play with the open-mindedness they would afford a magical spectacle or the marvellous tales of the Bible:

> . . . Por este miedo absurdo, y por el teatro en muchas ocasiones una finanza, la poesía se retira de la escena en busca de otros ambientes donde la gente no se asuste de que un árbol, por ejemplo, se convierta en una rosa de humo, y de que tres panes y tres peces, por amor de un mano y una palabra, se conviertan en tres mil panes y tres mil peces para calmar el hambre de una multitud.   (*OC* II: 376)[15]

Lorca's Autor senses that the audience will be displeased if they do not receive what they demand. Financial constraints are seen to condition the quality of crowd pleasing theatre ('por este miedo absurdo y por el teatro en muchas ocasiones una finanza'), while the audience is afraid of the author who brings poetry to the stage – expressed metaphorically as the magician conjuring up magical tricks. The Autor, in his attempts to please the audience, is dripping with flowery respect: 'respetable público' and '(*lleno de ironía*) Ustedes perdonen'. The question of the financial constraints on the

---

'el cine se entendía como una serie de cuadros, como un álbum de postales que se van posando [. . .] Adquiría el cine, pues, un aspecto mágico: consistía en la animación de lo inmóvil, en la vida de los muertos en el resucitar de lo que antes había estado vivo'. Hammond (1974: 8) writes that, 'the appeal of magic [in the cinema] was partly to be found in its thrilling coalition of polarities, and their careful manipulation to induce alternate feelings of well-being and disorientation in the spectator'.

14 Méliès's *Voyage dans la lune* (1902) may have provided the inspiration for Lorca's *Viaje a la luna*, a point that has been made by Monegal (1994a: 14) and Llafranque (1982: 81).

15 Wright (1927) explains that the scenes of magic appear in the religious drama of the seventeenth century, using legerdemain to illustrate Moses's miracles, for example.

theatre reflects Lorca's own feelings on the cultural climate, as demonstrated in the essay, 'Charla sobre teatro' (1935):

> Hay que mantener actitudes dignas, en la seguridad de que será recompensadas con creces. Lo contrario es temblar de miedo detrás de las bambalinas y matar las fantasías, la imaginación y la gracia del teatro, que es siempre, siempre, un arte excelso [. . .] vamos a tener que poner la palabra 'Arte' en salas y camerinos, porque si no, vamos a tener que poner la palabra 'comercio' o alguna que no me atrevo a decir.   (*OC* III: 460–1)

Commercial undercurrents are a common theme of these prologues. As he voices his anxieties about financial difficulties, the Autor switches from sycophancy to entreaty tinged with derision, in a violent change of register. Just as the eighteenth century English 'playwrights in prologues and actors on the stage courted, flattered and cajoled their aristocratic and plebeian patrons, for they knew that a disapproving audience could force a production's closure' (Brewer 1997: 353), so the *prologuistas* of these plays are depicted at the mercy of a demanding audience, anxious not to incite their displeasure.[16] In *Dragón*, an unfinished play which barely gets beyond the prologue, a *prologuista* (the Director) turns on a judgmental audience who have come demanding to be entertained while the Autores and Artistas console one another backstage:

> . . . Están ustedes sentados en sus butacas y vienen a divertirse. Muy bien. Han pagado su dinero, y es justo. Pero el poeta ha abierto los viejos escotillones del teatro sin preocuparse en hacerles a ustedes las clásicas cosquillas o los arrumacos de tontería que se hacen a ese terrible porra de pateo. Estas tablas han sido, hasta ahora, un suplicio para los autores. Cuando la obra empezaba a ser juzgada, los pobres autores ahí detrás (yo los he visto) tomaban tila y abrazaban tiernamente a las artistas, en medio del mayor desconsuelo.   (Llafranque 1987: 115)

The function of the prologue was traditionally often seen almost as an *apologia* for the play: the *prologuista* had to persuade the audience of the value and interest of the piece. In *El maleficio de la mariposa*, Mosquito, the *prologuista* cries: 'Ahora, escuchad la comedia. Tal vez os riáis al oír hablar a estos insectos como hombrecitos, como adolescentes.' This confrontation between audience and Autor will reach a climax in *El público* as the Director, 'alienates his audience by breaking both moral and dramatic conventions' (De Ros 1996: 101). This is a reflection of a contemporary debate regarding

---

16 The prologue written by Samuel Johnson for David Garrick in Drury Lane, 1747, sums up the delicate relationship between the prologue and the audience: 'The drama's laws the drama's patrons give,/For we that live to please, must please to live' (Brewer 1997: 353).

a crisis in Spanish theatre, where a bourgeois public clamoured for mimetic realism which did not challenge the hegemonic ideologies of the time, and in which, 'authors as ideologically diverse as Valle-Inclán and Benavente coincided in blaming the bourgeois mentality of Spanish audiences for the theatre's decadence' (De Ros 1996: 101). Rather than naturalism or realism, Lorca's *prologuistas* offer magical theatrical worlds and they anticipate the audience's resultant surprise and displeasure.

Thus, Mosquito, the *prologuista* of *Tragicomedia de don Cristóbal y la señá Rosita* (a farce revolving around the antics of Rosita and Don Cristóbal),[17] attacks the escapist genre offered by the theatre to bourgeois audiences:

> Yo y mi compañía venimos del teatro de los burgueses, del teatro de los condes y de los marqueses, donde los hombres van a dormirse y las señoras [. . .] a dormirse también. Yo y mi compañía encerrados. No os podéis imaginar qué pena teníamos.   (*OC* II: 105–6)

Mosquito is 'un personaje misterioso, mitad duende, mitad martinico, mitad insecto. Representa la alegría de vivir libre, y la gracia y la poesía del pueblo andaluz. Lleva una trompetilla de feria'.[18] Mosquito, and his travelling theatre troupe have come:

> . . . en busca de la gente sencilla, para mostrarles las cosas, las cosillas y las costillas del mundo; bajo la luna verde de las montañas, bajo la luna rosa de las playas . . .   (*OC* II: 106)

The *prologuista* now begs the audience to forget its usual expectations, to be open-minded and open themselves up to a new experience.

In *La zapatera prodigiosa*, Lorca's Autor-figure wants to bring poetry to the stage: 'la poesía se retira de la escena', by his creation of the world of the prodigious little shoemaker's wife, this new plane, this private magical world. Anderson (1991b: 11) tells us that in an earlier draft, Lorca named the piece, 'La zapatera fantasiosa'. Lorca may have been influenced in his use of the term 'prodigious' (the *OED* definition of which is portentous, ominous, wonderful, marvellous) by Calderón's 1637 play *El mágico prodigioso*.

---

[17] The *Tragicomedia de don Cristóbal y la señá Rosita* (like the *Retablillo de don Cristóbal*) is a farce which revolves around the marriage of the young and beautiful Rosita to the repugnant but wealthy Don Cristóbal. In the *Tragicomedia*, Rosita's suitors wait in the wings as she and Cristóbal are married and prepare for their wedding night. The suitors burst in and out of doors, one to be chased by Cristóbal, the other to embrace Rosita. Finally, the old man collapses from rage and is removed from the stage. The young lovers celebrate their love on stage.

[18] Lorca described Mosquito as 'el Puck de Shakespeare, mitad duende, mitad niño, mitad insecto'. From letter to Angel Ferrant, 1931 (Anderson and Maurer 1997: 703).

Another possible source is Catalan Russinyol's puppet piece of 1911, *The Prodigious Puppet*. Kaplan (1992: 49) has described that piece as 'a comic melodrama about Tofol's marriage to a countess who betrayed him, [and in which] human actors assumed the stereotyped roles of puppets'. In our case, 'prodigious' would appear to describe the fantastic world of the Shoemaker's Wife, a magical world created by the imagination of the Autor. The figure of the Autor as magician therefore on the one hand becomes a metaphor for the creative imagination of the poet. In a *conferencia* entitled 'Imaginacion, Inspiración, Evasión' (1928) Lorca expounded his concept of poetic imagination, defining it as 'sinónima de aptitud para el descubrimiento'. To imagine, therefore, is to 'llevar nuestro poco de luz a la penumbra viva donde existen todas las infinitas posibilidades, formas y números' (*OC* III: 259). The action of the poet is like that of the magician for, as Barbara Traister has written: 'magic and dramatic creation are similar; form matches content; magician and dramatist both work gracefully within the boundaries of their art' (Traister 1984: 144). The alignment of the *prologuista*/Autor with the magician becomes an allegory for artistic creation.

Lorca's essay on the imagination sets up a binary opposition between 'imaginación' on the one hand and 'evasión' on the other (with 'inspiración' as the means to achieve 'evasión'). Imagination emerges as the aptitude to discover unexpected connections, which spawn metaphor, bringing together disparate elements from the world in a process governed by the human logic of reason.[19] As Anderson (1991a: 152), writes, 'by shunning – or even subverting mimetic conventions and leaving the real world behind (one sense of "evasión") the "gift" of inspiration liberates the poet and enables him to discover or invent mysterious and inexplicable "hechos poéticos", free-standing images devoid of any analogical meaning whose creation, internal functioning and interrelations are now determined only by a "lógica poética" '. 'Evasión' can therefore take one further than 'imaginación', which is limited by human experience to a new poetic logic, a new version of the world, unrestrained by normal conventions: 'evasión de la realidad por el camino del sueño, por el camino que dicte un insólito que regale la inspiración' (*OC* III: 261). Language, thus, is taken to the limits in these discussions of poetic logic, new images are created through juxtaposition and paradox, but the creative imagination is always bound by the edges of language. What we seem to find in Lorca's discussions of language is a sense in which a gap is inserted between these words of poetic logic and their signifiers, thereby imposing a limit to language and a desire to look beyond to some meaning

[19] Lorca writes, 'pero la imaginación está limitada por la realidad: no se puede imaginar lo que no existe; necesita de objetos, paisajes, números, planetas, y se hacen precisas las relaciones entre ellos dentro de la lógica más pura. No se puede saltar al abismo ni prescindir de los términos reales. La imaginación tiene horizontes, quiere dibujar y concretar todo lo que abarca' (*OC* III: 259).

which escapes language. But while these linguistic games reveal the absurdity of the close adherence to the rules of language, at the same time, the games of inversion and juxtaposition also serve to reinforce the rules of language: the former is impossible without the latter. Where poetic language seems to involve the transgression of the limit (Bataille [1962] writes that transgression is inherent in all language) such a transgression seems to imply merely the entry into another set of literary devices: metaphor, inversion, juxtaposition which in turn rely on their own strictly defined poetic logic. Thus the poet captures the same ambiguities as the magician, for 'magic and dramatic creation are similar; form matches content; magician and dramatist both work gracefully within the boundaries of their art' (Traister 1984: 144). Both the poet and the magician seem to appeal to a different order, but both are ultimately related to 'the paradox of superhuman power that is humanly limited' (Traister 1984: 1). Like the magician, the poet uses words to spin a web of artifice and illusion.

MANIPULATIONS AND PLOTS

The protagonist of *La zapatera prodigiosa*, the little shoemaker's wife, wants to spread her wings and make flights of imagination: 'la zapatera va y viene enjaulada, buscando su paisaje de nubes, de árboles de agua, y se quiebra las alas contra las paredes' (*OC* II: 376). Meanwhile, the Autor suggests that the struggle of the Zapatera (to break out of the confines of drab existence) is also that of the spectators. To the shoemaker's wife he exclaims: 'tu traje y tu lucha será el traje y la lucha de cada espectador sentado en su butaca, en su palco, en su entrada general, donde te agitas, grande o pequeña, con el mismo ritmo desilusionado' (*OC* II: 376–7). However, the theme of the power and beauty of the creative imagination is double-edged. Within the body of the play itself, imagination will be linked to love. The Zapatera builds up a fantasy image of her husband, which allows her to fall in love with him:

> . . . me miró y lo miré. Yo me recosté en la hierba. Todavía me parece sentir en la cara aquel aire tan fresquito que venía por los árboles. El paró su caballo y la cola del caballo era blanca y tan larga que llegaba al agua del arroyo.   (*OC* II: 417)

The ridiculousness of the fantasy image of the Zapatero is quickly belied by the Niño, who cries: '¡ja, ja, ja! Me está engañando. El Señor Zapatero no tiene jaca' (*OC* II: 416). There is something of the 'lovers' lunacy' of *A Midsummer Night's Dream* (Dent 1965: 115–29) in this play as the Zapatera falls in love with her old husband, but in this case a love potion is replaced by sheer imagination to work the magic of love.

What is borne out by the play itself is that although love is 'a many splen-

dour'd thing', linked to the poetic imagination, taking one to the limits of
human experience, at the same time indulging the imagination can make one
lose one's critical faculties, and make one open to manipulation by another
party. The shoemaker's wife has in fact been deluded, seduced by the fantasy
introduced by her husband. This notion is extended to the content of the
prologue. In the first place, there is a correlation drawn between the
Titiritero/Zapatero's presentation of his play-within-a-play and our prologue.
The Puppeteer introduces his playlet with the words: 'Respetable público:
Oigan ustedes el "romance verdadero y sustancioso de la mujer rubicunda y
el hombrecillo de la paciencia, para que sirva de escarmiento y ejemplaridad
a todas las criaturas de este mundo" ' (OC II: 429), which resonates with the
words of our prologue, opened with 'respetable público'. Within the play, the
Titiritero/Zapatero is able to pull at the heart strings of his wife just as he
manipulates the puppets. The ending of the play may surprise us in its joyful
celebration of the love felt by the shoemaker's wife for her husband as she
appears almost duped. We have witnessed no clear psychological development in her falling in love, but rather are invited to see a sort of magical
madness, with the Zapatero as miracle worker. In the case of the prologue, the
Autor is able to manipulate the Zapatera just as the puppet-master wields his
puppets. The Autor, like a magician, has created the Zapatera, dressed her,
and made her speak. But like Pirandello's six characters, or Unamuno's
Augusto Pérez, the Autor's character rebels against her creator:

> . . . pero ella lucha siempre, lucha con la realidad visible. Encajada en el
> límite de esta farsa vulgar, atada a la anécdota que el autor le ha impuesto,
> y amiga de gentes que no tienen más misión que expresar su paisaje de
> nubes, la zapatera va y viene enjaulada, buscando su paisaje de nubes, de
> árboles de agua, y se quiebra las alas contra las paredes [. . .] (Se oyen
> voces de la zapatera) ¡Ya voy! No tengas tanta impaciencia en salir!
>
> (OC II: 376)[20]

The Zapatera fights fantasy and reality at once, yet seems curiously acquies-
cent at the end of the play. But as we have already seen, her struggle is also
the struggle of the spectators: 'tu traje y tu lucha será el traje y la lucha de
cada espectador'. The public, the Autor suggests, should also acquiesce,
should become seduced by the magical poetical world of the shoemaker's
wife:

---

[20] This notion of the creator of characters conversing with his creations finds echoes
in the 'Dialogo del poeta y don Cristóbal', in which the poet Federico García Lorca and
the character Don Cristóbal appear on stage before the play begins. The Poeta announces
to Don Cristóbal: 'Usted es un puntal del teatro, don Cristóbal. Todo el teatro nace de
usted. Hubo una vez un poeta en Inglaterra, que se llamaba Shakespeare, que hizo un
personaje que se llamaba Falstaff, que es hijo suyo' (OC III: 455).

También amanece así todos los días sobre los campos y las ciudades y el
público olvida su medo mundio de sueños para entrar en los mercados
como tú en to casa, en la escena, zapaterilla prodigiosa.   (*OC* II: 377)

But the public should *olvidar su medio mundo de sueños*. The implication to
be derived from the lesson of the shoemaker's wife is that the audience, rather
than lapsing into sheer identification with character, must be as alert as
possible to this magical journey and not be manipulated by the
Autor/puppet-master.[21] The Autor is silver-tongued and sly, exposing speech
as a verbal masquerade designed to entice.[22]

In the prologue, the Autor will beg for pardon (in clearly ironic tones) for
his meddling in the God-like creation of the Zapatera:

> . . . el poeta pide perdón a las Musas por haber transigido en esta prisión de
> la zapaterilla, por intentar divertir a un grupo de gentes, pero les promete
> en cambio, más adelante, abrir los escotillones de la escena para que
> vuelvan a salir las copas falsas, el veneno, las bibliotecas, las sombras, la
> luna fingida del verdadero teatro.   (*OC* II: 376)

The correlation of the Autor with the magician/God, resonates with
Calderón's *El gran teatro del mundo* (the support piece to the 1930 production of the play [Anderson 1991b: 14]) in which the Autor is the incarnation
of God/Dios, who begins a conversation with The World/El Mundo. Lorca's
Autor seems to retain some sense of the omnipotent God-creator (even if he
himself is answerable to the Muses) in terms of the correlation between the
religious miracles and the creation of a magical theatrical world.

Furthermore, we may be reminded of Calderón's *El mágico prodigioso*,
which opens with a soliloquy from the Devil, and in which he tells us that 'he
has received permission from God to tempt a man and a woman in order to
see whether he can entice them both to Hell. The man, he continues, is
engaging his pagan mind in philosophical speculation about the nature of
God. The woman is a Christian and is determined to live an ascetic life. The
Devil will try to frustrate both intentions' (McKendrick 1992: 5). Our Autor
retains something of this flavour: he will manipulate his characters into a

---

[21] The Autor therefore shares elements of the unreliable narrator, examples of which
are manifold, particularly in picaresque literature. The unreliable narrator is like Bakhtin's
'image of the fool – either of actual simpleton or the mask of a rogue' (Bakhtin [1934–5]:
402).

[22] We might describe the ambiguity of the words of the Autor as an example of
'double-voicedness'. For Bakhtin, language is 'double-voiced', or 'dialogic'. He explains
these terms with reference to Dostoevsky's predisposition to dialogism: 'In every voice he
could hear two contending voices, in every gesture he detected confidence and lack of
confidence simultaneously; he perceived the profound ambiguity, even multiple ambiguity, of every phenomenon' (Bakhtin [1929]: 30). The Autor seems to highlight this
trickster-like 'split' in expression – we might say that the Autor facilitates the split
between signifier and signified.

series of suppositions, persuading the shoemaker's wife to fall in love and the shoemaker to stick by his wife. The intentions of the Autor may be benign or malignant but both attitudes speak of his omnipotence. Kernan has written on the correlation between poet/playwright and magician and sees the ambivalence of 'the magician Prospero' who reflects 'divided and distinguished attitudes towards theatre', mingled with, 'earlier Renaissance images of the poet as religious and secular saviour' or 'as the courtier in the palace of a great prince'. Thus a magician/playwright/poet is at once 'a philosopher who communicates with and commands spirits who control the universe', and simultaneously 'a mere trickster or sleight-of-hand artist' (Kernan 1979: 155). The master of ceremonies, the Autor dressed as a magician, presents a double-edged metaphor, for he may not be all that he seems. The Autor appears out of the trickster-like 'crack' between any meaning and its opposite and stands apart from the world, revealing it to be a construction much as a magician reveals his tricks. Culture and 'truths', his presence seems to suggest, are fragile constructions, strengthened and sustained by belief.

The ambiguous magician is at once 'a man whose horizons were both limitless and limited – a self-contained paradox' (Traister 1984: 1). In the Renaissance his image became fused with the explorations into new scientific fields of learning, becoming a metaphor for the ambiguous state of knowledge, the 'paradox of superhuman power that is humanly limited' (Traister 1984: 1) and seemed poised between rationalism and superstition. Lorca's Autor appears to have inherited this tradition. At once poet, philosopher and trickster, he symbolises power, but a power that seems humanly limited rather than divine.

AUTHOR(ITY) AND THE LAUGHTER OF SIGNS

The framing device of the prologue, presented by the Autor, inscribes a point of view. The Autor is presented as the creator of this marvellous world. But his claims to authority are systematically evacuated in a series of clues. In Velázquez's painting of *Las Meninas*, the inclusion of the painter himself seems designed to add credibility to an impossible painting while simultaneously belying the authority of the spectacle – the King and Queen reflected in the mirror do not exist in the painting thus revealing its fictitiousness (see Foucault 1970: 3–16). In this case, the inclusion of an Autor cannot be taken as a clue to the 'authority' of *La zapatera prodigiosa* but rather similarly engineers an anti-mimetic split – exposing the spectacle (the Autor included) as merely appearances.

Lorca's Autor seems likewise to include elements of both the cunning trickster and the mystical shaman. The shifting dialectics of creator/created; manipulator/manipulated are performed dazzlingly before our eyes so that what emerges is not an authorial intent with a public desperate to discern the author's meaning, but a dialogue between audience and Autor, more a Faustian pact than any notion of authority/submission.

What then of the letter, which the Autor carries on stage, and which is never opened? Does this contain the key to the meaning of the piece? The presence of the letter flaunts and mocks our desire to know the truth and at the same time frustrates it. This letter is like the purloined letter of Edgar Allen Poe's short story, which, as Lacan has pointed out (1972: 28–54), we know exceedingly little about:

> ... the tale leaves us in virtually total ignorance of the sender, no less than of the contents, of the letter [. . .] Love letter or conspiratorial letter, letter of betrayal or letter of mission, letter of summons or letter of distress, we are assured of but one thing: the Queen must not bring it to the knowledge of her lord and master [. . .] the letter is the symbol of a pact.

Perhaps the letter carried by the Autor is a letter of summons, and the Autor is about to be led off by the censors. Or perhaps it contains some other secret which has nothing to do with the play. The contents of the letter are in fact irrelevant. The letter is a presence which disguises an absence. Like Lacan's signifiers, it is not significant in itself, but rather its importance lies in terms of the dialectical relationships which are involved around it – like a catalyst. More important, then, is its position and relation to others in a 'symbolic circuit'. It becomes, 'a shifting pivot around which a pattern of human relationships rotates' (Muller and Richardson 1988: 59). It is symbolic of a pact, the relationship between audience and Autor as the audience enters the liminal theatrical space. The letter is a 'parade of erudition' (Lacan 1972: 37) designed to expose the Autor as a 'magician repeating his tricks before our eyes' (Lacan 1972: 37).

In an essay entitled, 'Narratorial Authority and "The Purloined Letter" ', Chambers (1988: 285–306) writes that: 'to tell a story is to exercise power (it is even called the power of narration), and authorship is cognate with authority'. But if the function of a dramatic prologue is traditionally to narrate the story/set the scene, as we have already seen, Lorca's prologues establish a gap between the narrative and the events on stage. Chambers' piece is interesting as it conceives of the art of narration as a dialogue between reader and author:

> ... authority is not an absolute, something inherent in a specific individual or in that individual's discourse; it is relational, the result of an act of authorization on the part of those subject to the power and hence something to be earned. (Chambers 1988: 285)

Chambers relates this relationship to the notion of a conversation. However, he points out that 'the act of narration is a process of disclosure'. For as soon as the knowledge of the narrator is imparted to the narratee, the narrator loses his privileged position of authority. Chambers refers to certain 'tricks of the trade' that a teacher must invoke to maintain interest: 'divulgence is never complete, the telling of the ultimate secret is indefinitely deferred – and it most often transpires, in art as in education, that there is no ultimate secret'. There is a sense then, maintains Chambers, that narration is a kind of seduction. The final irony in this seduction is the fact that 'there is no ultimate secret'. The Autor's letter flaunts and mocks, yet never satisfies, our desire to know the truth. Whatever it contains, the function of the letter is to extend a simple invitation to the play.

Turning for a moment to Lorca's *La sabiduría: El loco y la loca*, we find that the Maestro is fully compatible with this definition of pedagogy as a trickster-like drawing of the listeners into the argument, but supplying no 'narrative secret':[23]

Maestro:	(*Dentro de la escuela*) Ya os he enseñado la esfera armilar. El mar es celeste y la tierra es de todos los colores.
Niño:	¿Sin que se te olvida ninguno?
Maestro:	Ninguno. La tierra es extraordinariamente grande, pero se puede reducir su tamaño si nosotros queremos.
Los niños:	¿Cómo?
Maestro:	¡Silencio! La tierra tiene cuatro puntos cardinales. ¡Oh maravilla! Norte, Sur, Este y Oeste.
Los niños:	Norte, Sur, Este y Oeste.
Maestro:	Nostros podíamos cambiar la superficie de la tierra si dijéramos: 'Hay cuatro puntos cardinales: Oeste, Este, Sur y Norte'.
Los niños:	Oeste. . .

The teacher then lowers his voice and, with a theatrical 'ssh!', draws the listeners in to hear the secret:

Maestro:	Chitón. Será peligroso. Y además ya se ha escrito la geografía.
Los niños:	Geografía es la ciencia que trata, etc., etc.
Maestro:	Muy bien. El Norte es una pera de cien kilos pintada de blanco. El Sur, una rueda de papel. El Este, un remo de cristal y el Oeste, un ala diminuta [. . .]
El Inspector:	(*Entrando*) ¿Qué está usted diciendo?
Maestro:	Explico geografía.
Inspector:	¿Qué geografía?

[23] I am grateful to John London for drawing my attention to the presence of the trickster (the Maestro) in this play. I am grateful to Manuel Fernández Montesinos for sending me a copy of the Spanish manuscript of this text.

Maestro: Mi geografía.
Inspector: Me veré obligado a dar parte a la superioridad. El Ministerio
                  de Instrucción Pública no tolera abusos.

The teacher divests language of its authority, divorcing words from their usual contexts within academic discourse to create poetic imagery. The Inspector declares that he will have to 'report you to the *authorities*'.[24] The teacher is abusing his position as the voice of authority, the voice who should hand out the official 'truth' by rote. Instead he provides no answers, only the play of signs, leaving the children to draw their own conclusions.

Returning to *La zapatera prodigiosa*, just as the letter provokes and frustrates our desire to know, the whole prologue delivered by the Autor serves to whet our appetite for what is to come afterwards. It creates a suspense within the audience, as it is a framing device which allows us to see only what is presented to us by the Autor. Hence the screams of the shoemaker's wife are slightly off stage, in a blind spot which is just out of our range of vision: '¡Ya voy!', while the Autor shouts back, 'No tengas tanta impaciencia en salir'. The framing device of the prologue therefore presents us with the threshold of the 'unseen yet', with the encroaching danger. It is a curiously seductive device. We want to know more, to see more. If this gap is predicated on an absence then we want to fill that absence with meaning. The prologue therefore incites the scopophilic and epistemophilic drives – a process that we shall also see at work in the scene of the Duendes in *Amor de Don Perlimplín con Belisa en su jardín* (this scene is discussed at length in chapter two).[25] The function of the prologue is therefore to draw the audience into the story. But the depiction of the Autor as magician (in a parallel with the puppet-master and his play-within-a-play which manipulates the Zapatera) holds out a warning: we should not be hypnotised into acquiescence with all that we behold. As Soufas (1996: 51) notes, 'a figure who has pretended to be an authoritative spokesperson for theater at this moment looks very like a vaude-ville magician who has just performed a trick'.

Lorca mentioned in some interviews his view that 'authority' should be reassigned to the playwright. Lorca's understanding of 'authority' in this case seems to involve an increased commitment or engagement on the part of the audience. The audience is lazy, and it should be made to react. Lorca's notion of 'authority in the theatre' therefore involves having the authority to stage a dialogue, which works on different levels, and which demands attention from the spectators.

The prologue to *La zapatera prodigiosa* appears to open in the middle of a

24 From London's (1996) translation of the play.
25 The duendes here may remind us of the magicians of the *Commedia dell'arte*. Mowat (1981: 281–303) writes that the *Commedia* magicians 'use charms to cudgel and torment their enemies'.

conversation. We, the audience, have just spoken. We have addressed the Autor, accusing him of presenting us with a play which is not to our taste. His opening line is a response to our supposed address:

> Respetable público [. . .] (*Pausa*) No; respetable público, no; público sola-
> mente, y no es que el autor no considere al público respetable, todo lo
> contrario, sino que detrás de esta palabra hay como un delicado temblor de
> miedo y una especie de súplica para que el auditorio sea generoso con la
> mímica de los autores y el artificio del ingenio.   (*OC* II: 375–6)

The Autor anticipates the fear and disgust of the implied audience. We cannot help but respond – either we agree with this supposition of our views, this putting words into our mouths, or we do not. In Manet's *Bar at Le Folies-Bergère* we discover that we are looking at the barmaid, who is blushing in recognition of a remark just directed at her by ourselves, from the position of a French bourgeois gentleman of the late nineteenth century. We find that we are being reflected back in a particular subject position, as part of a dialogue where our position and ideas are being inferred. In this case, we are immediately engaged in conversation with the Autor. Yet just as the Autor anticipates the fear and displeasure of the audience, he simultaneously irritates by suggesting that, whether the audience like it or not, he is the Author-God, and we must submit to his reason. This tack is clearly provocative and marks one instance of a series of ways in which Lorca seeks to elicit response from the audience throughout his theatre in order encourage participation. Thus, rather than a mimetic reflection of Lorca himself, we should view the Autor as a provocative figure who challenges us to defy him. The prologue is therefore haunted by the spirit of the trickster-like drawing in of the audience, as the Autor sets up a dialogue between Autor and spectators, and between audience and the rest of the plot, and then theatrically disappears to watch the results.

Dragón, dated 1928 or later (Llafranque 1987: 114–17), is unfinished, and consists of just the prologue delivered by the Director, who is 'vestido de frac': 'Me atrevo a presentar a ustedes una comedia del amor. Una nueva comedia del amor mágico. Su realidad es absoluta si ustedes la meditan un poco' (Llafranque 1987: 115). Once again, the *prologuista* wants the audience to enter into a new type of reality:

> . . . Vienen ustedes al teatro como van por la vida, procurando no romper
> las sutilísimas paredes de la realidad de cada día. Abrazados con vuestras
> mujeres, con vuestras hijas, con vuestras novias, sin atreveros a sacar la
> mano al aire prodigioso y libre de la realidad verdadera.
>
> (Llafranque 1987: 115)

This is the 'evasión' from the world into a magical plane, where signs can be reconstituted through paradox and juxtaposition. The Director of this prologue seems more overtly aggressive than the Autor of *La zapatera prodigiosa*, and again the theme of the magician runs throughout:

> Pero yo, como director de escena, no estoy en este caso (*Hace un gesto raro y se quita el sombrero de copa. Mete la mano y saca tres palomas que echa a volar por los bastidores. Se lo vuelve a poner*) No. Yo podría decirles a ustedes varias cosas que les producirían disgusto, miedo, sí, miedo, pero prefiero ordenar mi comedia sin meterme en la vidas de los demás. Já já já [. . .] no me gusta veros tan seguros ahí sentados ¿seguros de qué? ¿De qué están ustedes seguros? (Llafranque 1987: 115–16)

The flamboyant, mocking arrogance of the Director in this case is a precursor to the flowery sarcasm of the later Autor. The aim is once more the engagement of the audience through anger and irritation. Like the magician of Thomas Mann's short story, 'Mario and the Magician' (1929), the audience is depicted as a comfortable, bourgeois mass, open to persuasion, while the Director is rendered a dangerous confidence-man. His contempt is provocatively clear as he remarks that, 'no quiero decir respetable público porque el director no respeta al público, señoras y señores. No me gusta. Además no sois eso, sino hombres y mujeres o mejor niños y niñas' (Llafranque 1987: 116), and he concludes with a flourish:

> Así pues, buenas noches (*Se oyen unos rugidos*). Já já já. Voy a echar azúcar a ése para que se porte bien durante el espectáculo [. . .] (*Se quita el sombrero de copa y éste ilumina por dentro con una luz erde. El director de escena lo vuelca y sale un chorro de agua encendida.*) Ustedes perdonen.
> (Llafranque 1987: 116)

Rather than being an indication of Lorca's presumed contempt for the audience of the 1920s and 1930s, the whole exchange is raised to the level of the performative. The Autor/ Director figure is playing out the trickster-function. The Autor/Director insults, cajoles and instructs loftily, and then withdraws to see the muddle he has produced. Rather than a mere mimetic depiction of Lorca's desires, the Autor/Director presents us with an elaborate and sophisticated performance, designed to provoke a response, to lead the audience, through the trickster-function, into the liminal theatrical space.

Retablillo de Don Cristóbal (underway in 1928) and *El sueño de la vida* (mentioned in two interviews in 1936), both feature prologues at the start of the play, which then open out to feature dialogue within the action of the plot between the *prologuista* and other characters. The theme of dialogue, beginning to be established in the plays we have already examined, is now finding full force as the characters enter into polemic with each other. The *Retablillo* is a comic farce which features Don Cristóbal as a doctor who kills off a patient for his money, and then marries Rosita (an arrangement engineered between himself and Rosita's mother). After the wedding, Cristóbal falls

asleep and Rosita entertains her lovers. The play descends into pure farce as
Rosita gives birth to quadruplets and Cristóbal chases her mother around the
room as Rosita continues to give birth. But before Cristóbal can punish his
wife, the Director, who appeared earlier in the Prologue, intervenes and
brings the action to a close. The play begins with a prologue in which the poet
begins:

> Hombres y mujeres atención; niño, cállate [. . .] Será necesario que las
> muchachos cierren los abanicos y las niñas saquen su pañuelito de encajes.
> (*OC* II: 675)

Then, looking around to see if he is being observed, he remarks that, 'quiero
deciros que yo sé cómo nacen las rosas y cómo se crían las estrellas de mar,
pero' (*OC* II: 676), and is suddenly interrrupted by the Director: 'Haga usted
el favor de callarse. El prólogo termina donde se dice: "Voy a planchar los
trajes de la compañía" ' (*OC* II: 676). The prologue is being extended to
encompass the whole play. Moreover, the *prologuista* is no longer a generic
poet/director figure, but has split into the arguing personae of the Poeta and
Director. The audience is witness to a discussion regarding the play's characters. The Director's solution is to round up the characters by brute force and
cart them off, thereby bringing an end to the dramatic action. But it is less
than clear as to where authority resides regarding the content of the play. The
notion of a dialogue with different narratorial positions is beginning to
emerge very clearly.

   El sueño de la vida (1936) (also known as *Comedia sin título*) is the articulation of a more pronounced dialogue between the author of the text and the
spectators. It takes the form of a dialogue between Author, Prompter,
members of the audience and the cast of Shakespeare's *A Midsummer Night's
Dream*. It opens with a prologue delivered by an Autor figure who offers the
audience a '¡sermón!, sí, ¡sermón! ¿Por qué hemos de ir siempre al teatro
para ver lo que pasa y no para ver lo que nos pasa?'. The Autor's assault on
the audience is much more violent that in *La zapatera prodigiosa*:

> Con toda modestia debo advertir que nada es inventado. Angeles, sombras,
> voces, liras de nieve y sueños existen y vuelan entre vosotros, tan reales
> como la lujuria, las monedas que lleváis en el bolsillo, o el cáncer latente
> en el hermoso seno de la mujer, o el labio cansado del comerciante.
> Venís al teatro con el afán único de divertiros y tenéis autores a los que
> pagáis, y es muy justo, pero hoy el poeta nos hace una encerrona porque
> quiere y aspira a conmover vuestros corazones enseñando las cosas que no
> queréis ver, gritando las simplísimas verdades que no queréis oír.
> (*OC* II: 1069)

The notion of opening up new possibilities in the poetic plane paves the way for Lorca to direct an attack on the audience. The Autor sees his role as *agent provocateur*:

> ... todo lo que hacéis es buscar caminos para no enterarse de nada. Cuando suena el viento, para no entender lo que dice tocáis la pianola; para no ver el inmenso torrente de lágrimas que nos rodea cubrís de encajes las ventanas; para poder dormir tranquilos y a callar el perenne grillo de la conciencia inventáis las casas de caridad. (*OC* II: 1070)

Rather than escapist entertainment, this type of theatre will force the audience to face up to things. The Autor wishes to place the audience in the street outside:

> La realidad empieza porque el autor no quiere que os sintáis en el teatro sino en mitad de la calle; no quiere, por tanto, hacer poesía, ritmo, literatura, quiere dar una pequeña lección a vuestros corazones, para eso es poeta, pero con gran modestia. (*OC* II: 1070)

Provocation is the means by which people are made to sit up and take notice. Art must take its place in politics and culture. Carlos Bauer tells us that this play alludes to a specific historical event that occurred several years after Lorca wrote *El público*: The Revolution of October 1934.[26] Bauer (1983: xix) writes that 'the events of that October profoundly affected García Lorca's generation, and the author's transformation on stage, from a man only interested in his art to a man who openly sides with the Revolution, parallels what happened to many artists of that generation. The Revolution of October 1934 was almost universally viewed as a moment in history when the artist had to forget "art for art's sake", had to take sides, had to support the people'.

If the poet has to take sides, then the audience are also encouraged to take issue with events:

> El espectador está tranquilo porque sabe que la comedia no se va a fijar en él, ¡pero qué hermoso sería que de pronto lo llamaran de las tablas y le hicieran hablar, y el sol de la escena quemara su pálido rostro de emboscado! (*OC* II: 1070)

In a dramatic parallel with Pirandello's plays, in this play spectators rise up

---

[26] London (1996: 14–15) writes that, 'in October 1934, a Socialist Workers' Alliance in Asturias rose in armed rebellion against a new national government considered fascist. The Foreign Legion and Moroccan troups were sent to put down the revolt and the uprising reached the proportions of civil war. Some 1,500–2,000 people were believed killed and 30,000 people were imprisoned on political charges. The European press reported on the atrocities committed by both sides. When the Woodcutter mentions the "moon in October" in his song, he therefore alludes to the Asturian revolt as well as a more famous episode in Revolutionary Russia'.

out of their seats and enter into dialogue with the actors. Two strands are becoming clearer now: an increased commitment to provocation of the audience, coupled with a sense of the theatrical space as an arena for ritual acts, where real life is played out to the full. At the end of the prologue, the Autor exclaims:

	Pero ¿cómo se llevaría el olor del mar a una sala de teatro, o cómo se inunda de estrellas el patio de butacas?
Espectador:	(*En butacas*) Quitándole el tejado.
Autor:	¡No me interrumpa!
Espectador:	Tengo derecho. ¡He pagado mi butaca!
Autor:	Pagar la butaca no implica derecho de interrumpir al que habla, ni mucho menos juzgar la obra [. . .]
Espectador 1:	La única ley del teatro es el juicio del espectador.

(*OC* II: 1071)

In this space, there is no authority, just the dramatic playing out of an interaction between Autor and audience. When the first spectator shouts out, 'la única ley del teatro es el juicio del espectador', Lorca is placing responsibility at the door of the spectator just as much as the author. In this emptying out of the theatrical space, authority is absent: we find merely the clash of different meanings.

The voices of the Autor and Espectador are joined by that of the Criado, a Voz, the Apuntador, the Actriz 1°, the Hombre, Leñador, Nick Bottom and others. At the end of the fragment we have available, the Tramoyista cries out that, '¡El pueblo ha roto las puertas!', and the theatre symbolically goes up in flames.

These strains of the importance of dialogue, provocation and the stage as a ritual arena find their fullest expression in *El público* (1930), in which the call to a revolution of theatre practices seems curiously to anticipate the events of October 1934. Lorca uses transgressive language to launch a violent assault on the sensibilities of the audience, using language to explore the taboos which issue from the body: namely, death and decay, and homosexuality. (These notions will be discussed further in chapter V.) Provocation highlights the desire for dialogue with the audience which may be seen as part of a growing sense of the need to incorporate social praxis into the theatre.

De Ros (1996) has written of *El público* that the 'disparity of interpretations is a sign of the text's polyphony, which subverts the monologic discourse of the author's voice'. *El público* and *El sueño de la vida* demonstrate a desire to move towards dialogism.[27] *El público* stages the playing out

---

[27] In Bakhtin's theory of dialogism, 'there is no existence, no meaning, no word or thought that does not enter into dialogue with the other, that does not exhibit intertextuality in both time and space' (Morris 1994: 247).

of different registers and different voices, but leaves it up to the spectator to muse as to meanings – this is described as *polyphonic*.[28] As the fourth wall is completely broken down, the stage becomes the site for the playing out of 'real concerns'. As the Autor remarks in *El sueño de la vida*: 'Por eso yo no quiero actores sino hombres de carne y mujeres de carnes, y el que no quiera oír que se tape los oídos' (*OC* II: 1073).

Whereas the Autor contained elements of both shaman and trickster, in *El público* these two are very firmly distinguished and their disparate voices are clearly differentiated. The trickster takes the form of the Prestidigitador, who, like the Director, is responsible for the 'teatro del aire libre', the spectacle of light and show. The Hombre 1°, on the other hand, wants to inaugurate the 'teatro bajo la arena'.[29] The idea of 'beneath the sand' contains elements of ritual. Hence the shaman/trickster notion becomes the struggle between Dionysiac and Apolline forces, with the Hombre 1° as sacrificial victim. This is a stage which is, 'a pageant without footlights and without a division into performers and spectators', which is how Bakhtin (1965: 7) describes the scenes of carnival (to be explored more fully in chapter five).

In this new theatrical space, which could be described as 'non-theological' following Derrida's gloss on Artaud, we find not the 'Author-God', but a liminal space where signs interact in a dialogical relationship. Cunliffe (1997: 347–65) compares Bakhtinian dialogism with Derridean deconstruction – both are 'eminently playful, and [. . .] have similar aims and objectives'; namely to 'shatter the foundations of tradition, ideology or any kind of closure'. Like Bhabha's (1983) definitions of a 'hybrid text', this is a space in which, 'the insignia of authority becomes a mask, a mockery', and diegetics are replaced by dialogics. The theatrical space becomes dialogistic, a liminal space where actor and spectator are on an equal footing, and signs and meanings blend and clash.

---

[28] Bakhtin's notion of polyphony is distinguished from monoglossia which is characterised by a stable, unified language. Polyphony can also mean the simultaneity of official and non-official discourses within the same language.

[29] Two articles by Lorca are relevant here. The article entitled, 'Sol y Sombra' (*OC* III: 391–2), which speaks of the importance of the bull-ring in terms of ritual; secondly, the 'Juego y teoría del duende' (*OC* III: 306–18), in which 'duende' is derived from ritual, and manifests itself as a magical power to be tapped into and be felt by artists, linked to life and death.

SECTION II

THE TRICKSTER, GENDER AND MASQUERADE

II

PERLIMPLÍN'S SEDUCTION: FEMININITY, MASQUERADE AND THE *TROMPE L'OEIL*

> One face, one voice, one habit, and two persons,
> A Perspective, that is, and is not.
>
> William Shakespeare, *Twelfth Night*, v., i., 224

'The *femme fatale*', writes Mary Ann Doane, 'is the figure of a certain discursive unease, a potential epistemological trauma. For her most striking characteristic, perhaps, is that she never really is what she seems to be' (Doane 1991: 1). The *femme fatale* is larger than life, crudely drawn in large, sweeping strokes which seem to beckon one to peep beyond their surface to the dark, unknown world beneath. In this chapter, I argue that the same is true of García Lorca's 1926 play, *Amor de Don Perlimplín con Belisa en su jardín*.[1] This 'boceto de un drama grande', as Lorca termed the work in 1933, with its scanty stage directions and teasingly ambiguous comments from the author, is a seductive enigma, a dangerous mystery to be 'revealed, unmasked, discovered' (Doane 1991: 1).

Critics have been divided in their analyses and interpretations of this play. Most view it as a reflective piece on the nature of love – with spiritual love thrown into relief by carnal desire. But while some interpret Perlimplín's death as an altruistic sacrifice born of his love for Belisa (Honig 1944; Gasner 1954; Lima 1963; Lewis 1971),[2] others cite Perlimplín as a 'viejo verde', or *viejo celoso*, by his own admission a 'monigote sin fuerza', who takes revenge on a young girl out of anger at her rejection of him and due to the fear she inspires in him (Allen 1974; Bacarisse 1992).

The farcical tones, coupled with Lorca's comments that the play was merely 'el boceto de un drama grande' (*OC* III: 521) which he later intended to expand, 'con toda la complejidad que tiene' (*OC* III: 521),[3] have often led

---

1 In Ucelay's (1990: 130–1) excellent companion piece to the play, she suggests that the work must have been finished in 1926 as García Lorca read it to Dalí and Buñuel at that time.

2 For example, Lewis (1971: 248) writes '[Perlimplín's] love for Belisa is so selfless that he has created the image by which she can discover love [. . .] he gives his life that she will learn the meaning of love'.

3 From 'Una interesante iniciativa: El poeta Federico García Lorca habla de los clubs teatrales', *El Sol*, 1933 (*OC* III: 519–22).

this piece to be regarded as a minor farce (Fergusson 1957; Brown 1972; Edwards 1980).[4] G. G. Brown (1972), furthermore, suggests that Lorca was still 'searching for the right formula and balance when he wrote this piece'. The play is seen as a minor experiment *en route* to the great tragedies. I would contend, however, that the play is in fact deeply complex, and also a 'creación clave' in Lorca's dramatic output.[5] Bacarisse (1992: 72) suggests that the play's unpopularity[6] may be due to the difficulty in locating its import and remarks that 'if this is so then some blame must be laid at the door of the creator and it *should* therefore be labelled minor'. However, I suggest that the difficulty of locating an ultimate meaning is a function of a text in which univocal referential meaning is constantly undermined by a play of plurivocal signifiers. Neat categorisations are resisted, giving rise to a disconcerting surface tension produced by the collision of referential meanings. Doueihi (1993: 193–201) writes that such a process is characteristic of trickster narratives, in which: 'language becomes profound. On the other hand, the story loses its solidity and breaks down into an open-ended play of signifiers' (199). Thus:

> . . . the illusion of a clear, unique, referential meaning given by the rhetorical body of the discourse is precisely what the trickster, as discourse, is able to conjure forth . . .   (Doueihi 1993: 199)

At the same time, however, the 'trickster, as discourse', for Doueihi (1993: 199), is able to open us 'to the way our minds function to construct an apparently solid but ultimately illusory reality out of what is on another level a play of signs'. Multiple readings are sustained by the multilayered discourse of *Amor de Don Perlimplín* – a discourse whose profundity is represented by the motif of the veil. The perpetual unmasking or unveiling of meanings in this

---

4   Edwards (1980: 31–59) includes the play under a section entitled, 'The Minor Plays'. He cites the tradition of farce, 'a rich and long established one in Spanish literary history' (40).

5   Ucelay (1990); Bacarisse (1992) and Fernández Cifuentes (1986) likewise argue that the play should not be seen as a minor work. Fernández Cifuentes (1986: 116) suggests, furthermore, that the play constitutes a major step towards the author's 'teatro irrepresentable'.

6   Buñuel states in his memoirs (1982: 104) that at a reading of the play given by Lorca himself: 'de la concha del apuntador sale un gnomo que dice: "Pues bien, respetable público, entonces don Perlimplín y Belisa". Yo interrumpo la lectura dando una palmada en la mesa y digo: " – Basta, Federico. Es una mierda". El palidece, cierra el manuscrito y mira a Dalí. Este, con su vozarrón, corrobora: "Buñuel tiene razón. Es una mierda". No llegué a saber cómo terminaba la obra'. However, Isabel García Lorca (sister to the poet) maintains that the play was her brother's favourite ('predilecta') (from a private personal interview at the Fundación Federico García Lorca, Madrid, 12 February 1990). Certainly in interview Lorca claimed that the play, 'a mí me divierte mucho', in 'Un estreno de García Lorca en el Español en gran función de gala' (*OC* II: 518).

play will be seen to be a function and effect of this complex, tiny masterpiece.

On the surface of things, the plot of *Amor de Don Perlimplín con Belisa en su jardín* (1926) is deceptively simple. The characters are stock figures of farce (drawn from the eighteenth-century *aleluyas*)[7] and the story is a variation on the age-old theme of adultery and revenge. Don Perlimplín, after years of devoting himself solely to his books ('yo con mis libros tengo bastante' [*OC* II: 461]), is persuaded by his maid, Marcolfa, to contemplate betrothal to Belisa, his junior by many years. Belisa's mother, splendidly dressed in 'una gran peluca dieciochesca llena de pájaros, cintas y abalorios' (*OC* II: 464), agrees to the match, adding to Belisa that, 'Don Perlimplín tiene muchas tierras' (*OC* II: 465). Perlimplín is aroused by the secrets whispered by Marcolfa to entice him into marriage ('el matrimonio tiene grandes encantos, mi señor. No es lo que se ve por fuera. Está lleno de cosas ocultas' [*OC* II: 461]) seduced by the verbal repartee ('-¿Sí? -¡Sí!; -Pero, ¿por qué sí? -¡Pues porque sí!' [*OC* II: 459]) and later sexually excited by the idea and anticipation of Belisa ('está mi casa llena de rumores secretos y el agua se entibia sola en los vasos' [*OC* II: 468]). However, he is simultaneously terrified: 'cuando yo era niño una mujer estranguló a su esposo. Era zapatero. No se me olvida. Yo con mis libros tengo bastante' (*OC* II: 461). In his imagination, Don Perlimplín renders Belisa a *femme fatale* – she has quite literally become the incarnation of death for him. Consequently, after the intervening marriage and betrayal, he creates the fantasy Joven de la Capa Roja, tailor-made to Belisa's requirements, with the purpose of satisfying Belisa by proxy. Apprehensive that he will never satisfy Belisa (she hyperbolically commits adultery with five men, 'representantes de las cinco razas de la tierra' [*OC* II: 480]), Perlimplín seeks escape through transgressive madness and then death. His final act is to kill the Joven de la Capa Roja and himself – his revenge being to leave Belisa endlessly searching for the lost lover that she will never find: '¿dónde está el joven de la capa roja? [. . .] Díos mío. ¿Dónde está?' (*OC* II: 496). While the play parades as a farce, it has deadly serious undertones.

The image of the veil, with its suggestive dialectic of surface and depth, will be seen as a persistent trope in this discussion of *Amor de Don Perlimplín*. Veils have traditionally been the prerogative of feminine seduction and feminine allure. In the play, femininity (in its expression here as the archetypal veiled *femme fatale*, embodied in the character of Belisa), can be seen as an allegory for Perlimplín's journey into the world of his dreams. The *femme fatale* also represents Perlimplín's fear of the feminine and, through

7 As Helen Grant (1964) illustrates, the Spanish *aleluyas* were a kind of vignette or comic strip of the eighteenth century. Ucelay (1990: 13–31) expounds on this theme. Lorca subtitled the play 'aleluya erótica'.

displacement, his fear of approaching death. Veiling will be seen to represent the desire for discovery, the epistemological drive in relation to the visual and its limits, the equation of seeing and knowing which is accepted as the logic of Western thought.[8] Hence the play articulates the process of the tearing away of layers of meaning, on the part of the audience as well as Perlimplín, in an attempt to reveal the truth of the plot and of life. The *femme fatale*, and her accoutrement the veil, suggest the seductiveness as well as the deceptiveness of the visual medium.[9] The twin concepts of masquerade and unmasking or unveiling (characteristic of the trickster-figure) provide the key to a new understanding of this play whose theme is epistemology and its relation to the visual medium. Two plots can be seen to operate in relation to this theme. A plot motivated by the nature of truth, epistemology and the visual masquerades as the surface text of a farce concerning love, adultery and revenge.

THE IMPORTANCE OF THE ROLE OF THE *DUENDES*

The scene of the Duendes, in the *cuadro segundo* has been largely overlooked by critics,[10] yet close analysis of it produces fresh perspectives on the significance of the whole piece. The Duendes are trickster-figures, who emerge out of the twilight ('penumbra'), that liminal time between night and day, reflected by the grey curtain they draw over the stage. These trickster-figures are sprites or goblins – fantastical, unreal creatures who may almost be a trick of the imagination. The Duendes sit '*en la concha del apuntador, cara al público*', occupying the liminal area that lies between the action of the play and the space of the spectators. They do not participate in the action, but rather comment on the events taking place behind the curtain: the *noche de bodas* of Don Perlimplín and Belisa. The Duendes do not actively meddle in the plot, but through suggestion insinuate cruel events and mishap: 'mañana

---

[8]　This point has been made often. See for example Rorty (1980) who believes that this visual metaphor has generated all sorts of deep errors and should be discarded. Some femininist studies also decry the pervasiveness of visual metaphors in epistemology on the grounds that vision is a peculiarly masculine sense; for example Grotowski and Fox-Keller (1983).

[9]　My reading of Belisa is indebted to Mary Ann Doane's (1991) book on the *femme fatale* of *film noir*. She depicts the *femme fatale* as a symbol of visual deceptiveness and seductiveness and the elusiveness of 'truth'.

[10]　Most critics merely describe the Duendes as little goblins. Allen (1974: 49–51) does engage with the scene, observing that their 'remarks disclose that disguise (or suppression) is the best stimulus to curiosity'. Allen is interested in the sexual connotations of their speech. He describes them as the 'phallic aspect' of Perlimplín's 'ego consciousness'.

lo sabrá toda la gente'. They present themselves as a diversion, a showy distraction, a screen behind which the real drama rages:

Duende 1°:	¿Cómo te va por lo oscurillo?
Duende 2°:	Ni bien ni mal, compadrillo.
Duende 1°:	Ya estamos.
Duende 2°:	Y qué te parece. Siempre es bonito tapar las faltas ajenas.
Duende 1°:	Y que luego el público se encargue de destaparlas ...

(OC II: 473)

They simultaneously hint, however, that the distraction they flaunt may be nothing more than an elaborate and empty charade, and that the noise they make drowns out nothing but silence:

Duende 2°:	Porque si las cosas no se cubren con toda clase de precauciones [. . .]
Duende 1°:	No se descubren nunca.
Duende 2°:	Y sin ese tapar y destapar [. . .]
Duende 1°:	¡Qué sería de las pobres gentes!
Duende 2°:	*(Mirando la cortina)* ¡Que no quede ni una rendija!
Duende 1°:	Que las rendijas de ahora son oscuridad mañana *(Ríen)*.
Duende 2°:	Cuando las cosas están claras [. . .]
Duende 1°:	El hombre se figura que no tiene necesidad de descubrirlas.

(OC II: 473–4)

Like forerunners to Beckett's Vladimir and Estragon (Beckett 1952), their sound, fury and verbiage suggest action and presence but disguise absence and inaction: the whole play may, after all, be no more than a dream. Through showy display, the Duendes mask the events (or conversely the absence of events) taking place behind the curtain.

The Duendes perform the trickster-function in that they bring the spectators into self-consciousness, implicitly drawing attention to the audience's presence and taunting them for their desire to know what is happening behind the curtain. The Duendes mock the spectator's desire to know/see ('cuando las cosas están claras/El hombre se figura que no tiene necesidad de descubrirlas'). As the audience is engaged in spectating, relying on the visual to piece together the plot, the Duendes turn the play into a quest for meaning.[11]

As they are marginal and peripheral, the Duendes become nothing more than an empty screen which illuminates the workings of the plot and presents the implied projections of the audience. It is the desire to see/know (the scopophilic/epistemophilic drives) that urges the narrative forward. The Duendes insinuate, but it is the participation of the audience that creates the

11 Hynes (1993b) describes the association of the trickster with 'psychic explorers and adventurers'.

doubt: 'comentario quiere decir mundo' is the Duendes' pronouncement. The audience is given a role to play in the drama : they are rendered the *el qué dirán*, suspicious, plotting and driven by curiosity.

The scene of the Duendes is delightfully compact, but it has ramifications for the whole play. The Duendes are meta-players and revealers – through their mockery of the spectators' reliance on the logic of the visual for the production of truth, they simultaneously question that truth. The Duendes, I suggest, are a manifestation of Descartes' 'malicious demon of the utmost power and cunning', who employs all his energies in order to deceive: 'I shall suppose that the sky, the earth, the air, colours, shapes, sounds and all external things are merely the delusions of dreams which he has devised in order to ensnare my judgement' (Cottingham, Stoothoff and Murdoch 1985: II, 15).[12] In *Amor de Don Perlimplín*, the Duendes draw the audience's attention to the potential deceptiveness of the visual medium, suggesting that it is all too easy for us to be ensnared by what may be, after all, no more than a dream or delusion. The visual is persistently revealed as both seductive and deceptive throughout the play: there is danger and disorientation for the audience in this journey into the unknown as, through the destabilisation of the visual medium, truths are divested of their authority, rendered merely truths. Truth is therefore revealed to be 'but a surface: it would only become more profound, naked and desirable by the effect of a veil – that falls over it' (Derrida 1979: 59).[13]

In summary, through the trickster-function, the play becomes an effect of the epistemological drive, and is rendered a seductive enigma to be unmasked and revealed. What emerges in this philosophical quest for knowledge is a sense in which the epistemological search is illusory, although driven, and that there is no ultimate secret to be revealed. Artifice and masquerade are mere subterfuges or red herrings (showy displays or seductive veils) to disguise the relativity of truth and death.

[12] In the 'Juego y teoría del duende' (*OC* III: 306–18) Lorca writes of 'el otro melancólico demonillo de Descartes, pequeño como almendra verde'. A possible source for García Lorca's acquaintance with the writings of Descartes is the teachings of Ortega y Gasset. In a letter of 9 March 1923, Lorca writes to his family of his pleasure at being able to attend classes given by the philosopher at the Residencia de Estudiantes: 'además de asistir por gusto a la clase de Ortega y Gasset, pues aun cuando la asignatura que éste explica pertenece a la Facultad de Filosofía se aprenden, sin embargo, muchas cosas' (Anderson and Maurer 1997: 175). In Ortega y Gasset's 1923 publication *El tema de nuestro tiempo*, which develops his theory which can be described as 'perspectival epistemology' (Honderich 1995: 637), the philosopher writes at length of the theories of Descartes. For example, 'el entusiasmo de Descartes por las construcciones de la razón, le llevó a ejecutar una inversión completa de la perspectiva natural al hombre' (Ortega y Gasset 1923: 49).

[13] Derrida writes that, 'exhibiting, undressing, unveiling, denuding' are 'the familiar acrobatics of the metaphor of truth' (Derrida 1975: 175).

THE DREAM OF LIFE: DISTORTED VISIONS

After falling asleep on his wedding night, Don Perlimplín begins to dream. We are presented with nothing more than a figment of Perlimplín's imagination, a nightmare or hallucination precipitated by the fear he experiences in anticipation of union with Belisa. This may explain Lorca's ambiguous comments that: 'Don Perlimplín es el hombre menos cornudo del mundo. Su imaginación dormida se despierta con el tremendo engaño de su mujer; pero él luego hace cornudas a todas las mujeres que existen' (*OC* II: 993). Perlimplín is awakening into a new plane: 'me parece que han transcurrido cien años. Antes no podía pensar en las cosas extraordinarias que tiene el mundo'.[14] I argue, therefore, that the garden of the title is the symbolic space of Perlimplín's dream. The balconies erected in the *cuadro primero* are the allegorical gateways to a different level of consciousness. This is a dreamscape where black paper birds can fly through the air. In the *cuadro segundo*, the furniture is painted onto the green backdrop, and in the *cuadro tercero*, the *comedor de Perlimplín*, we are told that:

> *las perspectivas están equivocadas deliciosamente. La mesa con todos los objetos pintados como en una 'Cena' primitiva.* (*OC* II: 480)

The scene has been drawn like a piece of naive art. The table on stage looks 'real' but, were we to try to sit at it, we would discover it to be nothing but surface – a gap is inserted between the representation and the reality it depicts. Stage setting was important to Lorca: Ucelay (1990: 140–78) gives a description of the stage design intended for the productions of this play directed by the poet.[15] Therefore, while critics have posited the reference to the 'Last Supper' as evidence of the connotations of Perlimplín as a Christ-figure, in addition to the undeniable religious overtones,[16] attention should be paid to the description of the set in visual terms. The scenery in this set is a

14 This entry into the dream-world may be seen to coincide with Perlimplín's sexual awakening and initiation: Perlimplín cries out to Marcolfa: '¿en qué mundo me vas a meter?' Perlimplín's sexual awakening is symbolised by his thirst. His plaintive cry, '¿Y qué es esto que me pasa?', could be seen as a (humorous) reference, as Balboa Echevarría (1982: 105) writes, to Perlimplín's experience of his first erection.

15 Lorca's first attempt to stage *Amor de Don Perlimplín* in 1929 was thwarted by censors, but it eventually reached the stage under Lorca's direction with Pura Ucelay in 1933. Lorca paid close attention to stage-setting for his plays: he asked Salvador Dalí to design the scenery for a 1927 production of *Mariana Pineda*.

16 McDermott (1995: 211–12) provides an excellent account of the religious aspects to the play: 'as a victim of love, the enigma of Perlimplín's desire is cloaked in the red of passion and martyrdom, a profanation of the Host as a sacrifice for human love' (212).

'parodic contestation'[17] of Leonardo da Vinci's painting of the *Last Supper*, in which the perspectives are so carefully laid out for the viewer. As John Berger writes, perspective in European art since the Renaissance centres everything on the focal point of the eye of the beholder: 'the visible world is arranged for the spectator as the universe was once thought to be arranged for God' (Berger 1972: 16). By ruining the line of perspective in the stage setting, the central viewing position for the audience is disrupted as well as the focal point from which all truth emanates – all truth which relies on the visual.

We might describe this inversion of perspective as anamorphic – the technique of distortion used by Holbein for the anamorphic skull in his painting *The Ambassadors* (see Berger 1972: 89–97). For Jacques Lacan, anamorphosis gives a glimpse of what 'geometral researches into perspective allow to escape from vision' (Lacan 1979: 87). Lacan links this to a fascination with the annihilation of the subject. The distortion of perspective in this play signifies Perlimplín's (and the audience's) metaphorical entry into the chaotic world of dreams (that which is normally allowed to escape from vision, but is so patently linked to the visual medium through its expression in visual terms) – a topsy turvy dream-world where the most latent of fears can be articulated. This piece is therefore a journey into the liminal space, a *Spielraum*[18] where perspective is inverted. For the audience this signifies the entry into disorientation and danger where, armed only with eyes, ears and the imagination, they are robbed of the truth generally perceived to be afforded by the visual medium: quite literally they are deprived of their usual sense of perspective and awakened into a new way of viewing the world.[19]

We might relate the threatening distortion of perspective to events happening around the turn of the century in Spain and the rest of Europe. The end of the nineteenth and early twentieth centuries witnessed the destabilisation of the self or ego as depicted in theoretical accounts due to a conflation of new theories and themes. In the first place, the emerging field of psychoanalysis was involved in investigations into 'uncontrollable drives, the fading of subjectivity and the loss of conscious agency' (Doane 1991: 2). Awareness of the self, the ego was at once literally gaining consciousness, but simultane-

[17] Just as Magritte's famous *Ceci n'est pas une pipe* is a 'parodic contestation of earlier problematic forms' (Hutcheon 1985: 2), so this parody of the Last Supper inserts a gap between the original and the copy, rendering both dubious fictions.

[18] Barbara Babcock-Adams (1978: 32) designates the *Spielraum* as the *mundus inversus*, a world where disorder reigns.

[19] Thus the Duendes are fully compatible with Hynes' description of the trait of the trickster as being related to 'inverse perspective', where the trickster is viewed as disrupter, spoiler and thief (Hynes 1993b: 215–16). My approach to the play highlights the importance of the visual medium. Language is also undeniably important with its changes of registers and lyricism. For a discussion of the lyricism of the play see Fergusson (1957: 85–97).

ously the stable self was being decentred. The women's movements and theories emerging from psychoanalysis regarding human sexuality gave rise to shifts in the understanding of sexual difference. Advances in technology also precipitated fears surrounding the role of the human self in the universe. In addition, as Jonathan Crary observes, investigations into technologies of seeing and viewing – photography, cinema, the science of optics – meant new ways of viewing the world: 'in the texts of Marx, Bergson, Freud, and others the very apparatus that a century earlier was the site of truth becomes a model for procedures and forces that conceal, invert and mystify truth' (Crary 1990: 29). As Buci-Glucksman (1994: 129) puts it, this was 'a moment in history when the great certainties of the modernist philosophies of Progress were crumbling (Reason, Subject, linear Time, Science of a transparent reality)'. In what later became known as a 'crisis' of modernism, notions of what could be known about the world, how to gain access to truth and what constituted subjectivity received new foci and engineered a radical reordering of the world.

Perlimplín's dream can be seen as the symbolic space for the articulation of fears surrounding the destabilisation of the self, fading subjectivity and loss of control, which have been precipitated by Perlimplín's fear of ageing and approaching death. Perlimplín, immersed in a world of books ('yo con mis libros tengo bastante'), has never before noticed his advancing age. However, his betrothal to Belisa makes him sense his death for the first time, in the dual sense that her youth makes him realise his own decay, and because she represents castration.[20] Perlimplín faces his existential fears by veiling them in the form of the fearful feminine.[21] The motif of the veil becomes symbolic of the fear felt at the deceptive and seductive feminine; ideas about sexual difference and ambivalence toward the other; and also the meaning of death. Through a process of visual slippage (metonymy and metaphor),[22] the feminine (Belisa), whose accoutrement is the veil, comes to signify fears

[20] Freud (1908) writes that the fantasy of castration arises out of the child's puzzlement at anatomical differences between the sexes (the presence or absence of the penis): the child attributes its absence to the fact of its having been cut off. The boy then fears castration: a paternal threat which results in a profound castration anxiety. On a mythical level, female figures have often been associated with the threat of castration. Freud's (1922) article on Medusa relates the fear of tendrils of hair to the female pubic hair and the fearful vagina.

[21] A possible influence on Lorca of images which align the visual and death in feminine form was the work of Nietzsche (see Buci-Glucksman [1994: 129]), whose ideas were popular in Spain in the 1920s (see Sobejano 1967).

[22] Lacan (using Jakobsen's linguistic theories) uses *metonymy* and *metaphor* where Freud used *displacement* and *condensation* to refer to the slippage which takes place in a dream between one signifier and the next. I have chosen Lacanian terminology for this discussion, rather than the more historically relevant Freudian ideas, because Lacan brings together dream-work, symbols and language. *Amor de Don Perlimplín* expresses clearly

surrounding sexual difference, loss of stability, perceptual ambiguity and its implications, the inability to locate a final truth, and irrefutable death.

The audience is drawn into this imaginary quest to sift through the layers of metonymic meanings to reach the truth. Through the trickster-function, the various investigations into truth become the dangerous sites of conflict for the audience to engage with and, through the distortion of the visual medium, to experience. In *Amor de Don Perlimplín* the desire to know/see involves endless drawing back of the veil in a metonymic chain of signifiers,[23] and in the distortion of the visual in the play these signifiers are exposed. The tricksterish Duendes may have left the stage, but their influence remains. Trickster-figures are agents of chaos, but they do not stay around to take the blame for the disruption they have caused. They are best known, after all, by their entanglements. The symptom of the presence of the tricksters is expressed in the play as the highlighting of the split between signifier and signified. As the perspectives slide, the traces of lost signs are revealed and flaunted and the edges of the cultural masks are laid bare.

FEMININITY, MASCULINITY AND THE MASQUERADE

On the surface of things *Amor de Don Perlimplín* presents a plot involving adultery and revenge.[24] It can also be seen as an expression of Perlimplín's fears concerning sexual difference. The story (the marriage of the ugly old man and the beautiful young girl) is 'as old as the hills' (Cueto 1991: 93). We find versions of this plot in such diverse works as the *Cupid and Psyche* tale, Edmund Rostand's *Cyrano de Bergerac*, Crommelynck's *Le Cocu magnifique*,[25] Abbé Prévost's *Manon Lescaut* (1731),[26] *Pygmalion*

the relationship of language to knowledge and truth; whether in terms of the persuasive rhetoric used by Marcolfa; Perlimplín's creation of the Joven de la Capa Roja through whispered suggestion; or the network of signs and signifiers at play. Lacan's ideas of language seem to unite these meanings: his assertion that 'the unconscious is structured like a language' is relevant to our discussion of Perlimplín's dream.

[23] For Lacan, desire is metonymic as it involves the endless deferral and substitution of the object.

[24] The theme of adultery and the reworking of the honour code is an important motif. Lorca wrote that Perlimplín was 'español y calderoniano'. One of the motives for the censorship of the performance and confiscation of the text in 1929 was the fact that Lorca had a retired police officer on stage wearing horns: considered taboo at the time. See Ucelay (1990: 145).

[25] For the similarities between Lorca's *Don Perlimplín* and Crommelynck's *Le Cocu Magnifique* (1921) see Francisco García Lorca (1980: 319) and Carlos Feal Deibe (1970: 403–9).

[26] In this story, the protagonist attempts to keep his maiden imprisoned in a forest, so that she will remain untainted by the outside world. Abbé Prévost (1971) *Manon Lescaut*, trans. Leonard Tavistock, London: Penguin, 1991.

and Galatea[27] and in the Mme Leprince de Beaumont version of *Beauty and the Beast*, which can be seen as variations of 'a founding myth of sexual difference' (Warner 1994: 274).

The plot of *Amor de Don Perlimplín* has resonances of ancient themes, afforded by layer upon layer of versions of a basic story but, as soon as we attempt to grasp a familiar theme, we find it slipping away from us with each turn in the plot. As Feal Deibe (1989: 122) puts it, in *Amor de Don Perlimplín* '[el drama] construye y desconstruye de modo incesante la red de sus posibles interpretaciones'. The play is like an finely worked piece of intricate lace, with strands which separate and interweave at every turn: 'lo que me ha interesado en Don Perlimplín', wrote Lorca, 'es subrayar el contraste entre lo lírico y lo grotesco y aun mezclarlos en todo momento' (*OC* III: 521). The audience is then drawn into the plot, enticed further into the allegorical subtext to find a meaning, and simultaneously forced to reconsider attitudes towards the characters and themes. In most versions of the Beauty and the Beast tale, this 'classic tale of transformation [. . .] places the male lover, the Beast, in the position of the mysterious, threatening, possibly fatal unknown, and Beauty, the heroine, as the questor who discovers his true nature' (Warner 1994: 275). The Beauty and the Beast story is a quest to face the unknown other, and most modern versions have the heroine emerge with the joyous discovery that her Beast is in fact a beautiful young man, who is not at all to be feared. In the case of *Amor de Don Perlimplín*, however, Perlimplín is the questor who is afraid of the feminine.

Cupid and Psyche is also a moral tale about the dangers of trusting too much to appearances. It is suggested that what is within is what counts, that surface aesthetics are unimportant. Psyche loses her beloved Cupid because she is seduced by the desire to look at him while he sleeps (which she has been forbidden to do). He turns out to be beautiful, but also disappears immediately, leaving her endlessly mourning this lost image (See Warner [1994: 275]). This finds an echo in Marcolfa's speech to Belisa at the end of *Amor de Don Perlimplín*: 'El hermoso adolescente al que nunca verás el rostro.' Belisa: 'Sí, sí, le quiero, le quiero con toda la fuerza de mi carne y de mi alma. Pero ¿dónde está el joven de la capa roja?'. Like *Cupid and Psyche*, *Amor de Don Perlimplín* deals with the twin themes of sexual difference and perceptual ambiguity.

Belisa is an imaginary construct, a symptom of Perlimplín's fears surrounding female sexuality,[28] and thus becomes for Perlimplín the embodi-

27 In Ovid's *Metamorphoses* (18 AD), Pygmalion's relation to the statue of Galatea is at first set within the imaginary order: 'a creation of *trompe l'oeil* deceptiveness, where he treats the statue as if it were alive' (Brooks 1993: 22–3).

28 Allen (1983: x) writes that the *femme fatale* became popular in the art and literature of the end of the nineteenth century, a phenomenon she attributes to fears surrounding the greater sexual and political freedom accorded women at that time. Doane (1991: 2)

ment of a *femme fatale*,[29] or castrating Medusa. The *femme fatale* has been described as 'a male fantasy, as is most of our art' (Place 1978: 35) and (as Warner [1985] writes) has roots stretching back as far as Salome, the mythical Medusa, and even Eve. We may be reminded of Lorca's drawing *Epitalamio* (meaning 'marriage song', from the Greek *thalamos*, bridal chamber), which depicts what appears to be a 'vagina dentata' complete with tendrils of hair like those of Medusa. Likewise the drawing, *Sirena*, displays a similar preoccupation with the seductive deadliness of flowing locks. In this drawing the mermaid is a little black hole, which, like the sloping line dividing the picture, signifies disappearance and death for the ship and sailors.[30] Perlimplín views Belisa as a dangerous and deadly mystery that he can never get close to. He continually fetishises her, in an attempt to hold her at a distance.[31] She becomes a spectacle, unknown, gazed at from afar. Belisa always passively *appears* in this play.[32] When we first see her she appears semi-naked at her window: she is 'medio desnuda', and she has 'el pelo suelto y los brazos desnudos' (*OC* II: 468).[33] As she seductively combs her hair she is lost in self-absorption, her gaze is inward looking, while the male gaze, that of Perlimplín, is fully present. Later she is framed by the keyhole of the bedroom door as Perlimplín watches her dress. It is the distance between them which awakens Perlimplín's desire for her as he voyeuristically spies her through the keyhole of the bedroom door:

suggests that the *femme fatale*'s connotations of 'uncontrollable drives, the fading of subjectivity and the loss of conscious agency' were 'all themes of the emergent theories of psychoanalysis'. The *femme fatale* can therefore be seen as the incarnation of fears surrounding the shifting sands which were at that time related to theories of sexual difference and the self.

[29] Bacarisse (1992: 76–7) also views Belisa as a *femme fatale*. Binding (1985: 107) suggests that Belisa is the vivid articulation of a homosexual's misogynistic desire. Conflating the action of the play with imagined biographical detail, he claims that this is due to 'Lorca's resentment at having been placed outside the "normal" world of Granadine people, at being, possibly, mocked by girls for his failure to correspond to their images of malehood'. I would contend that the play is far more complex than this one-sided account suggests. The emphasis on systems of viewing reveal Belisa as a construction of femininity, caught up in a game engineered entirely by Perlimplín.

[30] Elena of *El público*, as well as *la máscara* and *la mecanógrafa* of *Así que pasen cinco años*, are also punishing females.

[31] Bacarisse (1992) compares Belisa with the subject of Lorca's poem 'Balada triste' from 1918: 'Ella era entonces para mí el enigma/estrella azul sobre mi pecho intacto' and also 'La mujer lejana: Soneto sensual', also from 1918: 'Todas las mil fragrancias que manan de tu boca/ Son perfumadas nubes que matan de dulzura'.

[32] Belisa is an example of what early film theorists called 'to-be-looked-at-ness', taken from Laura Mulvey's seminal essay, 'Visual Pleasure and Narrative Cinema', which spawned a debate surrounding the construction of femininity in cinematic discourse (Mulvey 1975: 19).

[33] Ucelay (1990: 150) writes that in 1929 the text was confiscated and placed in the 'departamento de la pornografía' of the 'Dirección General de Seguridad'.

Me casé [. . .] ¡por lo que fuera!, pero no te quería. Yo no había podido imaginarme tu cuerpo hasta que lo vi por el ojo de la cerradura cuando te vestían de novia. Y entonces fue cuando sentí el amor, ¡entonces!, como un hondo corte de lanceta en la garganta. (*OC* II: 471)

At the same time, this distancing can be seen as part of Perlimplín's attempts to control Belisa by restricting her to her visual image. The Duendes have alerted us to the centrality of viewing in the play. Here, as she is a mere figment of Perlimplín's imagination, at the mercy of his gaze, Belisa appears to be trapped by her visual image: Belisa is tied to the image of the *femme fatale*. In Lorca's plays, the imprisonment, immobility or tragic fixity associated with a character's situation is often expressed visually in terms of physical or visual restrictiveness. The decline and death of Rosita, protagonist of *Doña Rosita la Soltera*, is symbolised by the image of the rose, as it turns from red to white. The play simultaneously sends up the courtly traditions of depicting femininity as a delicate, passive flower. As the poem of the 'rosa mudable' is told to us in the first act, 'cuando se abre en la mañana/roja como la sangre está' (*OC* II: 888), it seems as if her visual and physical decline are inevitable and irrevocable. We learn that the rose turns white and, 'se comienza a deshojar' (*OC* II: 970), while Rosita appears wearing a white dress on stage.

In *La casa de Bernarda Alba*, Adela's revolt is likewise plotted visually – in this case by her green dress, while each of her sisters appear to be trapped by the frames of the windows. Adela is parodied by María Josefa, the mad old grandmother whose nightdress mimics wedding attire and who dreams of escape to live by the sea. María Josefa and Adela both 'make a spectacle of themselves'[34] in an attempt to express their revolt in visual terms. But Adela still positions herself on the side of spectacle as she sits at the window to attract Pepe el Romano. As Smith (1989: 122) writes, interpreting the play in terms of a Foucauldian account of the politics of surveillance, 'her pleasure (her "transgression") derives from a sense of self which continues to be defined as the object, not the subject, of the look'. A further discussion of Lorca's writing on photographic images and their relation to entrapment and stasis can be found in the following chapter. Repeatedly, physical entrapment is expressed in visual terms in Lorca's theatre. In the case of *Amor de Don Perlimplín*, we might argue that Perlimplín appears set on pinning Belisa down to her physical image and in the process she is rendered a construct.

Belisa represents a construction of femininity, framed by Perlimplín as an enticing secret to be discovered. At the end of the play Perlimplín speaks of 'tu cuerpo [. . .] ¡¡¡que nunca podría descrifrar!!!' (*OC* II: 494). Although he

---

[34] Mary Russo (1986) suggests that women may redeploy the taboos which render the female body grotesque (the pregnant, ageing or irregular body) to create disorder through 'making a spectacle of oneself'.

never reaches a solution, during the course of this play Perlimplín is therefore
anxious to discover the truth about femininity. He is asking the question,
'what is femininity?'.[35]

Belisa is consistently linked with perceptual ambiguity. Her seductive
beauty and surface sweetness in fact hide an ugly spirit and carnal desire.
Belisa's mother hints at the dialectic between surface and depth associated
with Belisa when she says:

> ... Es una azucena. ¿Ve usted su cara? (*Bajando la voz*)
> ¡Pues si la viese por dentro! [. . .] Como de azúcar . . .
>
> (*OC* II: 465)

On her wedding night, Belisa commits adultery with five men, but she
sweetly calls her husband 'Perlimplinillo' and 'maridito' and denies her
infidelity:

Belisa: ¡Qué marido tan bromista tengo! (*En voz baja*) ¡Tú! ¡Tú me
               has besado!   (*OC* II: 478)

Rupert Allen (1974: 100) writes that Belisa has 'the kind of "personality"
granted characters in hard-core pornography. Her lack of character and
expostulations of limitless erotic appetite recall the sexual orientation of
pornographic literature'. This description seems to coincide with Jenkins'
(1981: 35) description of the *femme fatale* of *film noir* whose 'conception of
character is archetypal; these women personify destructive and violent erotic
drives, but they are never explored in any depth'. The alignment of Belisa
with the veil (the quest to discover the feminine) has the effect of rendering
Belisa two-dimensional, a construct, a mask of femininity.

The depiction of femininity as a mask also features elsewhere in Lorca's
work. The poem 'Carnaval: Visión interior' (de Paepe 1994: 150) includes
the following stanza:

> Las mujeres sonríen
> Con aire banal.
> Morenas, rubias, deliciosas
> Son las máscaras preciosas
> De mi carnaval.

[35] In Lacanian terms we could define Perlimplín as a hysteric: the structures between
neurotic and 'normal' subjectivity are the same according to Lacanian theoretical accounts
of subjectivity. Perlimplín seems to be asking the question 'What is a woman?', the question posed by hysterics, whether male or female. The hysteric appropriates another's
desire by identifying with them, but always on the condition that he/she is not the object of
that desire. Perlimplín creates the fantasy Joven de la Capa Roja as object of fantasy for
Belisa and identifies with him, but he does this so as not to have to face Belisa himself.
See Lacan (1955) and Evans (1996).

In the play *Así que pasen cinco años*, meanwhile, the character of *la máscara* is portrayed as sheer mask: a reference to the dehumanising quality of city life. She has, '*pelo de seda amarillo, cayendo como un manto, y máscara blanco de yeso; guantes hasta el codo, del mismo color. Lleva sombrero amarillo y todo el pecho sembrado con lentejuelas de oro*' (*OC* II: 567). Everything about this character is fake or assumed. With her counterpart the *maniquí*, who represents the marriage and the child *la novia* will never have with *el joven*, *la máscara* also represents sterility and cruelty. *La máscara* is pure mask, a constellation of the empty accoutrements to feminine seduction.

If Belisa's alignment with the veil/mask renders her a mystery to be explored, beckoning one to look beneath, it nevertheless makes no promises that there will be some essence to be discovered. The veil, after all, gives the illusion of depth. In their speech of the *cuadro segundo*, the Duendes reminded us that 'sin ese tapar y destapar [. . .] ¿Qué sería de las pobres gentes?' (*OC* II: 473). The image of surface and depth is echoed in a series of images throughout the play: 'no es lo que se ve por fuera' and 'está lleno de cosas ocultas' (*OC* II: 461), remarks Marcolfa about the delights of marriage; 'pues si la viera por dentro' (*OC* II: 465), La Madre teases Perlimplín with reference to Belisa, and 'Nunca creía que fuese tan complicado!' (*OC* II: 496), cries Belisa of Perlimplín. The Duendes point to the illusion of depth that the process of metaphorical or physical veiling can convey. The scene of the Duendes presents the visual in terms of the *trompe l'oeil*, the appearances which incite but can deceive, just as Perlimplín taunts Belisa with the image of the Joven de la Capa Roja: 'Acaba de volver la esquina' (*OC* II: 486). We might be reminded of Lacan's version of the tale of Zeuxis and Parrhasios. Challenged by his rival Parrhasios, Zeuxis draws a painting of grapes which attract birds who attempt to peck at them. But when Zeuxis demands that Parrhasios draw aside the veil which covers the painting, he discovers that the veil too is painted. Lacan writes, 'if one wishes to deceive a man, what one presents to him is the painting of a veil, that is, something that incites him to look behind it'. (Lacan 1979: 107). Here too, the veil gives the suggestion of presence, but may be no more than an optical illusion, disguising nothing but absence.

If femininity is a mask/veil which begs one to look beneath it in this play, then the question is posed – is there a truth or essence of femininity to be found? Within the text, Perlimplín rages about his desire to give Belisa a soul. Is Belisa therefore merely a construct, to be animated by the gaze of another?[36] What is the truth of femininity? This play seems to suggest that once the veils have been torn back, there is no essence to be discovered.

These questions find a parallel in the inquiries into femininity posed by

---

36 Kappeler (1986: 45) writes that 'the notion of women as objects of aesthetic perception, soulless until animated by the genius of the perceiver is grounded in the very definition of the aesthetic'.

psychoanalysis. In Joan Rivière's 1929 essay, 'Womanliness as a Masquerade' (Rivière 1929: 35–44),[37] she writes that, 'womanliness could therefore be assumed and worn as a mask [. . .] The reader may now ask where I draw the line between genuine womanliness and the "masquerade". My suggestion is not, however, that there is any such difference; whether radical or superficial, they are the same thing' (38). Lacan corrects Rivière's thesis to claim that masquerade, rather than merely describing a particular sort of femininity, in fact defines ('normal') femininity per se. Femininity is hollow, in Lacan's formulation, constituted only in reference to the masculine (as a reaction-formation against the masculine). Femininity is sustained only by its accoutrements: 'decorative veils, and inessential gestures' (Doane 1991: 34), which mask her lack. Femininity is 'variously veiled according to the epochs of history' (Irigaray 1983: 118).[38] In theoretical discourse, therefore, as well as in the play under discussion, femininity is contingent, staged, inessential.

On one level the reference to Belisa's soul can be seen (as some other critics have done) as a reflection on the nature of love – Platonic love is juxtaposed with carnal desire, and seen as an attempt to reach a spiritual understanding. At the same time, however, the preoccupation with Belisa's soul seems to suggest an anxiety that she may be pure appearance, and have no soul, no substance. As she is aligned with the veil, the suggestion that this play makes, is that there is no sense of an essence of femininity to be discovered beneath the mask. Is subjectivity therefore no more than an empty charade, sustained by its accoutrements? The dangerous threat posed by the alignment of femininity with the mask is the notion that, were we to look behind the mask of femininity, we might find mere absence.

If Belisa is depicted as an empty charade in this play, then Perlimplín is also consistently expressed in the terms of masquerade. Perlimplín finds himself trapped by his circumstances. This is expressed in visual terms as Perlimplín looks in despair at what he perceives to be his useless, wasting body. He therefore determines to become the master of his own script – he will write and perform a new identity for himself, masquerading a new subjectivity. In Lacanian terms, Perlimplín performs the entry into language (symbolised by his awakening into the language of fantasy and the imagination: '¡Perlimplín no tiene honor!' are the words of this new transgressive language) and the divisiveness of self necessary for the entry into (male)

[37] Rivière cites the case of a female academic who adopted exaggeratedly feminine gestures, 'flirting and coquetting with [the males in the audience] in a more or less veiled manner' after her lectures, in an attempt to ward off the retribution she feared from men for her usurping of the masculine role (the intellectual stance).

[38] Irigaray, in her critique of Nietzsche's alignment of femininity with truth, writes that femininity is 'by virtue of her inexhaustible aptitude for mimicry – the living support of all the staging/production of the world. Variously veiled according to the epochs of history' (Irigaray 1983: 118).

subjectivity.[39] In the language of his imagination, Perlimplín can be whatever he wants to be. He creates the fantasy of Joven de la Capa Roja, tailor-made to Belisa's desires. Perlimplín provides the merest glimpse of a red cape, and Belisa projects the rest:

Belisa: Tampoco he conseguido verlo. En mi paseo por la alameda venían todos detrás menos él. Debe tener la piel morena y sus besos deben perfumar y escocer al mismo tiempo como el azafrán y el clavo. A veces pasa por debajo de mis balcones y mece su mano lentamente en un saludo que hace temblar mis pechos.   (*OC* II: 481)

Perlimplín uses the techniques of masquerade to create the perfect fantasy object of desire for Belisa. The Joven de la Capa Roja is a fetish, sustained merely by accoutrements (in this case the cloak which veils, seduces and deceives). The Joven de la Capa Roja demonstrates the play of slippery Lacanian signifiers at work in the sexual relationship. Don Perlimplín has the *phallus*, the control and the mastery, but on his wedding night the insinuation is made that Perlimplín is unable to perform sexually. Rather than be exposed as a fraud, Perlimplín creates the fantasy lover. As this is no more than an empty charade, he uses the cloak to veil his lack: 'why not acknowledge that if there is no virility which castration does not consecrate, then for the woman it is a castrated lover or a dead man (or even both at the same time) who hides behind the veil where he calls on her adoration' (Lacan 1964: 95). Lacan's playfully ambiguous comments suggest that for him all men are symbolically castrated, and all men masquerade. '¡Nunca creí que fuese tan complicado!' (*OC* II: 486), cries a distraught Belisa. If femininity is a masquerade, then so too is masculinity.[40] The relationship between Perlimplín and Belisa is reflected in terms of the play of masks, a farce based on seduction – the empty courtship rituals which depend upon the play of appearances.[41]

The Joven de la Capa Roja is a screen for the projection of fantasies of both Perlimplín and Belisa. Like a trickster-figure, this fantasy image is a charged, potent space which highlights the constructed nature of the relationships around him. Perlimplín creates the fantasy lover because of his inability to get close to Belisa, to avoid contact with her. The Joven de la Capa Roja is

[39] Doane (1991) for example, criticises Lacan's assertion that masculinity is constructed through divisiveness (a reworking of Freud's assertion that the little boy looks at his body and perceives that he has the phallus) whereas femininity is defined by closeness and presence to the image. For Doane, masquerade, the excess of femininity associated with the *femme fatale*, may provide femininity with a form of distance from her own image, which may lead to a reworking from traditional discourses of femininity.

[40] See Holmlund (1993) for a discussion of male masquerade in Hollywood film.

[41] Lacan writes that masks define the sphere of sexuality more than any recourse to essence. The emphasis upon appearing therefore 'has the effect that the ideal or typical manifestations of behaviour in both sexes, up to and including the act of sexual copulation, are entirely propelled into comedy' (Lacan 1958: 84).

therefore a diversionary tactic, giving the illusion of action while disguising tragic immobility. The Joven de la Capa Roja presents an example of Girard's notion (1961) of 'triangular desire': desire mediated (his term is 'mimetic'), an example of desire as 'desire according to the Other'. Girard asserts, speaking of the adulterous relationship, that the intervention of the third person is a result of this mediated desire, that rivalry is necessary for desire to function. This rivalry can escalate into violence – hence the classic tale of revenge associated with adultery. The Joven de la Capa Roja presents an example of such mimetic desire which is exposed as having a mere diversionary or mediatory function. There is no adulterous lover, after all – he is merely a figment of the imagination of the other characters. The Joven de la Capa Roja creates the interest, however – without him there would be no plot, no scandal, no intrigue (we are reminded of the Duendes' mocking of the audience's desire for scandal). But the Joven de la Capa Roja is ultimately nothing more than an empty charade.

The relationship between Don Perlimplín and Belisa is mediated at every turn. While Belisa poses at the window, Perlimplín wraps a cloak of deceit around himself and creates a fantasy lover. Relationships take place at a remove, and anticipation is all: 'it is a better thing to travel hopefully than to arrive', as Robert Louis Stevenson had it. Masquerade, fetishism and seduction are constituent parts of this game of courtship. The swirl of the cape promises much but delivers nothing. As in a Lacanian relationship, this entry into the symbolic and language renders love adulterous at every turn. Desire is metonymic, writes Lacan, so every love is adulterous (based on a chain of substituted *object a* signifiers) as it is filled with the ghosts of lovers past, present, future and imagined. The influence of the trickster-function (in this case the audience's entry into a new perspective) creates in this play an anamorphic vision of the sexual relationship. As the perspectives slide, those elements which are generally not glimpsed – the excesses of vision, fears and desires crystallised into form – appear, and we are presented not only with the edges of the masks (the constructed nature of identity) which appear at every turn, but also the laying bare of the mechanisms, the ghosts of a metonymic chain of signifiers, held together by masquerade, threat, danger and fear.

VEILING DEATH

> Death is the veil which those who live call life;
> They sleep, and it is lifted.
>
> P. B. Shelley.

On one level, *Amor de Don Perlimplín* is a tale of adultery and revenge, but if we tear back the layers of meaning in the trickster-function, we discover that the adultery plot is nothing but a seductive charade, and what parades as one thing is in fact a disguise for another sort of plot altogether.

The tale of revenge and cuckoldry is revealed to be nothing more than the dream of Perlimplín, precipitated by the fears he feels when faced with Belisa. Perlimplín is persuaded to consider marriage to Belisa by the verbal game he enters into with Marcolfa. We have the feeling that they often engage in this verbal repartee, with Marcolfa cajoling Perlimplín into marriage, but this time Marcolfa's words actually goad Perlimplín into some kind of realisation of his advancing age:

Perlimplín:	¿Sí?
Marcolfa:	Sí
Perlimplín:	Pero, ¿por qué sí?
Marcolfa:	Pues porque sí.
Perlimplín:	¿Y si yo te dijera que no? [. . .]
Marcolfa:	Veinte y veinte son cuarenta [. . .]
Perlimplín:	(*Escuchando*) Adelante.
Marcolfa:	Y diez, cincuenta.
Perlimplín:	Vamos.
Marcolfa:	Con cincuenta años ya no se es un niño.
Perlimplín:	Claro.
Marcolfa:	Ya me puedo morir de un momento a otro.
Perlimplin:	¡Caramba! (*OC* II: 459–60)

Contemplation of his impending marriage to Belisa makes Perlimplín aware of death for the first time in his life: he says of Belisa, '¿Será capaz de estrangularme?' (*OC* II: 467). His erotic awakening is synthesised with an awareness of his approaching death. The whole play can be seen as a reaction to death, an attempt to create the illusion of action, while simultaneously warding off resolution/death. Therefore, the surface text of adultery disguises another, more significant question for Perlimplín: what is the truth of existence?[42]

The distortion of vision in the play ('las perspectivas están equivocadas deliciosamente') therefore can be seen as symptomatic of Perlimplín's fear of fading subjectivity and the destabilisation he feels in the face of death. Where

---

[42] In the slippage of signifiers, we might also define Perlimplín as an obsessional neurotic, rather than an hysteric. The question the obsessional poses is: 'To be or not to be?' 'Am I dead or alive?' and 'Why do I exist?'. The obsessional is neither male nor female, or both at once: we could say that Perlimplín's identification with Belisa in the creation of the fantasy object and his claims that 'estoy fuera del mundo' may reflect a desire to transcend gender boundaries. The obsessional neurotic's questions about existence and death have consequences for his attitude to time: this can be either perpetual procrastination while waiting for death, or considering oneself immortal because one is already dead (Lacan 1955: 179–80). Perlimplín's cloaked fantasy lover can be seen as an attempt to put off union with Belisa (the incarnation of death) and his killing of the lover can be seen as a belief in his own mortality: he is in part successful in this because Belisa will endlessly search for the Joven de la Capa Roja, thereby keeping him alive in her mind.

identity seems to rely so heavily on the visual medium for its construction and confirmation, the implication seems to be that if the perspectives slide sufficiently, perhaps the subject can be made to disappear altogether.[43] Perlimplín appears to be plagued by the kind of doubts that afflicted Descartes concerning existence and philosophy. Significantly, Descartes makes claims for the existence of matter based on geometry but holds that sensible attributes (such as colour) can be activated solely by an observer. In *Amor de Don Perlimplín*, the table is two-dimensional, but attempts to give the appearance of having three-dimensions. We imagine the table to exist: 'cogito ergo sum' is taken to extremes. Following Berkeley, this play seems to suggest that everything in the world may be just a delusion, a trick of the imagination.

Like Descartes before him, Perlimplín meditates on the relationship between the mind and the body. Perlimplín begins to view his body in terms of a wasting decrepitation. It is not under the control of his mind. He also views Belisa in terms of corporeality – her carnality requires a young lover to satisfy her: 'el cuerpo de Belisa era para músculos jovenes' (*OC* II: 495). The Joven de la Capa Roja writes letters to Belisa which speak of her body: 'Hablan de mí [. . .] de mi cuerpo' (*OC* II: 485). Perlimplín wonders whether corporeality could provide the answer to the play of transient signifiers which threatens to make identity disappear in a sideways glance. However, his body is defying him – he is a 'monigote sin fuerza' (*OC* II: 495), whose body is decaying and dying. Perlimplín's reflections on the soul/body dialectic which runs throughout the play can be seen as a quest for immortality. If Perlimplín can create a fantasy image of himself in the mind of another (Belisa), then perhaps he may attain a kind of immortality – this would be the 'triunfo' of his imagination (*OC* II: 356). The creation of the fantasy lover is therefore an attempt to freeze life into visual form, as a defence against the passage of time, an attempt to 'embalm the dead', to use André Bazin's (1967: 9) term for the visual image.

However, in this search for the elixir of youth, something has to be sacrificed by Perlimplín. Critics have drawn attention to the connotations of Perlimplín as a Christ-figure and martyr in relation to Belisa. For example, Feal Deibe (1989: 121) writes that, 'la frase, referida a Perlimplín, "Míralo por dónde viene" procede del lenguaje de las saetas de Semana Santa y, como tal, está dirigida al Nazareno, al Hijo. Muerto ya Perlimplín, las palabras de Marcolfa apuntan en igual sentido: "Belisa, ya eres otra mujer. Estás vestida por la sangre gloriosa de mi señor". La "sangre gloriosa" es, por antomasia, la de Cristo'. Bacarisse points out that 'aleluya' is associated with Easter

---

43 This may remind us of the ideas of Berkeley who mused as to whether a rose that grew in the desert unseen by anyone else could be said to exist. His notion of 'esse est percipi' involved the 'rejection of any distinctions between sensation on the one hand and sensible qualities on the other' (Berkeley 1975: x).

(Bacarisse 1992: 87) which would seem to render the whole play a biblical tale. I suggest that the theme of self-sacrifice is extended to Perlimplín's creation of the Joven de la Capa Roja – in order for the fantasy young man to live, he must sacrifice his own life. In Blanchot's rendering of the Lazarus story, behind the resuscitated Lazarus (the Joven de la Capa Roja in our case) lies another, 'less palatable' Lazarus, who is a reminder of the truth of death (our Don Perlimplín). In the Blanchot version, 'not just one but two Lazaruses are summoned forth' (Gregg 1994: 59): 'the first Lazarus who emerges is the one held together by clean, white, tightly bound bandages, and the other much less palatable Lazarus is the one whose partially decomposed body would be revealed were the bandages to come undone' (59). For Blanchot, the *Lazare veni foras* is performed in order to give evidence of the human possibility of death. I would suggest that Perlimplín's intention in his creation of the fantasy lover is to give evidence of the possibility of resurrection and immortality. However, he is ultimately let down by the irrefutable physicality of his decaying body.

In a final attempt to gain immortality, Perlimplín must kill himself, so that the fantasy may remain intact:

Perlimplín: Perlimplín me mató [. . .] ¡Ah don Perlimplín! Viejo verde. Monigote sin fuerza, tú no podías gozar el cuerpo de Belisa [. . .] el cuerpo de Belisa era para músculos jovenes y labios de ascuas [. . .] Yo, en cambio, amaba tu cuerpo y nada más [. . .] ¡tu cuerpo! [. . .] pero me ha matado [. . .] Con este ramo ardiente de piedras preciosas.   (*OC* II: 495)

Belisa is left endlessly searching for the lost lover: 'pero, ¿dónde está el joven de la capa roja? ¿Dónde está?' (*OC* II: 496). Perlimplín has gained a form of immortality, for at least as long as Belisa lives. Of course Belisa's confusion at the end of the play, '¿Dónde está el joven de la capa roja?', signals that while the fantasy lover remains, Perlimplín is very much dead and buried. It is as if Perlimplín's 'creation' has taken on a life of its own, has become detached from its creator and lives on after Perlimplín's death. In visual terms, Perlimplín's actions have led him to enter a new plane, symbolised by the distortion of the perspective, but this transgression ('estoy fuera del mundo y de la moral ridícula de las gentes')[44] ultimately will result in a different set of rules which entrap him. As Balboa Echevarría (1986: 98–9) writes, 'la transgresión a los diferentes textos construye un espiral que aprisionará finalmente al personaje'. In order to keep the fantasy alive, he must kill himself: death is the only way out of this triumph of his imagination.

Perlimplín's impending marriage to Belisa has precipitated his fear of

_____

[44] Perlimplín's transgression could be described as 'wearing the cloak of shamelessness' (*anaideien epieimene*) which comes from the trickster-myth *Hymn to Hermes* (see Hyde 1998: 321).

death and she becomes a *femme fatale*. In a sense, the play has resonances of
many fairy tales where the beautiful young woman is wearing a mask to hide
the ugly old hag, symbolic of death. Perlimplín's quest to discover the feminine, is thus also a quest to discover the truth about death.

Nietzsche writes of such a quest in reference to a poem by Schiller entitled
'Das verschleierte Bild aus Saïs' in which a young adventurer, 'compelled by
the thirst for knowledge' (which reminds us of Perlimplín's description of his
thirst), travels to Egypt to confront a veiled statue of Isis.[45] In Schiller's
poem, the protagonist is told that the veil conceals the very form of truth, but
also that there is a divine decree prohibiting its disturbance. The youth trans-
gresses, pulls aside the veil and looks.[46] Schiller does not tell us what is
found behind the veil, but as Lévy (1992: 617) writes: 'in the final analysis it
is the actual pursuit of the unveiling which takes over from its fulfillment, in
a work where everything is subordinated to the quest'. Nietzsche (1882: 38)
expounds his theory that the veils are evidence of the human desire to know
(incarnated here in feminine form). They entice one to look beneath them,
but as we have already seen, they issue no promises that anything can be
found beneath them. For Nietzsche, the truth behind the veil is death. He
maintains that this is a truth which we prefer to disguise in life: the desire to
know too much can only result in death. He writes that:

> We no longer believe that truth remains truth when the veils are withdrawn;
> we have lived too much to believe this. Today we consider it a matter of
> decency not to wish to see everything naked, or to be present at everything,
> or to understand and know everything.   (Nietzsche 1882: 38)

Nietzsche seems to suggest that we pull the wool over our own eyes, a notion
suggested by Perlimplín's veiling of death in the form of Belisa. Thus while
life is no more than a series of veils to obscure death, at the same time 'truth'
is rendered no more substantial than a deceptive veil. Behind the veil is
merely the absence which is death. Perlimplín's quest likewise ends in death.

The difficulty on the part of critics to locate a meaning in this work is a
function and effect of this slippery play where meanings co-exist and are
supported simultaneously within the piece, and, as when faced with a seductive enigma, the harder one looks, the more one can read into it. This notion

---

45 Lévy (1992: 611–18) writes that Isis is a symbol of fertility, magic and also resurrection as she managed to bring her dead husband back from the dead (in Egyptian
mythology). Furthermore, in Apuleius' tale of *The Golden Ass*, the unveiling of Isis was
the reward for initiates to the cult of Isis in ancient times: 'the very act of initiation
includes a voluntary death and salvation obtained through grace'. Isis is therefore associated with rebirth, resurrection, salvation and magic.

46 'No mortal', she says, 'Sets this veil aside until I myself raise it, /And anyone who
with/an impure, guilty hand/Raises the holy, forbidden veil sooner,/ [. . .] Will', said the
goddess [. . .] 'Yes?', 'He will see the truth'.

finds a parallel within the text itself, as Perlimplín attempts to help Belisa to see the light, to see the truth, but at the end there is no revelation and illumination for Belisa, merely more layers of confusion and deception: '¿Dónde está el joven de la capa roja?' and '¡Nunca creí que fuese tan complicado!'. *Amor de Don Perlimplín* is presented in the form of Perlimplín's, and through the trickster-function, the audience's, quest to discover the truth about Belisa (femininity) and, in a metonymic slippage, the truth about life and death, rendered obscure by a process of veiling. When the masks are drawn away, we find only absence – the trace of a lost presence. Femininity (Belisa) comes to represent the conflation of themes surrounding discovery and duplicity. Themes surrounding truth and deceptiveness have rendered the feminine as 'other', as the object of a voyage into the unknown. Through the Duendes' mockery of our desire to know/see, the audience is also engaged on a quest to sift through the signifiers and likewise enters a journey of discovery. This play reveals that life can be seen as a series of flimsy red herrings to disguise the constant presence of death. The play simultaneously mocks our desire to know the truth and suggests that perhaps we would be wise not to look too closely. Our search for knowledge is nothing more than a game of the imagination where the only certainty is physical decay and death.

III

ASÍ QUE PASEN CINCO AÑOS. LEYENDA DEL TIEMPO: MASOCHISM AND THE LIMITS OF MASCULINITY

> Arlequín: El sueño va sobre el tiempo
> flotando como un velero. Nadie
> puede abrir semillas en el
> corazón del sueño.
>
> Federico García Lorca, *Así que pasen cinco años*.

The trickster can be found at the crossroads where past, present and future meet briefly to go their separate ways. The trickster articulates a liminal time above, beyond and between real time – neither *compás* nor *contratiempo*, but somewhere in-between. In this chapter I argue that *Así que pasen cinco años* expresses this trickster-like liminal time, that it is located above, betwixt and between temporal limits.

Así que pasen cinco años (1931) belongs to the fruitful and exciting period that García Lorca spent in the United States. Lorca remembered his stay in New York (June 1929 – March 1930) as 'one of the most useful experiences' of his life (Maurer 1988: ix).[1] Inspired by the 'new' forms of theatre he saw there,[2] he was to begin his project to 'crear un nuevo teatro, avanzado de formas y teoría',[3] which he would later name, 'teatro del porvenir' (Ucelay 1995: 11).[4]

---

[1] Andrew Anderson (1991a: 149–73) writes that 1928 was a crucial year in Lorca's life. A failed relationship with the sculptor Emilio Aladrén, negative reviews of *Romancero Gitano*, perhaps above all the criticism he received from Salvador Dalí and a growing interest in Surrealism, may have prompted Lorca to undertake the trip to New York and also to explore new avenues in his work. Lorca was working on *Así que pasen cinco años* and *El público* during his trip to Cuba (March–June 1930). Both of these plays are markedly different in tone from his earlier and later works.

[2] Lorca wrote to his parents from New York, 'el teatro aquí es muy bueno y muy *nuevo* y a mí me interesa en extremo. Aquí el teatro es magnífico y espero sacar gran partido de él para mis cosas' (Maurer 1986: 59, 69). Although Lorca gave few clues as to the plays he saw there (he does make mention of 'teatro chino', for example), Andrew Anderson draws on and enlarges upon Maurer's piece to construct a picture for us of those plays in performance in New York during the time Lorca spent there, and the plays he is likely to have seen. See Anderson (1993: 135–48).

[3] Anderson (1993) and Rodolfo Gil Benumeya, Estampa de Federico García Lorca', in *La Gaceta Literaria*, 15 January 1931, reprinted in *OC* III: 502–5.

[4] *Poeta en Nueva York*, *El público*, the film-script *Viaje a la luna* as well as new

The play is intense, complex and deeply enigmatic. A young man (Joven) is to wait five years to marry his fiancée (Novia) who is away on a journey. In the meantime, he fuels his desire with fantasy images of her. Yet upon her return, the fiancée tells him that she no longer loves him and subsequently runs off with a rugby-player she has met in the interim. Recalling the amorous advances of his typist (Mecanógrafa), the young man seeks her out and declares his love for her, but she informs him that he must wait five years for their love to be consummated. Two friends and an old man (Viejo) offer advice to the young man and events are also interrupted by the arrival of a series of non-naturalistic characters: a dead cat, a dead child (Niño), a mannequin (Maniquí) from a shop-window; a girl (Muchacha) whose lover has drowned; a yellow mask (Máscara), and a clown (Payaso) and harlequin (Arlequín). Rejected for the second time, the young man arrives home to find a poker game in action. On producing the ace of hearts the young man clasps his hands to his chest and dies.

Critical attention has focused on the psychoanalytic, filmic and expressionistic elements of this play (Anderson 1992b; Edwards 1981; Huélamo Kosma 1989).[5] Most critics concur that the play gives form to a journey into the psyche of the play's protagonist, the Joven. My study will begin by positing the play as a liminal space for the exploration of the twinned concepts of time, and the representation of masculinity. I shall examine the young man at the centre of the drama against the model set out by Deleuze (1989) for male masochism, a paradigm which explodes the stereotype of conventional masculinity in a variety of interesting ways. I shall then consider the ways in which the structure of the text, with its deferral, circularity and repetition constitutes a form of 'frozen progression', which has striking similarities with the model of Deleuzean masochism set out earlier. Lastly, as the audience was a vital consideration for Lorca in the development of his plays, I shall consider what are the pleasures of this text in performance. These pleasures – deferral, fetishism and repetition, among others (vital constituent parts of the theory of masochism) – implicate the audience in a paradigm (through the trickster-function) which questions received notions of pleasure and perversion.

At the centre of *Así que pasen cinco años* is the figure of the Joven. Like Augusto Pérez at the start of Unamuno's *Niebla*, our young man is poised at the threshold of the rest of his life. He is caught, immobile, frozen with indecision. He seems to exist in a state of perpetual limbo. The motivating force behind his indecision is fear of action, of death, of sexuality, of the cruel

versions of *Amor de Don Perlimplín con Belisa en su jardín* and *La zapatera prodigiosa* were all underway at this time.
5   Anderson (1992b) draws out the expressionistic strains; Edwards (1981) finds similarities between the play and *Un Chien Andalou* by Buñuel and Dalí. Huélamo Kosma (1989) constructs a Freudian reading.

consequences of life. In an attempt to control the frightening unpredictability
of life, to impose some sort of order on the system of fate, chaos and ultimately death (which we shall see exemplified in the fatal poker game at the
end of the play), the Joven has retreated into the inner world of illusion. This
retreat is symbolised by the references to dirt and unruliness outside the
house in the street:

> Ruido, ruido siempre, polvo, calor, malos olores. Me molesta que las cosas
> de la calle entren en mi casa. (*Un gemido largo se oye*) Juan, cierra la
> ventana.   (*OC* II: 502)

Internal and external space is clearly delineated. While chaos reigns outside,
the Joven feels safe within the confines of his house. In symbolic terms, he
retreats into the inner world of the psyche, rather than having to cope with the
pressures of action in the world.

This play is the incarnation of the dream-world of the Joven. All temporal
and spatial restraints have therefore been suspended. Characters appear to the
Joven from his past, present and potential future, while past, present and
future are blended with disorientating abandon. Time often seems to be
projected forward into a potential future time. Hence at the beginning of the
play we are told that the Joven is to wait five years before he can marry the
Novia. Later, when he is rejected by the Novia, the Joven declares his love for
the Mecanógrafa, but she too insists that he wait five years for their union to
be consummated. Time is therefore often also postponed or repeated. The
play begins with the six chimes of the clock, and ends with six chimes to
signal that clock-time has not advanced. The entire action of the play has
taken place within the mind of the protagonist.

The play therefore operates within the confines of a liminal space – it is
the articulation of a time between, above and beyond temporal limits.[6] There
is a tension between the potential time, the events which may occur, and the
past, the traces of lost memories. It is the expression, then, of a 'perpetual
allusion', what Mallarmé (1897) defined (speaking of mime), as the illustration of:

> . . . but the idea, not any action, in a hymen (out of which flows Dream),
> tainted with vice yet sacred, between desire and fulfilment, perpetration
> and remembrance: here anticipating, there recalling, in the future, in the
> past, under the false appearance of a present. That is how the mime

6   The concept of Time received a radical reordering at the turn of the century in
Europe through the ideas of Freud on memory, and before that through the concepts of
Henri Bergson. Both seem to deal with time which cannot be rendered in clear linear
terms (e.g. Bergson's 1903 article 'Introduction à la métaphysique' and Freud's 1900 *The
Interpretation of Dreams*).

operates, whose act is confined to a perpetual allusion without breaking the ice or the mirror: he thus sets up a medium, a pure medium of fiction.

(Mallarmé 1897: 175)

Like the trickster-figure, the play is also a medium of fiction through which to explore and enact the facing of limits: in this case the subversion of linear time and the limits of masculinity. The fluidity of this potential time presents the promise of great freedoms: in this limbo the protagonist (and the audience) can flit through time, exploring different subject positions, shape-shifting and time-switching. The fluidity of potential forms is represented within the play by the Arlequín and Payaso. The former wears masks which he changes at will as he dances on to the set. The Arlequín is the guardian of the liminal space, having emerged from a theatre which has sprung up in the middle of the wood. But his sidekick the Payaso, who has emerged from a travelling circus, gives the impression of a skull. These two figures, it soon emerges, far from symbolising freedoms, represent death and stasis. The circus is blocking the path of the young man, and the Arlequín attempts to coax the Joven to join him there: '¿No quiere entrar señor?' (*OC* II: 571). The circus represents the entrapment and death associated with the stasis and fixity of types – it is 'lleno de espectadores definitivamente quietos' (*OC* II: 571). Hence there is a tension here between the potential possibilities expressed by the notion of a liminal space, and the symbolic death presented by types and the fixity of identity. The trickster-figures (Arlequín and Payaso) perpetually dodge the fixity of form by their bewildering play of masks, but their power is not complete – rather, it is double-edged. As mediators, 'pure fictions', like the play as a whole they present the potential for the Joven, and likewise for the audience through the trickster-function, to explore the pleasures of facing the limits of culture. But at the same time, they represent replaced action, presenting inaction which poses, masquerades and parades as action. They present themselves as red herrings, sent to trip up the protagonist and ourselves in this game of life so that we are so occupied with the appearance of action, that nothing is in fact achieved. Or perhaps all achievements are nothing more than appearances: these are the questions that this play meditates upon. If *Así que pasen cinco años* explores the way that we take pleasure in the continual facing of the limits of culture, then what emerges is a sense in which life can be seen as a series of attempts to court and face death, and there is pleasure in this.

In this dream-world created by the Joven, each of the characters can be seen as aspects or projections of the mind of the young man.[7] As such, they

---

[7] Lorca may well have been acquainted with the ideas of Freud from his stay at the Residencia de Estudiantes in Madrid which organised lectures and seminars on the major ideas and thinkers of the time. For a Freudian reading of this play, see Huélamo Kosma (1989: 59–83).

present us with fragmentary elements of a masculine psyche. The Viejo lives constantly in the past, his life has now passed by and he is left with just his memories. In fact, he delights in the pastime of recalling the past: 'Me gusta tanto la palabra recuerdo. Es una palabra verde, jugosa. Mana sin cesar hilitos de agua fría' (*OC* II: 571). He represents what the Joven will become if he does not grasp life to the full while he has the chance.[8] The oral introjection suggested by the word 'jugosa' (the implication being that time can be eaten whole), is qualified by 'verde', which can mean lush and verdant, but also may signify fruit that is unripe, immature: or represent gangrenous decay and death.

If the Viejo represents the dying embers of a life wasted, then the Niño is a life which has been cut off before it really had a chance to flower. In terms of the motif of masculinity, the Niño can be seen as a representation of the threshold of masculinity. He is dressed in white as for the First Communion (a garb which interestingly parallels the bridal gown – symbolic of a different sort of ritual threshold – of the Maniquí in the second act). The dead child wears a crown of white roses and is carrying a candle and a ribbon of golden flowers. This pathetic, innocent creature has died, we learn later, of malnutrition before he has had a chance to reach maturity. '¡Quiero ser niño, un niño!' (*OC* II: 520), is his pitiful cry. The Viejo and the Niño seem to represent two extremes of a spectrum of masculine subject positions – what binds them is their shared inability to indulge in life, to live on anything other than nostalgic yearnings for what might have been.

The Amigo 1° and Amigo 2° can also be seen as projections of the young man. The Second Friend is delicate and hypersensitive, while the First Friend is a boisterous Don Juan figure. In the case of the Amigo 1°, with his dizzying list of female conquests, he seems to encapsulate very well the traditional Don Juan figure:

Amigo 1°:   Ayer hice tres conquistas y como anteayer hice dos y hoy una
              pues resulta [. . .] que me quedo sin ninguna porque no tengo

---

8   My reading therefore differs from that of Soufas (1996: 69–77), for whom the protagonist is the Viejo as he looks back on his life which is now wasted. Harris Smith (1984: 113) writes that the Viejo and the Joven represent 'a basic conflict between halves of a Self, the Young Self (El Joven) and the Old Self (El Viejo), whose memories about a shared past differ'. Harris Smith writes that 'as they argue, their memories are enacted by masked figures, mannequins and other dream images'. I would suggest that rather, it is the Joven who is the protagonist, while the Viejo represents what the Joven will become if he continues along this path, much as Scrooge is presented with the ghosts of Christmas Past, Present and Future in Dickens's *A Christmas Carol*. From this point of view, the Viejo is like Dante's Virgil, attempting to lead the young man and guide him through this journey into the depths of the psyche. It seems obvious, however, that the shifts in time in this play encourage readings on different levels and both readings of the Viejo (as protagonist, or as projection) can operate simultaneously.

	tiempo. Estuve con una muchacha [. . .] Ernestina ¿la quieres conocer?
Joven:	No.
Amigo 1°:	Nooo y rúbrica. Pero si vieras ¡¡tiene un talle!![. . .] No [. . .] aunque el talle lo tiene mucho mejor Matilde.

(OC II: 510)

He represents the stereotype of the *Don Juan* archetype – that traditional symbol of masculine sexual prowess. I shall explore the Amigo 1° and Amigo 2° in greater detail further on.

To complete this spectrum of masculinity, the Jugador de Rugby is the epitome of virility. As the Novia throws herself into his arms, he stands silently and smokes, occasionally blowing smoke into her face: '*no habla, sólo fuma y aplasta en el piso el cigarro*' (OC II: 396). But with his 'rodilleras' and 'casco' in the garb of American football, even his muscular body is enhanced artificially (a predecessor of the body builder, perhaps). He represents hyper-masculinity, the empty spectacle of the men of Hollywood cinema.[9] In some ways he seems to suggest Pepe el Romano, of *La casa de Bernarda Alba*. Pepe el Romano is described as 'un gigante'. He is symbolised by the stallion in the courtyard, kicking down the stable walls, yet he never appears on stage, leading the audience to suspect that perhaps this specimen of virility has been enhanced by the imaginations of the women within the house. In the case of the Jugador de Rugby, he seems likewise to have been 'created' by the imagination of the Novia (alternatively, we could view the figure as a creation of the mind of the Joven – the Jugador de Rugby is a foil to the young man, epitomising all that the Joven feels he ought to aspire to in order to please the Novia).[10] The Jugador de Rugby never speaks, and the Novia projects her feelings onto him:

> Porque eres como un dragón (*Le abraza*). Creo que me vas a quebrar entre tus brazos porque soy como una diminuta guitarra quemada por el sol y no me quiebras. (*El jugador de rugby le echa humo en la cara.*) (OC II: 532)

The bitter-sweet humour of this passage stems from the empty, mask-like figure of the Jugador de Rugby and the mismatch with the gushing romanticism of the situation by the Novia. The rugby-player, with no personality of his own, is symbolic of the hollowness of the traditional image of masculinity.

The play's presentation of masculinity as fragmentary (in these differing projections of the psyche), split and vulnerable, challenges the traditional

9 See Cohan and Hark (1993) for a discussion of Hollywood masculinities.

10 This reminds us of Don Perlimplín's creation of the fantasy Joven de la Capa Roja for Belisa in *Amor de Don Perlimplín con Belisa en su jardín*, and the Zapatero's refashioning of himself for the Zapatera in *La zapatera prodigiosa*.

perception of masculinity as a monolithic, stable entity. As David Buchbinder
has written in his 1994 book on masculinity:

> Masculini*ties*? A *plurality* of masculinity? Twenty years ago such an idea
> would have been, to say the least, unusual. And twenty years before that,
> unthinkable. Masculinity has traditionally been seen as self-evident,
> natural, universal; above all as unitary and whole, not multiple or divided.
> (Buchbinder 1994: 1)

The multi-faceted Joven therefore presents us with a view of masculinity in
this play as unstable, divided and vulnerable. The Joven, with his awareness
of the sort of masculinity he feels he should aspire to, and his sense of failure
at not doing so (we have only to think of the Novia's accusatory, '¿Y no
jugabas al rugby? [. . .] ¿Y no llevabas un caballo de las crines y matabas en
un día tres mil faisanes?', and the Joven's shamed reply, 'Nunca' [*OC* II: 546]
to perceive this sense of failure) could be seen as an example of what Mark
Breitenberg (1996) has termed 'anxious masculinity'. Breitenberg writes
that, paradoxically, the term 'anxious masculinity' is in fact redundant,
because all masculinity is 'anxious':

> masculine subjectivity constructed and sustained by a patriarchal culture –
> infused with patriarchal assumptions about power, privilege, sexual desire,
> the body – inevitably engenders varying degrees of anxiety in its male
> members.   (Breitenberg 1996: 1)

The Joven is clearly 'anxious' about his body (the antithesis of the rugby-
player); about his lack of sexual prowess (the antithesis of the First Friend)
and about his lack of strength and intellectual prowess (the Viejo can be seen
to represent Wisdom – another traditional masculine symbol). The portrayal
of the masculine psyche which emerges from this play is therefore one which
encapsulates very well the notion of 'anxious masculinity'. It challenges the
traditional view of conventional masculinity in subtle and interesting ways.

ASÍ QUE PASEN CINCO AÑOS . . .

The young man of *Así que pasen cinco años* is in love with the Novia, but
is to have nothing to do with her, by his own consent, until five years have
passed. Meanwhile he is free to enjoy the image he has of her, imprisoning
her in his mind within the idea of the sweet young girl who will never grow
old:

Joven: Usted quiere apartarme de ella. Pero yo concozco su
              procedimiento. Basta observar un rato sobre la palma de la
              mano un insecto vivo, o mirar al mar una tarde poniendo

atención en la forma de cada ola, para que el rostro o llaga que llevamos en el pecho se deshaga en burbujas. Pero es que yo estoy enamorado como ella lo está de mí y por eso puedo aguardar cinco años en espera de poder liarme de noche, con todo el mundo a oscuras, sus trenzas de luz alrededor de mi cuello. (*OC* II: 503)

The Joven jealously guards his fantasy-image of the Novia, and reacts angrily when the Viejo tries to introduce some element of reality into his dreams, which threatens to distort the perfect image he has constructed in his imagination:

Viejo: Me permito recordarle que su novia [. . .] no tiene trenzas.
Joven: (*Irritado*) Ya lo sé. Se las cortó sin permiso naturalmente y esto [. . .] (*con angustia*) me cambia su imagen. (*Enérgico*) Ya sé que no tiene trenzas. (*Casi furioso*) ¿Por qué me lo ha recordado usted? (*con tristeza*) Pero en estos cinco años las volverá a tener. (*OC* II: 504)

The Joven sees the Novia as if she were a painting created by himself – but it is an image that he struggles to keep hold of :

Joven: ¡Pues si me pongo a pensar en ella! La dibujo, la hago moverse blanca y viva, pero de repente, ¿quién le cambia la nariz o le rompe los dientes o la convierte en otra llena de andrajos que va por mi pensamiento monstruosa como si estuviera mirándose en un espejo de feria? (*OC* II: 505)

The Joven has created a fantasy image of the Novia so that he can *cope with the idea*. It is essential to him that he maintains a certain distance from her, hence his desire to call her 'muchachita', rather than 'novia', the latter suggesting more involvement with her:

Joven: [. . .] Novia [. . .] ya lo sabe usted, si digo novia la veo sin querer amortajada en un cielo sujeto por enormes trenzas de nieve. No, no es mi novia (*hace un gesto como si apartara a la imagen que quiere captarlo*) es mi niña, mi muchachita.
                                                                        (*OC* II: 505)

Any suggestion of proximity to the Novia seems to fill the Joven with anxiety and fear. It is for this reason that when the Novia rejects him – telling him she is in love with the Jugador de Rugby – he is more distraught about losing his ideal love, than about the reality of living without her: 'No es tu engaño lo que me duele. Tú no eres mala. Tú no significas nada. Es mi tesoro perdido. Es mi amor sin objeto' (*OC* II: 549). The whole scenario with the Novia has been invented, I argue, within the imagination of the Joven. He cannot

conceive of the couple ever coming together, being too frightened to get close
to the Novia, and so engineers the split as the only solution within his mind.
In contrast to Edwards (1980: 95–6) for whom the character of the Joven is
tied to 'all the female figures who, in Lorca's poems and plays wait and
dream of a love that never comes', I argue that the young man's waiting is
entirely self-imposed. The whole play comes to be seen as a figment of the
imagination of the Joven – the endless waiting game is created by the character and corresponds to his desires. So that when the Joven is rejected by the
Mecanógrafa in the Third Act (in spite of her burning passion for the Joven
earlier on in the play, she now insists that they can only marry, 'así que pasen
cinco años'), once again it is because the Joven is so fearful of entering into a
relationship that this outcome, invented in his mind, is the only solution:

> Mecanógrafa: ¡Me iré contigo! [. . .]
> Joven: ¡Amor!
> Mecanógrafa: Me iré contigo (*Timida*) ¡Así que pasen cinco años!
> Joven: ¡Ay!   (*OC* II: 581)

According to my reading of this play, the Joven's relationship to the Novia
and the Mecanógrafa is characterised by a need to distance himself from
them. Their rejection of him is in fact a product of his imagination. The Joven
says of the Novia:

> Aun está más vivo lo de adentro aunque también cambie. Mire usted, la
> última vez que la vi no podía mirarla muy de cerca porque tenía dos arru-
> guitas en la frente que, como me descuidara [. . .] ¿entiende usted? le
> llenaban todo el rostro y la ponía ajada, vieja, como si hubiera sufrido
> mucho. Tenía necesidad de separarme para [. . .] ¡enfocarla!, ésta es la
> palabra, en mi corazón.   (*OC* II: 506)

The Joven appears to be caught within a cycle which will not allow him to get
close to any of the female characters.

MALE MASOCHISM

In my view, the Joven has actively constructed the scenarios of rejection
between himself and the female characters. In his active seeking out of
suffering and humiliation, the Joven could be seen as an example of male
masochism. Masochism acquired its name after the German author Leopold
von Sacher-Masoch and the term was created by Richard von Krafft-Ebing
(1886: 132) in his 1886 study on sexual aberrations entitled, *Psychopathia
Sexualis*. For Sigmund Freud, who explored these ideas further, in *Three
Essays on Sexuality* (1905a), sadism and masochism are two poles of a

'perversion' involving 'the desire to inflict pain upon the sexual object, and its reverse'. Freud writes:

> . . . other writers have preferred the narrower term 'algolagnia'. This emphasises the pleasure in *pain*, the cruelty, whereas the names chosen by Krafft-Ebing [sadism and masochism] bring into prominence pleasure in any form of humiliation or subjection.   (1905a: 157)

Freud examined masochism in several essays: 'Three Essays on the Theory of Sexuality' (1905a); 'Instincts and Their Vicissitudes' (1915a); 'A Child is Being Beaten' (1919a); and 'The Economic Problem of Masochism' (1924). In the last of these, Freud distinguishes between three forms of masochism: erotogenic, moral and feminine masochism.[11] In the case of all of these, masochism derives from an initial Oedipal conflict. Freud therefore implicates the father as the prime mover in a fantasy in which a fear/love of a powerful mother figure is actually nothing more than the child's repressed wish, *I am being beaten by the father*, which in turn stands for *I am being loved by my father*. 'In both cases [Freud contends that the same case applies for male and for female masochists] the beating phantasy has its origin in an incestuous attachment to the father' (Freud 1919a: 198). Masochism is nothing more than the reverse of sadism, with sadism and masochism two sides of a pairing of opposites: aggressiveness/passivity.[12] Gilbert explains masochism thus:

> Masochism has the self as its object and works through fantasy: a fantasy which can be seen as introducing death as the ultimate sexual event, a death which is always about to occur but is always kept at a distance, anticipated. The essential feature of the scenario is suspense, waiting, deferred fulfilment of desire.   (Gilbert 1993: 165)

Gilles Deleuze challenges Freud's definition of masochism as resulting from Oedipal conflicts in his book, *Masochism: An Interpretation of Coldness and Cruelty* (Deleuze 1989). In it, he makes the point that this perversion takes its name from a literary work – Sacher-Masoch's *Venus in Furs* (Sacher-Masoch

---

11 Laplanche and Pontalis (1988: 244–5) define erotogenic masochism as involving the sexual perversion; moral masochism as deriving from a sense of guilt, whether sexual or not, and 'feminine' as involving 'the expression of the feminine essence', although this type of masochism affects male subjects.

12 Freud writes, 'Sadism and masochism occupy a special position among the perversions, since the contrast between activity and passivity which lies behind them is among the universal characteristics of sexual life', in 'Three Essays on the Theory of Sexuality' (1905a). Freud has been criticised for his alignment of male/female with aggressive/passive within this framework. However, once Freud conceived of a Death Instinct, *Thanatos*, there is some evidence that he believed that masochism cannot adequately be explained as a turning-around of sadism against itself.

1870), and that, by attaching the Marquis de Sade's and Sacher-Masoch's names to distinct perversions, psychoanalysis took, 'a major linguistic and semiological step' in that 'a proper name is made to connote signs' (Deleuze 1989: 16).[13] According to Deleuze, sadomasochism [as a single concept] is a semiological and clinical impossibility, for:

> as soon as we read Masoch we become aware that his universe has nothing to do with that of Sade [. . .] We must take an entirely different approach, the *literary approach*, since it is from literature that stem the original definitions of sadism and masochism [. . .] In place of a dialectic which all too readily perceives the link between opposites, we should aim for a critical and clinical appraisal able to reveal the truly differential mechanisms as well as the artistic originalities.   (Deleuze 1989: 13)

Deleuze not only challenges the sado-masochistic link, but also perceives that masochism is derived not from Oedipal conflict, but from a much earlier period in the child's development. Deleuze also challenges Freud's theories by asserting that it is the mother who is the crucial influence in the psyche of the masochist.

Furthermore, Deleuze stresses that masochism is not restricted to the arena of sexual conflicts, but is to be perceived in many areas of culture and language. As Gaylin Studlar asserts:

> Deleuze considers masochism to be a phenomenology of experience that reaches far beyond the limited definition of perverse sexuality. Similarly, the masochistic aesthetic extends beyond the purely clinical into the arena of language, artistic form, narrativity and the production of textual pleasure.   (Studlar 1988: 14)

I would like to examine how far our protagonist could be seen as an example of Deleuzean masochism, and how far the play corresponds with the definition of masochistic fantasy as outlined by Deleuze's theories.

The masochian fantasy involves 'an indefinite awaiting of pleasure and an intense expectation of pain' (Deleuze 1989: 71):

> Sacher-Masoch's fictional heterocosm is mythical, persuasive, aesthetically oriented, and centred around the idealising, mystical exaltation of love for the punishing woman.   (Studlar 1988: 18)

But unlike Sade's misogynistic violence towards women, masochian fantasy involves the contractual agreement of the female. The female is 'called upon by contract to play her role' (Studlar 1988: 22). *Así que pasen cinco años* can

---

[13] For a full discussion of the difference between Freudian and Deleuzean models of masochism, see Studlar (1985).

be interpreted as a masochian fantasy surrounding love for the 'punishing female'. In the scene between the Mecanógrafa and the Máscara, they speak of nothing but their love of taunting men. As a figment of the imagination of the Joven, this scene has been created by him, they merely deliver their side of the bargain, or contract set out by him:

Mecanógrafa:	Yo me fui de su casa. Recuerdo que la tarde de mi partida había una gran tormenta de verano y había muerto el niño de la portera. El me dijo: "¿Me habías llamado?"; a lo que yo contesté cerrando los ojos: "NO". Y luego en la puerta, dijo: "¿Me necesitas?"; y yo le dije: "No. No te necesito".
Máscara:	¡Precioso! (*OC* II: 567)

In this fantasy, the women collude in their punishment of the male characters.

In Deleuze's conception of masochism, the hero neither destroys the real nor idealises the real, but instead disavows the real and introduces the ideal with fantasy, an intermediary realm midway between the real and the ideal. Unlike Sade's descriptions of violent sexual scenarios, those of Masoch tend to avoid obscenity, serving instead to create, 'a strange and oppressive atmosphere, like a sickly perfume', in which the only things to emerge are suspended gestures and suspended suffering. This description seems to recall the stultified atmosphere of *Así que pasen cinco años* and the curiously oppressive dream-like atmosphere generated by these characters who appear as if out of nowhere and then disappear almost as quickly in a disorientating blend of past, present and future. In Masochian fantasy, as set out by Deleuze, sexual pleasure itself is disavowed, the scene of ritualised torture leading towards a frozen stasis, a pure waiting comprised of an 'indefinite awaiting of pleasure and an intense expectation of pain'. This seems to sum up very well the action of this play which features the repetition of the scene of torture when the Joven is rejected by both the Novia and then subsequently by the Mecanógrafa:

Joven:	Dime.
Mecanógrafa:	¡Me iré contigo! [. . .]
Joven:	¡Amor!
Mecanógrafa:	Me iré contigo. (*Tímida*) ¡Así que pasen cinco años!
Joven:	¡Ay! (*Se lleva las manos a la frente*)
Viejo:	Bravo. (*OC* II: 581)

The repetition of the phrase 'así que pasen cinco años' makes the words ring with a dreadful inevitability. Living in fear of consummation, the Joven must obsessively recreate the conditions of fear to assure himself that he is in control and 'safe'.

In the waiting game, Deleuze (1989: 33) writes that, 'Masoch's heroes are literally suspended (hanged, crucified, and so on) and the gestures and poses of the female torturer are often arrested, the torturer identified with a statue, painting or photograph'. Interestingly, the Joven's fantasy-image of himself involves just such a scene of hanging or suspension: 'sus trenzas de luz alrededor de mi cuello':

Joven:	Pero es que yo estoy enamorado como ella lo está de mí y por eso puedo aguardar cinco años en espera de poder liarme de noche, con todo el mundo a oscuras, sus trenzas de luz alrededor de mi cuello.
Viejo:	Me permito recordarle que su novia [. . .] no tiene trenzas.

(OC II: 503–4)

Deleuze cites coldness as a central component of the representation of femininity in the Masochian fantasy. In this play there are frequent references to coldness as well as to death. The Joven speaks thus of the Novia:

. . . si digo novia la veo sin querer amortajada en un cielo sujeto por enormes trenzas de nieve. *(OC* II: 505)

Furthermore, the hands of the young man are described as being 'waxen' ('una mano fría. Una mano de cera cortado'), which has resonances of the plaster cheek of the Maniquí and the Máscara and the pallid complexion of the Niño. Masochian coldness, according to Deleuze, signifies the disavowal of sensuality and the ascent to the ideal. Hence, 'the masochist is therefore able to deny the reality of pleasure at the very point of experiencing it, in order to identify with the "new sexless man" ' (Deleuze 1989: 33). Coldness is an expression of the distance which maintains the fantasy, but in this play it is even more sinister as it is linked to death.

In addition to a correlation between the feminine and coldness in this play, as in the Masochian fantasy set out by Deleuze, female characters in this play are often represented in terms of static images such as a painting, a statue or photograph. The Maniquí is a plaster mannequin from a shop-window; the Máscara is the mere mask of femininity; while the images of femininity constructed for us by the two friends equally involve the restriction of the feminine to frozen, static images.

The Maniquí takes the form of a dummy from a shop-window. She appears towards the end of Act Two, shortly after the Novia has rejected the Joven. She is the mannequin that has stood in the bedroom of the Novia, displaying the wedding dress, among the decoration of angels and pink hearts which adorns the boudoir. The Maniquí enters wearing 'el vestido de novia':

. . . *este personaje tiene la cara gris y las cejas y labios dorados como un maniquí de escaparate de lujo. Lleva peluca y guantes de oro. Trae puesto con cierto embarazo un espléndido traje de novia blanco, con larga cola y velo . . . (OC* II: 552)

The mannequin has stepped straight out of a shop-window in the glittering arcades of the city. The mannequin is dehumanised, empty and cold. She is a reflection of the mixture of fascination and repulsion that Lorca felt for the large metropolis of New York. All of the characters of this play seem to reflect these mixed feelings. They cry out in anguish, yet their tears are as artificial as the sequins covering the dress of the character of the Máscara. Lorca juxtaposes what he sees as utopian attempts to drag the city into the future, with this creation of a glittering dream-world populated by characters who are hollow and dehumanised. The play is infused with an apocalyptic vision of the city: the city is portrayed as decaying, the phantasmagoria hiding the brittle fragility of dehumanisation. The character of the Maniquí, therefore, a product of this city, is frozen, lifeless and sterile. Walter Benjamin wrote of the arcades of the 1920s in Europe:

> . . . in the window displays of beauty salons are the last women with long hair. They have rich, undulating hair masses with a 'permanent wave' – fossilised hair curls.[14]

The Maniquí, like the women in these beauty salons, appears 'fossilised' – her features have been permanently fixed on her body. Furthermore, in that she represents the wedding that will now never take place between the Joven and the Novia, her presence on stage represents an absence. She is 'what might have been, but was not':

Maniquí: (*Canta y llora*) ¿Quién usará la plata buena
                   de la novia chiquita y morena?
                   Mi cola se pierde por el mar
                   y la luna lleva puesta mi corona de azahar.
                   Mi anillo, señor, mi anillo de oro viejo,
                   se hundió por las arenas del espejo.
                   ¿Quién se pondrá mi traje? ¿Quién se lo pondrá?
                   Se lo pondrá la ría grande para casarse con el mar.
                                                    (*OC* II: 552)

The Maniquí is the dress that will never be worn – as such she represents the absence of the body. As Roland Barthes has written, the body gives existence to the dress, 'for it is impossible to conceive of a dress without a body [. . .] the empty garment without head and limbs [. . .] is death, not the neutral absence of the body, but the body mutilated and decapitated':[15]

14 Benjamin (1982), *Das Passagen-Werk*, vol. 5, ed. by R. Tiedemann, Frankfurt am Main: Suhrkamp Verlag, cited in S. Buck-Morss (1995: 4–26).
15 Barthes (1985), *The Responsibility of Forms*, New York: Hill and Wang, cited in Gaines and Herzog (1990: 2).

Maniquí: Yo canto
                muerte que no tuve nunca,
                dolor de velo sin uso,
                con llanto de seda y pluma.
                Ropa interior que se queda
                helada de nieve oscura.   (*OC* II: 552)

To complete the picture of cold loss and sterility, the Maniquí mourns for the
children that she will never have:

Maniquí: Un trajecito
                que robé de la costura.
                (*Enseña un traje rosa de niño*)
                Dos fuentes de leche blanca
                mojan mis sedas de angustia
                y un dolor blanco a abejas
                cubre de rayos mi nuca.
                Mi hijo. ¡Quiero a mi hijo!   (*OC* II: 555)

She clasps the child's suit as if it were a baby and hugs it to her. The picture
of anguished sterility is complete. But given that the Maniquí is a projection
of the fears of the Joven, she also represents the child that he will never have,
owing to his inability to consummate the relationship with the Novia. The
child he would have had, is potentially now dead, making a correlation with
the character of the Niño – the child who will never cross the threshold of
maturity and become a man, but remains suspended in time like the ghostly
figure of an angel.[16]
    At the end of the act, the mannequin's dance is disturbed by the entrance of
the maid:

> *La luz es de un azul intenso. Entra la Criada por la izquierda con un cande-*
> *labro y la escena toma suavemente su luz normal, sin descuidar la luz azul de*
> *los balcones abiertos de par en par que hay en el fondo. En el momento que*
> *aparece la Criada, el Maniquí queda rígido con una postura de escaparate.*
> *La cabeza inclinada y las manos levantados en actitud delicadísima.*
>
> (*OC* II: 557)

Her magical dance (like the coming to life of the toys in the Nutcracker Suite)
must now come to an end, and she is once again rigid, fossilised, petrified.
    The frozen image of femininity represented by the Maniquí is repeated by
the character of the Máscara. This character:

---

[16] For J. A. Valente (1976: 195) in his article 'Pez luna', the motif of the 'niño no
engendrado' is central to this play.

... viste un traje de 1900 amarillo rabioso con larga cola, pelo de seda amarillo cayendo como un manto y máscara blanca de yeso con guantes hasta el codo del mismo color. Lleva sombrero amarillo y todo el pecho de tetas altas ha de estar sembrado de lentejuelas de oro. El efecto de este personaje debe ser el de una llamarada sobre el fondo de azules lunares y troncos nocturnos. Habla con un leve acento italiano. *(OC* II: 567)

Everything about this character is fake or assumed. With a face of white plaster and false yellow hair, this character is the personification of the mask – she represents the stultified outer signs of femininity. Although we later learn that her persona of the Countess where she danced with the Count Arturo is now a dream to mask the pathetic reality of her dreary life as the concierge (she is also the mother of the dead child), she nevertheless represents an image which has been frozen into outer accoutrements which signify an inner hollowness. It is the repetition of these images of femininity as frozen, static and stultified, that adds impact.

The Máscara, in the image of frozen subjectivity she presents, appears to resemble what Otto Fenichel (a Marxist psychoanalyst of 1930s Berlin) referred to as the 'fossilisation' of femininity. According to his reading of some forms of masculinity, a fear of the feminine can at times manifest itself as a desire for an androgynous girl – or a girl who may have a phallus, which, when fetishised, can create the girl into a phallus itself. He writes that fright paralyses: 'Inhibitions in the realm of motility may mean, "I am frightened"; very often they mean, "I am paralysed by a frightening sight", that is, by a sight that makes one face the possibility of castration or death' (Fenichel 1949: 310). The masculine subject's fear of the castrated and castrating woman can in some cases lead him to conceive of a woman who *is* a phallus. For Fenichel, this often results in the image of femininity being petrified, or turned into stone (we may be reminded of the statue of Galatea, created by Pygmalion [in Ovid's *Metamorphoses*]) – she is literally, a 'little phallus'. The masculine subject repeatedly converts the female object of his desire into 'stone' – this being the only way that he can approach her. This would seem to fit at least partly with our images of frozen femininity in this play.[17] The Joven 'fossilises' the women he meets so that he can overcome his fear of them.

Two friends call on the Joven to offer him advice. They present us with two very different portraits of masculinity. They both speak to the young man about their fantasies and interactions with women. The Amigo 2° does not seem to correspond to any traditional ideals of masculine subjectivity. The stage directions inform us that this part can be played either by a young boy

17 According to Fenichel's formulation, the fact that the masculine subject always knows that the girl is/has not really got the phallus, means that the only way out of this set of affairs is death (Fenichel 1949: 303–21).

or else by a girl, which lends the character a delicate sensitivity. The Second
Friend:

> . . . *viene vestido de blanco, con un impecable traje de lana y lleva guantes y*
> *zapatos del mismo color. De no ser posible que este papel lo haga un actor*
> *muy joven lo hará una muchacha. El traje ha de ser de un corte*
> *exageradísimo, llevara enormes botones azules y el chaleco y la corbata serán*
> *rizados encajes.* (*OC* II: 526)

This garb seems to have resonances of the white-suited pierrot. The Amigo 2°
explains that as a child he indulged in the fantasy of keeping a tiny woman
suspended within a raindrop:

Amigo 2°:   La lluvia es hermosa. En el colegio entraba por los patios y
                estrellaba por las paredes a unas mujeres desnudas, muy
                pequeñas que lleva dentro. ¿No las habéis visto? Cuando yo
                tenía cinco años [. . .] no cuando yo tenía dos [. . .] ¡miento!
                uno, un año tan solo. Es hermoso ¿verdad? ¡un año! cogí una
                de esas mujercillas de la lluvia y la tuve dos días en una
                pecera.
Amigo 1°:   (*Con sorna*) ¿Y creció?
Amigo 2°:   ¡No! se hizo cada vez más pequeña, más niña, como debe ser,
                como es lo justo hasta que no quedó de ella más que una gota
                de agua. (*OC* II: 527)

The fantasy image of femininity for the Second Friend is, like that of the
other male characters, one of a woman suspended, perfect, unsullied and
frozen in time and space. This passage has fascinating implications for our
reading of the play according to Deleuze's theory of masochism. Whereas
Freud maintained that masochism is the result of Oedipal conflict, Deleuze
believes that it derives from a pre-Oedipal, oral stage, which highlights the
subject's relationship with the mother. Studlar writes:

> . . . in Deleuze's construct, the mother becomes the familiar dual symbol of
> creation and death who crystallises infantile ambivalence in the maso-
> chistic ideal of 'coldness, solicitude and death'. She is the figure of the cold
> oral mother who represents the good mother from the infantile stage of
> imagined dual unity or symbiosis between mother and child.
>
> (Studlar 1988: 16)

In the speech of the Amigo 2° above, we can see that this fantasy of femininity began very early in the life of the Second Friend. 'Cuando tenía cinco
años [. . .] no cuando yo tenía dos [. . .] ¡miento! uno, un año tan sólo'. This
fantasy involving 'una de esas mujercillas de lluvia', began in the oral stage
of the life of the character. The Amigo 2° was in complete control of this
fantasy woman – she shrank until she was no more than a drop of rain,

completely at the mercy of the Amigo 2°. The Amigo 2° finds the image comforting – it harks back to a time before maturity.[18] Studlar paraphrases Deleuze thus:

> The masochist's disavowal of phallic power calls for the suspension of orgasmic gratification and the conditioning of its arrival with pain. This is the price paid for a mature genital sexuality that is at odds with infantile desire.   (Studlar 1988: 16)

The Amigo 2° remains locked within a dreamy time between childhood and maturity. His white suit represents the temporal limbo in which he finds himself. He is one more element of a psyche (that of the Joven) which displays many of the elements of masochism. What this play articulates is the continual suspension of gratification in a ritualised scene of torture involving the Joven and his psychical counterparts. He can therefore be seen to represent an example of Deleuze's theory of masochism.

The Amigo 1° bursts on stage, complaining about the silence of the house. The Amigo 1° and the Joven tussle and rub noses, reacting guiltily when surprised by the Viejo. We have intimations, therefore, of an intimate, sexually-charged relationship between the two which is not publicly acknowledged. The Amigo 1° has had many encounters with women. He explains to the Joven that he keeps photographs or portraits of the women he has slept with, and demands of the Joven:

| | . . . ¿Y dónde están en esta casa los retratos de las muchachas con las que tú te acuestas? Mira (*se acerca*): te voy a coger por la solapa, te voy a pintar de colorete esas mejillas de cera [. . .] o así restregadas. |
| Joven: | (*Irritado*) ¡Déjame!   (*OC* II: 510) |

The Amigo 1° is constantly in a hurry:

	(*Sentándose y estirándose en el sofá*) ¡Ay! ¡mmm! Yo en cambio [. . .] Ayer hice tres conquistas y como anteayer hice dos y hoy una pues resulta [. . .] que me quedo sin ninguna porque no tengo tiempo. Estuve con una muchacha [. . .] Ernestina ¿la quieres conocer?
Joven:	No.
Amigo:	Nooo y rúbrica. Pero si vieras ¡¡tiene un talle!! [. . .] No [. . .] aunque el talle lo tiene mucho mejor Matilde. (*OC* II: 510)

---

18 There seems to be a correlation between the Niño and the Amigo 2° in that both are suspended in their youth. Of course both carry resonances of death. The Niño, the dead child (and the references to the First Communion) can be said to represent stifled and denied sexuality.

The First Friend is rushing around, he has so many conquests to make:

> . . . no tengo tiempo, no tengo tiempo de nada, todo se me
> atropella. Porque ¡figúrate! Me cito con Ernestina (*se
> levanta*) las trenzas aquí, apretadas, negrísimas y luego [. . .]
> (*El Joven golpea con impaciencia los dedos sobre la mesa*).
>
> (*OC* II: 511)

The Amigo 1° keeps a photograph album filled with pictures of the women he
has slept with. In this way, he keeps the women distanced, objectified so that
they become mere memories, locked into images from the past. Although the
Amigo 1° therefore seems to be the antithesis of the Joven, it soon becomes
clear that he too is unable to commit himself to any woman. According to
Otto Rank, the *Don Juan* complex:

> . . . is based on the unattainability of the mother and the compensatory
> substitute for her.[19]

The Don Juan figure has been seen as an individual, 'suffering from
attenuated development who attempts to bind himself ever more closely to a
mother figure' (Mandrell 1992: 235). This constant searching for the ideal
woman (the impossible dream) has been seen as a diversionary tactic, to
disguise homosexuality.[20] This theory would seem to be suggested in our text
with the hints of a sexually-charged relationship between the Joven and the
Amigo 1°. Returning to Deleuze's theory of masochism as it might be applied
to the Joven, we find that in the case of the Amigo 1° we are dealing with a
fantasy image of femininity that is distanced, objectified, frozen into a visual
image.

Interestingly, the Amigo 1° seems to fit with the stereotype of Don Juan as
the Sadean libertine.[21] Following Barthes in *Sade, Fourier, Loyola* (1971) we
note that the language used by the Amigo 1° is clipped and chopped up into
short sections. In addition, the images of femininity he presents are dismembered, cut up into a jumble of limbs and hair, tokens and statistics. However,
the relationship between this character, who distances women in this way, and
the masochistic young man is clear: they are related in that they both attempt
to manipulate time in different ways. Deleuze writes that both the Sadist and

[19] Otto Rank, *The Don Juan Legend* (1975: 95) cited in Mandrell (1992: 235).
Possible sources for the ideas of Don Juan for Lorca were the theories of Ortega y Gasset,
whose 1923 text, *El tema de nuestro tiempo*, includes a long section on Don Juan, and also
Unamuno's *El hermano Juan* of 1928.

[20] Cf. Mitchell (1990) for whom Don Juan should rather be seen as a (heterosexual)
male hysteric.

[21] See Didier, 'Sade et Don Juan' (1981: 67–81); Schumacher (1981: 67–74) who
draws links between Don Juan and Thomas Shadwell's *The Libertine*; and Kossovitch,
'Don Juan e Sade' (1988: 77–82).

the Masochist are concerned with repetition, but: 'in Sade it is a function of acceleration and condensation and in Masoch it is characterized by the "frozen" quality and the suspense' (Deleuze 1989: 34).

These two figures seem to share both a willingness to court and simultaneously defer death.[22] In Shoshana Felman's excellent book *The Literary Speech Act: Don Juan with J. L. Austin or Seduction in Two Languages* (1980), Felman depicts the Don Juan figure as a character integrally related to time. Thus, Molière's myth of Don Juan features a 'struggle, or dramatic confrontation, between two cutting instruments: Time's scythe, and Don Juan's sword'. Thus, 'in making cuts, the Donjuanian performance is seeking above all to cut off the advance of Death, to escape Time, to cut away from its cutting edge: it strives to cut out Time's cutting' (Felman 1980: 45). Hence the string of broken promises which are characteristic of the Don Juanesque language of seduction are nothing more than a 'flight in the face of death' (47), and a flight from death.

Felman argues that Don Juan's promises are, following Austin's theory of speech acts, 'performatives', that is, 'expressions whose function is not to inform or describe, but to carry out a "performance", to accomplish an *act* through the very process of their enunciation' (Felman 1980: 15). Hence the scandal of the seduction perpetrated by Don Juan is the scandal of broken promises, but furthermore, they are acts which have been violated. I suggest, then, that the masochistic Joven and the Don Juanesque Amigo 1° are structurally and symbolically linked in that, while the Amigo 1° makes promises he knows he will not keep, the Joven wants promises to be made to him that will not be kept. The performative promise is therefore, like Mallarmé's mime, operating in a liminal time 'between perpetration and remembrance'. It stands in place for an action, giving the illusion of action, while disguising inaction. I suggest that both the Joven and the Amigo 1° are caught up in a game of repetition which continually courts death in an attempt to feel the fear of death, and somehow to defer its arrival.

I shall now examine the structure of the play in the context of these ideas about Deleuzean masochism. *Así que pasen cinco años* does not obey the unities of Aristotelian structure, but instead seems to play around with notions of past, present and future.[23] Narrativity, or the advance of plot, is halted by the disorientating shifts in time. For example, the intriguing tense used by the Viejo, 'se me olvidará el sombrero', and the delicious mixture of

22 Deleuze (1989: 35) writes: 'The first representation [Sadism] is a speculative and analytical manner of apprehending the Death Instinct – which, as we have seen, can never be anything given – while the second [Masochism] pursues the same object in a totally different way, mythically, dialectically and in the imaginary'.

23 Edwards (1980: 100) writes that, 'in evoking a world of dreams the play exposes its precariousness before the advance of time and suggests in doing so that what is true of the future is true of the present too, for the future is inevitably the present, the present the past, the whole a shifting process in which, in terms of illusions, the only certain end is death'.

tenses in this exchange between the Joven and the Mecanógrafa with a love which is constantly projected forward and backwards but can never take place in the present:

Mecanógrafa:	¡Te he querido tanto!
Joven:	¡Te quiero tanto!
Mecanógrafa:	¡Te querré tanto!
[. . .]	
Mecanógrafa:	¡Te he querido, amor! Te querré siempre!
Joven:	Ahora [. . .]
Mecanógrafa:	¿Por qué dices ahora? (*OC* II: 576–7)

The repetition of details of plot, but with certain tiny differences (such as the rejection of the Joven by both the Novia and the Mecanógrafa and the repetition of the phrase, 'así que pasen cinco años') also create an image of liminal time – always projecting forwards or back. These elements serve to disorientate the spectator.

The structure of the play, then, seems to involve the advance of the narrative, interspersed with elements which halt the narrative. These glitches in the narrative movement mean that the structure of the play mimics the progression of masochism, which involves, not, 'the mechanical cumulative fashion of Sade' (Deleuze 1989: 34), which accelerates movement, but 'a sort of frozen progression' (cascade) that creates a type of static reiteration (Deleuze 1989: 34).

If we think of the play in visual terms, we seem to jolt from one photographic image to the next, again, in a sort of 'frozen progression'. The characters appear often limited to hollow visual images, rather like photographs.[24] We have only to think of the one-dimensional Jugador de Rugby to see evidence of this.

The motif of photography interested Lorca very much. As Marie Llafranque (1987) has documented, Lorca, in a letter to Melchor Fernández Almagro, spoke of an as yet secret project, consisting of 'cuatro cuartillas de otro tamaño que el de *Posada*, iguales de dos en dos. Una triple referencia fotográfica en los títulos, con leves variantes, sugiere tres proyectos distintos

---

[24] Other critics have discussed the play's debt to cinematic images (but none so far has seen them as photographic images), for example Edwards (1981: 128–41). Ucelay (1995) points out that Fritz Lang's *Metropolis* was shown in Madrid in 1928 – she sees parallels between that film's Grim Reaper and the final scene of this play, in which poker players seal the fate of the young man. Deleuze (1989: 31) writes of masochism that it involves a fetish which is 'not a symbol at all, but as if it were a frozen, arrested, two-dimensional image, a photograph to which one returns repeatedly to exorcise the dangerous consequences of movement'.

en versiones sucesivas' (Llafranque 1987).[25] Lorca's description of the proposed play is as follows:

Los personajes son ampliaciones fotográficas y están fijos en un momento del cual no pueden salir. Tienen grandes bigotes y adoptan posturas de pose fotográfica. El sentimiento de los personajes es puramente exterior, lo que se ve y nada más. El drama oscuro y sordo corre delante del objetivo de las gentes. La escena ha de estar impregnada de ese terrible silencio de las fotos de muertos y ese gris difuminado de los fondos.

The description of these characters as 'lo que se ve y nada más', in fact, seems to sum up very well the characters of *Así que pasen cinco años*. They appear like photographs, or a pack of cards, frozen into types as they pass across the stage.

Roland Barthes (1980: 89–90) conceived of the photographic image as an example of stasis. He contrasts the photograph with the cinematic image and writes:

Like the real world, the filmic world is sustained by the presumption that, as Husserl says, 'the experience will constantly continue to flow in the same constitutive style'; but the Photograph breaks the 'constitutive style' [. . .] it is *without future* (this is its pathos, its melancholy).

He goes on:

In the Photograph, Time's immobilization assumes only an excessive, monstrous mode: Time is engorged (whence the relation with the *Tableau vivant*, whose mythic prototype is the princess falling asleep in *Sleeping Beauty*). That the Photograph is 'modern', mingled with our noisiest everyday life, does not keep it from having an enigmatic point of inactuality, a strange stasis, the stasis of an *arrest*.   (Barthes 1980: 90)

Barthes goes on to conceive of the photograph as an essentially dead image. Images in *Así que pasen cinco años* are 'posed', arrested in time – they point metaphorically to the halting and flow of the narrative. Banfield (1982: 257–74) has written of the difficulty in ascribing a tense to a photograph, while Baker (1996: 74) writes that photographs are 'torn *necessarily* between narrative and stasis'. Photographs attempt to pin time down to a visual image, but they belong to a liminal time, the mask of a present, hiding absence.

In the preceding pages we discussed the figure of the Maniquí and her

---

25 Llafranque (1987: 20). The plays concerned are *Ampliación fotográfica. Drama*; *Drama Fotográfico* and *Rosa mudable: Drama fotografiado*. The *dramatis personae* of *Drama fotográfico* includes la Novia, el Novio, el Sargento, el Hermano de América, el Niño Muerto and la Madre – suggesting a correlation with this play's list of characters.

lament for the wedding that will never take place, and the child she will never
have. Like the performative promise of Don Juan, she stands in for an event
which will not take place, pointing forward to a potential future time.[26] She
represents unfulfilled desire and longing – she has become an empty signifier. The emphasis on masks, fake pieces and various accoutrements to
gender (think of the 'cascos' of the rugby-player; and the 'peluca' of the
Máscara) seems to point endlessly elsewhere. These elements are locked into
a 'perpetual allusion' (Mallarmé). The Viejo likewise refers endlessly to a
time past, the Niño to a potential future time (his life as a child/growing into a
man) which will now never take place. In this 'perpetual allusion', some of
the characters are borrowed straight from the shadowy world of mime and
Commedia dell'arte. The Arlequín and Payaso have drifted onto the set from
a travelling circus nearby, in the wood.[27] In the sense that all of the characters
seem to be referring elsewhere, either in terms of allusions to stereotypical
characters, or else to a different space in time, the play seems to articulate
that liminal area between fulfilment and desire; between perpetration and
remembrance of the event, above and beyond the limits of linear time.

Mime and this liminal time figure strongly in the final scene of the play.
Three poker players appear on stage dressed in smoking jackets. The first
player mentions Venice, evocative of masks and disguise, and sits down to
play poker with the Joven. When the ace is drawn from the pack, we are told:

Joven: ¡Juego!
(*Pone la carta sobre la mesa*)
(*En este momento, en los anaqueles de la biblioteca aparece un gran as de
'coeur' iluminado. El Jugador 1° saca una pistola y dispara sin ruido con una
flecha. El as desaparece y el joven se lleva las manos al corazón*).

                                                                    (*OC* II: 594)

The production of the ace of hearts signifies the death of the young man.[28]
The first player produces a pistol but fires a silent arrow. The manner of death
of the Joven (which borrows from Symbolism) is fitting for this dream which
takes place in liminal time, somewhere between living and death, between
waking and sleeping. The arrow reminds us of Bergson's attempts to capture

---

[26] We might draw a correlation between the Maniquí and Marcel Duchamp's 'delay' in
glass, *The Bride Stripped Bare by Her Bachelors, Even*, part of the project for the *Large
Glass* of 1923 (Duchamp 1923). As Hyde (1998: 305) writes, 'to continue the sexual
analogy of the window-gazing note, the bride represents a kind of arousal without
consummation, which is best represented by the "delay" '.

[27] For a discussion of the influence on the play of the characters of the *Commedia
dell'arte*, see David George (1995: 143).

[28] Bakhtin (1965: 235) writes that, 'games are also related to time and to the future.
The basic accessories of games, dice and cards are often used as the accessories of
fortune-telling'.

l'expérience vécue, the flow of immediate subjective experience ungraspable by thought and its relation to time through Zeno's Paradox.[29] At the end of the play the clock strikes six and is immediately followed by another six chimes. The second series of chimes may constitute an echo, or repetition of the first. No time has taken place since the beginning of the play, but at the same time, time has been repeated. An echo repeats the words of the Joven:

Joven:	Lo he perdido todo.
Eco:	Lo he perdido todo [. . .]
Joven:	Mi amor [. . .]
Eco:	Amor. . . (*OC* II: 595)

To sum up then, the narrative structure of this play seems to involve glitches which halt the advance of the narrative and turn it into a sort 'frozen progression', punctuated by circular routes, detours and repetitions, which has clear resonances of Deleuze's conception of masochism and its ritualised suspension and denial of gratification.

Given that performance was such an important element in Lorca's conception of his plays, an examination of spectatorship is important for an analysis of this play. My reading is indebted to Gaylin Studlar's analysis of 'the masochistic aesthetic' in her analysis of film theory (1988).

Roland Barthes, in *Sade, Fourier, Loyola* (1971), wonders what are the pleasures of Sade's writing and concludes that it produces pleasures which are 'structurally linked to crime and sex'. Studlar (1988: 18) draws the conclusion that the novels of Sacher-Masoch must therefore produce pleasures involving 'formal and narrative patterns structurally linked to self-abasement and suspended desire':

> Masochism tells its story through very precisely delimited means: fantasy, disavowal, fetishism, and suspense are its formal and psychoanalytic foundations. (Studlar 1988: 18)

We have already looked at the ways in which the narrative structure seems to mimic the formal structures of masochism, with its narrative structure of 'frozen progression'. In terms of the relationship of the Joven to the women in his life, we follow the anguish of the Joven when he is rejected by the Novia , but there is a certain satisfying circularity about the repetition of the event through the Mecanógrafa: the repetition of the phrase 'así que pasen cinco años' is at once frustrating and satisfying for the audience.

The plot of *Así que pasen cinco años*, like the Masochian text, is 'mythical, persuasive, aesthetically oriented, and centred around love for the

---

29 Russell and Barratt (1990: 59) document the attempts of Russian modernist theatre to put Bergson's ideas on the stage, to recreate, 'the dramatic flux of personal life'.

punishing woman' (Studlar 1988: 18). The pleasures of this text are therefore related to fantasy, disavowal, fetishism and suspense, constituent parts of the pleasures of masochism.[30] If there is pleasure in this text for the audience, I would suggest that through the contractual trickster-function the audience is perpetually led vicariously to experience the thrill of the limit, to court and simultaneously to defer death. If there is pleasure in this text, it is masochistic.

[30] Cf. Murray (1997: 14–22) for whom (using a theory of mimesis) all theatre is masochistic and involves disavowal.

IV

THE RIDDLING OF DIFFERENCE:
REPRESENTATIONS OF THE ANDROGYNE

Carnaval perpetuo en mi corazón.

Federico García Lorca, *Carnaval*, 1918.[1]

For spirits, freed from mortal laws, with ease
Assume what sexes and what shapes they please.

Alexander Pope, *The Rape of the Lock*, 1711.

The trickster is the shape-shifter for whom no boundary is sacred. The trickster can change sex and gender at will, and is therefore both polytropic[2] and deceptive.[3] The trickster is transformative and performative, and gender as a result becomes unstable and contingent. In the play of signs of gender-markers, the trickster is androgynous (many traditional tricksters such as Harlequin are depicted as androgynous), arising out of the fissure between gender divisions and revelling in the playfulness of change, flux and undecidability.

The androgyne bodies forth a visual and ontological riddle, an aporia, a conundrum. While the hermaphrodite denotes the physiological combination of male and female sexual organs, the androgyne is rather a question of appearances (gender-markers). Hermaphrodite refers to the myth of Hermaphroditus (the joining of two separate bodies) and is therefore rooted in the physical, whereas the androgyne 'cannot be circumscribed as belonging to some being; it is more a question of a relation between a look and an appearance' (Pacteau 1986: 62). Pacteau writes that it is not possible to encounter an androgyne in the street; 'rather I encounter a figure whom I "see as" androgynous. That is to say, the androgyne does not exist in the real

---

1 From de Paepe (1994: 148–50).

2 Polytropus means 'turning many ways', from the Greek *polutropos*. See Hyde (1998: 52).

3 Hynes (1993a: 36–7) writes that, 'as shape shifter, the trickster can alter his shape or bodily appearance in order to facilitate deception. Not even the boundaries of species or sexuality are safe, for they can be readily dissolved by the trickster's disguises and trans-morphisms'. Minor shape-shifting may involve changing clothes, while some characters may actually change gender (see Dorje 1975: 16).

– and this presents us with a major stumbling block in trying to organize a meaning for androgyny, for the impression is always that androgyny *does* so exist' (Pacteau 1986: 62). Androgyny is born out of the liminal space between gender categories, since it is the incarnation of undecidability. Androgyny highlights the importance of the visual for our establishment of gender divisions.

Images of the androgyne abound in García Lorca's work, revealing a fascination with the form. Picasso, Dalí, Valle-Inclán and many of Lorca's contemporaries likewise depicted pierrots, harlequins, and other androgynous figures,[4] and artists and writers of the nineteenth century were likewise fascinated by the androgyne.[5] The nineteenth-century interest may be viewed as a reaction to discoveries in the fields of medicine and sexuality,[6] but androgyny is by no means restricted to this age and can be found in many of the religions and mythologies of the world that we have access to.[7] As the allusions in this study affirm, androgyny presents current epistemological questions, but can also be revealed in the founding myths of our culture.

Within the canons of the Western world, based on the structures of myth that we have access to, the androgyne has come to symbolise a fantasy of primordial totality and unity, forged out of a union of opposing forces. Aristophanes' conception of humanity, as related by Plato in *The Symposium* (c.375 BCE), can be described as a founding myth upon which our notions of androgyny are now based. Aristophanes' tales depict an originary three beings, each made up of the union of halves – one male (two male halves), one female (two female halves) and one androgynous (half-male, half-female). In this myth, Zeus was jealous of these mighty elemental human forms and cut each into two, thereby reducing their strength and increasing their number. Apollo gathered together the skin left hanging from Zeus' cut and fastened it into a knot at the navel, the 'memorial of the primeval state' (Plato 1994: 147). From this initial division and from the profound feeling of incompleteness that it produced, desire and love were born, sending each of the newly created beings in search of its other half:

4 See for example, Sheppard, 'Tricksters, Carnival and the Magical Figure of Dada Poetry' (1983: 116–25); George, 'Harlequin Comes to Court: Valle-Inclán's *La Marquesa Rosalinda*' (1983: 364–74).

5 As Busst (1967: 1–95) writes, in 'The Image of the Androgyne in the Nineteenth Century', the androgyne featured in novels such as Péladan's *L'Androgyne* (1891), the work of Gustave Moreau and many others.

6 For example, Edward Carpenter's *The Intermediate Sex: A Study of Some Transitional Types of Men and Women* (1908).

7 See for example, Halley des Fontaines' *Contributions à l'étude de l'androgynie* (1938) and Delcourt's *Hermaphrodite: Mythes et rites de la Bisexualité dans l'antiquité classique* (1958).

... and the reason is that human nature was originally one and we were a whole, and pursuit of the whole is called Love [. . .] We must praise the god Love, who is our greatest benefactor, both leading us back in this life back to our own nature and giving us hopes for the future, for he promises that if we are pious that he will restore us to our originary state and heal us and make us happy and blessed.   (Plato 1994: 147–8)

From this mythical origin, the androgyne is figured as a utopian ideal before the fall into division and sexual difference – a fall from grace which is told in the biblical story of human creation in the Old Testament. Some scholars in the Jewish esoteric religion maintain that Adam (and also God) was androgynous, before the fall into sexual divisions.[8] Furthermore, in psychological terms, the androgyne as archetype or fantasy has been associated with a repressed desire to return to what Freud terms the pre-Oedipal phase before sexual difference. In *Three Essays on Sexuality* (1905a) Freud implies an acceptance of the Platonic view of the origins of difference when he attempts to trace the path of sexual instinct from puberty to maturity. But he omits the apparently homosexual origins of the first and second originary beings (a point made by Heilbrun [1973: xiii] and Weil [1992: 3]), citing only the part of the myth referring to the androgyne – splitting is conceived of solely in terms of the split of the androgyne into its masculine and feminine attributes. In *Beyond the Pleasure Principle* (1920) Freud explicitly cites the Platonic myth, but once again he reinstates the popular view of androgyny as the basis of sexual difference and the origins of sexual desire.[9] The pre-Oedipal phase therefore precedes the split into difference for Freud, a period before castration which is theorised by Pontalis (1973: 16) in his article, 'L'insaisissable entre-deux', as a 'positive androgyny' – a time full of potentiality, plenitude and expectation.

In this chapter I examine certain examples of fantasies of androgyny within García Lorca's theatre. I explore the ways in which androgyny, as a liminal space, can be seen as paradoxically related in the first place to fruitful potential, and on the other to stasis and death. The dressing-room screen, brought on stage in *El público*, presents an example of the liminal space of

8   Heilbrun (1973: 17) writes that Luis Ginzberg, in his book *The Legend of the Jews*, refers to the myth that Adam himself was created 'androgynous'.
9   In *Three Essays on the Theory of Sexuality* Freud writes that, 'the popular view of sexual instinct is beautifully reflected in the poetic fable which tells us how the original human beings were cut up into two halves – man and woman – and how these are always striving to unite again in love. It comes as a great surprise therefore to learn that there are men whose sexual object is a man and not a woman, and women whose sexual object is a woman and not a man. People of this kind are described as having "contrary sexual feelings" or better, as being "inverts", and the fact is described as "inversion" ' (1905a: 136). Freud appears to discount the myth in the first place as not fully able to explain the origins of desire, and yet appears to use what he perceives to be its model of sexual difference to inscribe homosexuality as 'inverted'.

the undecidability of gender. The Amigo 2° of *Así que pasen cinco años* is examined in the light of an interplay between plenitude and stasis. Lastly, I examine the figure of the Moon of *Bodas de sangre*. This figure is viewed firstly in the light of fantasies of the androgyne and subsequently in terms of the ways in which this figure riddles the question of sexual difference in that play.

Central to the theme of theatricality which is developed in García Lorca's *El público* (1930) is a huge dressing-room screen which is brought on stage in the *Cuadro Primero*. Characters pass behind the screen and emerge transformed: they have variously changed their appearance, name, age, maturity, and often their gender:

> (*El Director empuja bruscamente al Hombre 2 y aparece por el otro extremo del biombo una mujer vestida con pantalones negro y una corona de amapolas en la cabeza. Lleva en la mano unos impertinentes cubiertos por un bigote rubio que usará poniendo sobre su boca en algunos momentos del drama.*)   (*OC* II: 607–8)

The visual accoutrements to gender (e.g. the detachable blond moustache, the feminine attire) convert gender identity into no more than a series of constructed visual signs, a mask to be put on or removed or a performance which relies on an observer for confirmation. In this parade of the imitations of gender, this sartorial éclat,[10] these scenes, 'implicitly reveal the imitative structure of gender itself – as well as its contingency' (Butler 1990: 338). The static accoutrements in the midst of movement and bewildering change convert gender into an arbitrary play of signs in these scenes.[11]

The theatrical cross-dressing inspired by the 'biombo' in *El público* is reminiscent of the masquerades of the eighteenth century, where the confusion of gender codes was sanctioned by the liminal space of the masquerade.[12] Likewise in the plays examined here, through the trickster-function, the audience is invited to indulge in the 'guilty pleasures' of cross-dressing.[13] Theatre's ties with cross-dressing have gone hand-in-hand with a history of anti-theatrical tracts, as Levine (1994) has documented. Shakespeare's theatre often featured

---

[10] Castle (1986: 57) writes of the masquerades of the eighteenth century, that, 'the travesties of masquerade represented a collective "making strange" – a play, at once disorientating and compelling, on the instability of sartorial signs'.

[11] For a discussion of the theme of transvestism in *El público*, see Monegal (1994b: 204–16), 'Unmasking the Maskuline [sic]: Transvestism and Tragedy in García Lorca's *El público*'.

[12] The masquerade shares with carnival a reversing of the governing structures. Zolla (1981: 91) writes that gender-switching is common in carnival where men can often perform pregnancy and a dramatic birth-scene. Thus, 'Harlequin and Polchinello are connected with Carnival rites. They are hermaphrodite lechers and prankish mourners who give birth'.

[13] See for example, Straub (1991: 142–66) on 'The Guilty Pleasures of Female

plots involving disguise and gender-switching, and young boys were often called upon to play the parts of female characters. The theme of cross-dressing in the theatre is extended in *El público* as the substitute Juliet is played by a youth:

> Estudiante 4°: ¿Pero no te has dado cuenta que la Julieta que estaba en el sepulcro era un joven disfrazado, un truco del Director de escena, y que la verdadera Julieta estaba amordazada debajo de los asientos? (*OC* II: 659)

This play suggests what Levine (1994) writes was the fear at the heart of Renaissance anti-theatricality, that costume could actually alter gender.[14] 'Theatre effeminates the mind', wrote Stephen Gosson in 1579 and Philip Stubbes in 1583 wrote of the fear, 'that boy actors who wear women's clothing can literally "adulterate" male gender. In the years of mounting [anti-theatrical] pamphlet war, this evolves into a full-fledged fear of dissolution, expressed in virtually biological terms, that costume can structurally transform men into women'.[15] *El público* articulates this dissolving of gender boundaries, a liminal, androgynous subject position in metaphorical terms. As in the case of Teiresias of Sophocles' *Antigone*, who 'both the man's and woman's joys by trial understood', or Woolf's *Orlando*, who could change gender without regard for temporal limits, the audience at the theatre can occupy a similarly privileged position in the liberatory flux, like the shape-shifter who 'continually alters her/his body, creates and recreates a personality [. . .] floats across time' (Smith-Rosenberg 1985: 291).

There is another liminal space involved, I suggest, which is the liminal space behind the dressing-room screen in *El público*. Like the androgyne, this is a potential space, charged and rich with potential meanings. Like the mythical Janus, it can face either way, now masculine, now feminine, on a whim. Like the trickster, is slips easily from one form into another. The space occupied by the androgyne is a mythical union of opposites – a playful, fertile area which can spawn new combinations and surprises. But, at the same time,

---

Theatrical Cross-dressing and the Autobiography of Charlotte Clark'. In the Book of Deuteronomy it is stated that, 'the woman shall not wear that which pertaineth unto a man, neither shall a man put on a woman's garment: for all that do so are abomination unto the Lord Thy God' (22.5).

14 Levine (1994: 3–5) writes that, 'at the heart of the Renaissance anti-theatricality lay a glaring contradiction. For at the root of the [anti-theatrical] pamphlet attacks lay the fear that costume could actually alter the gender of the male body beneath the costume'.

15 Gosson, S. (1579) *Playes Confuted in Five Actions*, in A. F. Kinney, *Markets of Bawdrie: The Dramatic Criticism of Stephen Gosson*, Salzburg: Institut für Englische Sprache und Literatur, 1974, and Philip Stubbes (1583), *The Anatomy of Abuses*, Netherlands: Da Capo Press, 1963.

this liminal androgynous space is a non-presence, an uncanny uncertainty, a
presence which is a non-presence: a stasis or a death.

Lorca's poem *Arlequín*, accompanied by a drawing of the same name, is a
fusion of opposites embodied in one:

> Arlequín
> teta roja de sol
> teta azul de la luna.
>
> Torso mitad coral.
> mitad plata y penumbra.

As Mario Hernández (1986: 156) has noted, 'lo definitorio del arlequín, su
traje, está aludido mediante contrapuestas de luz y de sombra'. Furthermore,
the *contrapuestas* are expressed in terms of physical opposites: 'teta roja de
sol/teta azul de la luna', a poetic rendering of the androgynous body.[16] The
Harlequin and similar androgynous figures unite and embody opposites.
These visual paradoxes (what Pacteau [1986: 75] refers to as 'the impossible
referent'), occupy a liminal realm which could be described, following
Fletcher (1967: 25) in his discussions of Pierrot, as 'that autonomous world,
the imaginary museum'. Androgynes offer themselves up as an aesthetic,
liminal space within which to discuss the binary oppositions which divide
and structure our world.

The Harlequin and Clown as they appear in Lorca's work are fully
compatible with the figure of the masquerading trickster. These are deriva-
tives of the mask, who play with and point up the deceptiveness of appearances. The drawing, *Payaso de rostro desdoblado*, 1927 (Hernández 1990:
[102]) for example, features a Harlequin figure with a mask, while the *Arlequín* of *Así que pasen cinco años* carries two masks, 'una careta de alegrísima
expresión', the other, 'de expresión dormida', which he changes at will. In *El
público* and *Viaje a la luna*, the Harlequin is pure 'traje', a suit that can be
worn or removed. Like the trickster-figure, these characters seem to stand
apart from the action – they occupy an autonomous liminal realm which is
neither fully part of the action nor separate from it. This notion is fully articulated in *Así que pasen cinco años*, as the Harlequin has emerged from a travelling circus stationed within a wood. There is a sinister air to the Clown and
Harlequin of *Así que pasen cinco años* – their visual androgyny points to a
slipperiness. They are difficult to pin down and to define, which makes them
seem menacing and dangerous.

The notion of a liminal realm prior to division and difference is important

---

[16] The reference to 'teta' rather than the more neutral 'pecho', is suggestive of the
eighteenth-century engraving, *Harlequin Breastfeeds Her Son*, an illustration in *La
Comédie Italienne*, by P. Ducharte, 1927, cited and reproduced in Pacteau (1986: 75).

for an analysis of the figure of the Amigo 2° of *Así que pasen cinco años*. As we saw in chapter III, the Second Friend represents the theme of the *Joven* as poised on the threshold of maturity – caught in a liminal realm before the plunge into castration, gender divisions and sexual difference. The Amigo 2° is dressed in a white suit, evocative of Pierrot, an attire which emphasises his androgynous appearance, and this is reinforced by the stage directions which inform us that this character can be played by either a boy or a girl. This figure does not wish to grow up: 'Porque no quiero estar lleno de arrugas y dolores como usted', he says to the Viejo (*OC* II: 527). Instead, he wishes to remain suspended in time like the little fantasy females he keeps within a raindrop. This figure therefore corresponds to the fantasy of the androgyne as:

> . . . also reminiscent of a more primitive imago of early childhood located prior to the recognition of sexual difference – the 'phallic' mother whom the child perceives as complete and autonomous [. . .] This image will be retained in spite of subsequent knowledge of sexual difference – an aspect of disavowal, a form of defence against castration anxiety.
>
> (Pacteau 1986: 71)

The Amigo 2° seems to confirm this view of the importance of the maternal for the pre-castration fantasy when he cries: 'cuando yo tenía cinco años [. . .] no cuando tenía dos, miento, uno, un año tan sólo. Es hermoso, ¿verdad?, un año cogí una de estas mujercillas de la lluvia y la tuve dos días en una pecera' (*OC* II: 527).

Through an analysis of the Amigo 2° we can see therefore that the fantasy of androgyny may represent a utopia of wholeness before the construction of sexual difference.[17] However, Lacan's discussions of the construction of identity, the very structures of language (its binary models, for example) reveal that the subject is constituted through language itself. The androgyne seems to represent a subject constituted within a binary system. But at the same time, the androgyne suggests another binary: that of the time *before* difference, the idyllic, pre-mature state, which according to Lacan, is an anomaly.[18] We might say, then, that presence of the androgyne on the scene of representation reveals and subverts the texts' structure of opposition as well as 'its use as a paradigm for the creation of hierarchy and meaning' (Weil 1992: 11). At the same time, the binary inscribed by the time *before* difference is revealed to be an anomaly. The playful blending of opposites within the figure of the

----

17 The notion of 'wholeness' seems to correspond to the biblical idyll of the Garden of Eden before the Fall and the acquisition of shame and knowledge.

18 However, the notion of a time *before* the inscription reveals a binary model. Lacan argues that a state of final wholeness and maturity is not possible for the subject, because the subject is irremediably split and the metonymy of desire is unstoppable. See Lacan (1956).

androgyne therefore reveals the construction of difference not just in terms of the outlines of gendered identity, but in terms of language and meaning itself.

The Amigo 2° is the embodiment of the androgyne as a fantasy of the comfort and safety of a time before the threat of castration and the inscription of sexual difference. But the Amigo 2° is caught, suspended, frozen (by fear) in time, unwilling to progress to maturity and so, is metaphorically dead. The linking of the figure of the androgyne with death is suggested also by the Payaso of *Así que pasen cinco años* whose head is described thus: '*su cabeza empolvada da una sensación de calavera*' (*OC* II: 563). He and the Arlequín enter the scene and try to intimidate the other characters. They have the exaggerated gestures of circus performers, but their playful air lends a sinister note to the scenes in which they appear. They attempt to persuade the Joven to follow them to the circus, where, 'allí están los carros y las jaulas con las serpientes'. In fact, the Joven is just as enclosed by the glittering stasis of the world he inhabits as he would be locked in a circus cage, but the correlation of the Arlequín and Payaso with death is clear – they simply know too much to be benign characters. They can enter the scene to meddle with the characters, and then withdraw once more.[19] They embody a sense of foreboding and the threat of evil omens. Hence the Arlequín, in Act Three, Scene One, appears to emerge out of a theatre which has sprung up in a clearing in the woods – and carries two masks, which he changes at will. His demeanour is playful, but his words are menacing. He tells the Muchacha:

> Tu amante verás
> a la media vuelta
> del viento y del mar.

While the girl cries:

| Arlequín: | (*Asustada*) Mentira.
Verdad
Ya te lo daré.   (*OC* II: 563) |

Androgyny therefore seems to suggest liminality, a standing apart from culture, but this separation can imply death just as much as potential. Androgyny may present a space from which to meditate upon the ramifications of difference, suggesting the possibility of escaping difference (to a liminal time before, after, beyond or above sexual difference), but ultimately the androgyne is related to stasis, undecidability and death. Participants in culture appear to be inextricably unable to escape difference – the alternative to this life appears to be non-life: death.

---

[19] This may remind us of the Shakespearean Fool (Williams 1979), whose foolishness may in fact hide deep wisdom and an ability to predict the outcome of the play.

THE FIGURE OF THE MOON

The elements which link death with seeing into the future, coupled with the suggestion of androgyny, become even more pronounced if we consider the character the Moon of *Bodas de sangre*. The play is a tragedy which features the abduction of a bride on her wedding day by her lover. Critical attention has tended to focus on the lyricism of the play; has found sources for the dramatic action in real events (the play is based on newspaper accounts of a real rural tragedy in Níjar, Almería); or else examines considerations of genre.[20] I shall 'liminalise' the play by focussing on the uncanny, anti-naturalistic figure of the Moon, with a view to producing a new reading of a familiar text.

The Moon appears in Act Three of the play, in a forest, where the lovers, Leonardo and the Novia have taken flight. The Moon is described as a 'leñador joven, con la cara blanca' (*OC* II: 776). Yet despite being represented by 'un hombre joven' and 'un leñador' (*OC* II: 776), the Moon refers to him/herself in the feminine: 'vengo helada' (*OC* II: 776) and speaks of 'los montes de mi pecho' (*OC* II: 777). This description may well remind us of T. S. Eliot's depiction of the character Tiresias in *The Waste Land* (1922):[21]

> I Tiresias, though blind, throbbing between two lives,
> Old man with wrinkled female breasts can see
> At the violet hour.

Garber (1995: 158) writes that Eliot (and, I suggest, possibly also Lorca) may have been influenced by the 1917 staging of the French surrealist play, *Tirésias* by Guillaume Apollinaire. Lorca's Moon shares with Eliot's (and Ovid's) Tiresias an ability to 'see at the violet hour'. The switching from male to female gendered identity – 'both the man's and woman's joys by trial understood' – has rendered this character the capacity to see into the future. This character (like a trickster-figure) now stands apart from society – a move which can serve to make him/her extremely powerful and therefore minatory. In *Bodas de sangre*, this ability to see at the violet hour is rendered as the moonlight flooding through the darkness of the trees:

---

[20] In his brilliant recent study of the play, Smith (1998b: 44–70) includes a review of the critical approaches to this play, which he describes as belonging to three 'perennial concerns [. . .] language, reference and genre' (44). Smith himself juxtaposes García Lorca's play with two English translations of the play (by José Weisberger and Langston Hughes) together with a reading of Freud to present a deft analysis of homosexual desire in the play.

[21] Angel Flores translated Eliot's *The Waste Land* into Spanish as *La tierra baldía* (Barcelona: Cervantes, 1930). Lorca met Angel Flores in New York on 29 June 1929, as a letter to his family records (Anderson and Maurer 1997: 616).

La Luna: No quiero sombras. Mis rayos
han de entrar en todas partes,
y haya en los troncos oscuros
un rumor de claridades,
para que esta noche tengan
mis mejillas dulce sangre,
y los juncos agrupados
en los anchos pies del aire.
¿Quién se oculta? ¡Afuera digo!
¡No! ¡No podrán escaparse!
Yo haré lucir al caballo
una fiebre de diamante.   (*OC* II: 777)

This figure is at once male and female, and as such is linked with both power, and death: 'mis mejillas dulce sangre' and '¡no podrán escaparse!'.

Anderson (1982: 58) has written of 'el hermafroditismo de la luna' and the blending of feminine and masculine adjectives used by the Moon to describe him/herself is evocative of Foucault's (1980: xiii) description of the nineteenth-century Hermaphrodite Herculine Barbin in which the protagonist switches from masculine to feminine adjectives in the first person. We might say that the Moon oscillates between androgyny and hermaphroditism – nothing is quite clear about the Moon, as it shimmers through the trees.

Weil (1992) relates her discussion of the androgyne and the hermaphrodite to the myths on which our modern conceptions of them are based. As we have seen, Aristophanes' myth of the androgyne is a utopian ideal, presenting 'an ideal, even Edenic state of being, a state of wholeness in which nothing is lacking' (Weil 1992: 18). In visual terms, this is portrayed as the 'perfect' symmetry between two halves, cleaved in two and then reunited. Weil continues: 'structurally and thematically, [Aristophanes'] story recalls the separation of Eve from Adam [. . .] and the biblical fall into disunity. Both in Genesis and Aristophanes' account, sexual division is regarded as the punishment for the fall. For Aristophanes it is also the remedy – the union of two sexes through divinely inspired love is the route towards regaining salvation' (Weil 1992: 18).

Weil (1992: 18) juxtaposes this view of androgyny with Ovid's story of hermaphroditism, from Book IV of the *Metamorphoses*: 'Whereas for Aristophanes androgyny precedes the fall, Ovid's hermaphrodite embodies the fallen state, especially because s/he blurs the distinction between male and female.' When Salmacis catches sight of the beautiful Hermaphroditus stepping naked into her pond, desire transforms her into an aggressive hunter ('she was on fire with passion to possess his naked body') and prays to the Gods that they never be separated. Her prayers are answered: 'when their limbs met in that clinging embrace, the nymph and the body were no longer two, but a single form, possessed of a dual nature, which could not be called either male or female, but seemed at once both and neither'. Weil writes that unlike Aristophanes' rendering of wholeness at the origins of love, Ovid's account features, at the origin:

> an unstable and frightening confusion from which there emerges not ideal love, but a power struggle between the sexes, each trying to establish a wholeness it never had [. . .] The resulting union does not produce wholeness, instead, it displaces the oppositions self/other and male/female between Salmacis and Hermaphroditus to reveal their confused manifestation within Hermaphroditus [. . .] In other words, Hermaphroditus' fallen state bodies forth the always fused and confused relation of male and female. (Weil 1992: 18)

Weil describes the figure of the hermaphrodite therefore as a figuring of the consequences of negative desire,[22] which posits confusion at the origin of desire. Desire is figured as a power struggle between the opposing forces of male and female.

Anderson (1982: 58) suggests that we find a power struggle within the language expressed by the Moon. The passages reflect an ambiguity between 'los papeles activos y pasivos, una sexualidad a la vez sádica y masoquista'. Anderson relates these positions to the differences between male and female, making reference to a description of the Moon by Juan Pérez de Moya written at the end of the sixteenth century and republished in 1928:

> Dicen ser la luna macho y hembra, porque unas veces tiene virtud activa, y ésta se atribuye en cosas de naturaleza al varón, y otras veces la tiene pasiva, que se atribuye a la hembra. (Anderson 1982: 58).

Furthermore, the speech of the Moon draws reference to the phallic knife, but oscillates between 'deja [. . .] abandonado' and 'acecho':

> La luna deja un cuchillo
> abandonado en el aire,
> que siendo acecho de plomo
> quiere de dolor de sangre.   (*OC* II: 776)

Anderson's equation pairs feminine desire with masochism and passivity, and masculine desire with sadism and aggressivity. These pairings have been common in Western thought until recent feminist studies sought to break

---

[22] Weil (1992: 19) posits the tale as the negative consequences of 'specifically feminine desire', which begins 'as a story of female desire' but 'ends as a tale of the fall of man, a fall from clear sexual division into sexual confusion'. Furthermore, the suggestions that the confusion is the origin of desire implies that 'the moral standard governing desire is the result of a power struggle in which phallic desire has won out over any other type of love that does not conform to it'.

down such binary pairings which often sublimate and restrict feminine desire. These juxtaposed and often conflicting drives are found within the ambiguous body of the Moon. On this site, these codes are confused and blended, so that masculine and feminine, active and passive and indistinguishable.[23] Notwithstanding, embodied within the figure of the Moon is a power struggle between male and female, to the death.

There appears to be a clear correlation within *Bodas de sangre*, of the figure of the Moon – representative of the union of masculine and feminine and the embodiment of the mythical origins of heterosexual desire – and the desire and flight of the characters of Leonardo and the Novia, the star-crossed lovers, hunted down by the (Diana-like) figure of the Moon.[24] Reed Anderson (1984: 97) hints at this correlation through his analysis of the denouement which views 'the tragic action purely as a consequence of the collision of antagonistic forces that are inevitably in opposition', but he does not link the androgyny of the Moon to the death of the main characters. Andrew Anderson (1982: 58) does make this link: 'la naturaleza sexual de la luna y la de su relación con los humanos es análoga a la situación emocional de Leonarda y la Novia'. For Anderson, this is a reflection of the ambivalent feelings Leonardo and the Novia have for one another:

> Tan pronto ella quiere suicidarse o que él la mate, él tiene que arrastrarla tras de sí, pero después ella le acompaña voluntariamente. En resumen, la ambivalencia sexual de la Luna refleja la ambivalencia de los sentimientos sexuales que experimentan Leonardo y la Novia y esto, a su vez, implica la interpretación del amor como una especie de muerte, una noción dominante explorada por la obra.   (Anderson 1992: 58)

I agree with Andrew Anderson that the Moon seems to figure as an echo of the relationship of the lovers but suggest that, rather than a simple equation of one with the other, the Moon instead acts as a space from which to 'make strange' the relationship of the lovers. It serves to open up a (liminal) space to place in question the heterosexual desire figured in this play. Its very uncanny presence seems to bring the notion of the naturalness of heterosexual desire into discussion and provides the opportunity for an examination of the figuring of desire within the plot.

The desire of Leonardo and the Novia for one another is figured in terms of a physical instinct that is stronger than both of them:

---

23 As, for example, in *Amor de Don Perlimplín con Belisa en su jardín*, where the codes of masculine and feminine attributes are confused – Perlimplín is meek, timid and masochistic, while Belisa is assertive and sexually adventurous. These roles are complicated even more towards the end of the play as Perlimplín exacts his revenge.

24 Diana is the Goddess of the Moon, thought to embody androgynous qualities as she is beautiful and has many suitors, but permits no man to enter her realm, preferring the sport of hunting to love. She is also associated with woods at night.

| Leonardo: | Callar y quemarse es el castigo más grande que nos podemos echar encima. ¿De qué me sirvió a mí el orgullo y el no mirarte y el dejarte despierta noches y noches? ¡De nada! ¡Sirvió para echarme fuego encima! Porque tú crees que el tiempo cura y que las paredes tapan, y no es verdad, no es verdad. ¡Cuando las cosas llegan a los centros, no hay quien las arranque! |
| Novia: | (*Temblando*) No puedo oírte. No puedo oír tu voz. Es como si me bebiera una botella de anís y me durmiera en una colcha de rosas. Y me arrastra y sé que me ahogo, pero voy detrás. |

(*OC* II: 743)

Leonardo and the Novia appear to be swept along by a physical and sexual drive. Interestingly, in an attempt to account for sexual desire, Freud turned once more to the Platonic myth of the androgyne in his 1920 essay, *Beyond the Pleasure Principle*. Here, it is not the metaphysical nature of love but the physical aspects of desire that interest him. He begins with an image of light and darkness: 'science has so little to tell us about the origin of sexuality that we can liken the problem to a darkness into which not so much as a ray of hypothesis has penetrated'. Freud finds the information he seeks, to light the way, 'in quite a different region', where:

> . . . it is true, we *do* meet with such an hypothesis; but it is of so fantastic a kind – a myth rather than a scientific explanation – that I should not venture to produce it here, were it not that it fulfills precisely the condition whose fulfilment we desire. For it traces the origin of an instinct to a need to restore an earlier state of things.   (Freud 1920: 57)

This time, Freud does not omit the sections of the Platonic myth referring to the homosexual models of desire, the male and female originary beings:

> What I have in mind is, of course, the theory which Plato put into the mouth of Aristophanes in the *Symposium*, and which deals not only with the *origin* of the sexual instinct, but also with the most important of its variations in relation to its object. The original nature was not like the present, but different. In the first place, they were originally three in number, not two as they are now; there was man, woman, and the union of the two [. . .] Eventually Zeus decided to cut these men in two, 'like a sorb-apple which is halved for picking'. After the division had been made, 'the two parts of man, each desiring his other half, came together and threw their arms about one another eager to grow into one'.   (Freud 1920: 57)

Freud maintains that sexual instincts are 'conservative' in that they 'seek to restore an earlier state'. He goes on to give a scientific rendering of the Platonic myth, saying: 'Shall we follow the hint given us by the poet-philosopher, and venture upon the hypothesis that living substance at the time of its coming to life was torn apart into small particles, which have ever since endeavoured to reunite through the sexual instincts?' He continues:

> . . . that these instincts, in which the chemical affinity of inanimate matter persisted, gradually succeeded, as they developed through the kingdom of the protista, in overcoming the difficulties put in the way of that endeavour by an environment charged with dangerous stimuli – stimuli which compelled them to form a protective cortical layer: that these splintered fragments of living substance in this way attained a multicellular condition and finally transferred the instinct for reuniting, in the most highly concentrated form, to the germ cells? – But here, I think, the moment has come for breaking off.   (Freud 1920: 58)

Curiously, although Freud cites the passage as an explanation of an originary wholeness which is then spilt, Aristophanes' tale in fact begins with a split or division between the sexes (the two halves). Freud uses the passage in his argument that instinct is linked to the death drive. As the death drive is expressed in terms of 'a desire to return to an anterior state', then we might go so far as to suggest that the androgyne has become intertwined in the notion of death. The androgyne would figure, then, as an undifferentiated state much like death, the time after the splitting into difference, when male, female, self and other become merged into an undifferentiated mass that is death. It is certainly not difficult to link desire, death and the androgyne in *Bodas de sangre*. They appear in the figure of the Moon. But it becomes clear that Freud's notion of the death drive is founded upon a concept of splitting and reunion that is figured in the myth of the Platonic androgyne. Lacan also refers to Aristophanes' androgyne to explain the origins of sexuality and desire. For Lacan the notion of loss or lack involved in the first division of the sexes pervades sexual life (Lacan 1954). And, where sexuality signifies loss for Lacan, sexual union (and specifically heterosexual union) offers the one (false) hope of retrieving that origin.

STAR-CROSSED LOVERS. . .

> From forth the fatal loins of these two foes
> A pair of star-crossed lovers take their life.
>   William Shakespeare, *Romeo and Juliet*, the Prologue, 5–6.

I argue that the figure of the Moon prefigures the heterosexual desire of the lovers, hinting at their fate (death) long before the dénouement. Through the image of the Moon it at first sight seems clear that what we are dealing with in the figure of the Moon is a *Liebestod* fantasy – a desire to achieve perfection in death – the perfect union of male and female counterparts in death. The term *Liebestod* was introduced into psychoanalytic literature in 1953 by Flügel, as Gediman (1995: 2) has documented, but *Liebestod* fantasies, the fantasy of dying together, have origins in a more distant myth. From Wagner's *Tristan and Isolde* to Dante's Paolo and Francesca, or even Dante and Beatrice, the *Liebestod* fantasy has strong roots. Max Klinger after Edvard Munch depicted 'Lovers locked in a postmortem amidst a sea of darkness' (1881). Sir Edward Burne-Jones vividly depicts a *Liebestod* fantasy in 'The Depths of the Sea' (1887). For Gediman (1995: 6) in the *Liebestod* fantasy, 'the sexual climax of orgasm was rejected in favour of the transcendental bliss of a joint death'. Also, as Gediman (1995: 6) writes, *Liebestod* is 'characterized by the wish for "merger", symbiosis and other forms of identification with the loved object'. Other than in terms of sexuality and orgasm, writes Gediman, love is a narcissistic phenomenon: 'not only is it based on a foolish idealization of the loved one, but as Plato said, on a feeling of insufficiency, wanting and longing' (Gediman 1995: 15). The songs of the troubadours, she writes, 'substituted a consummation at the point of joint death for the bliss of orgasm' (Gediman 1995: 15). For Flügel (1953), *Liebestod* fantasies of love, death and dying together, express a wish not for a cessation of life, but for 'intrauterine omnipotence', for Nirvana, a life of peace after death.

My view, then, is that the presence of the Moon in *Bodas de sangre* prefigures the relationship of the lovers, Leonardo and the Novia as a *Liebestod* fantasy. The Moon embodies a dreadful but fitting inevitability. In addition the union of male and female attributes within the figure of the Moon suggests that in death the lovers can reach a perfect union, a symbiosis in death.

However, within the plot, this 'idyllic' *Liebestod* is never achieved. It is not the two lovers who die under the light of the Moon, but rather the two males: the Novio and Leonardo. This could be seen as a reworking of the revenge tragedies, where two male rivals duel for the love of a woman. But if we follow the paradigm of homosocial desire set out by Kosofsky Sedgwick, we could see that this death complicates the heterosexual *Liebestod* paradigm quite substantially. We are told that, 'se mataron los dos hombres del amor'. Furthermore, this was achieved, 'con un cuchillo, con un cuchillito' – the phallic knife seems to provide the climax to the play and the *Liebestod* fantasy, except that it is a climax between two men that is figured in this paradigm. We might agree then, with Ángel Valente (1976: 200) that the play should be seen as the expression of homoerotic desire. Hence, 'el tema de las bodas es secundario'. It is not the Novia and Leonardo who are united in death beneath the light of the Moon (who elsewhere in Lorca's work is associated with homosexuality through the image of the 'pez luna' [Valente 1976]), but rather the two men, 'que se acoplan [. . .] en una lucha a muerte que es la única expresión real del eros en *Bodas de sangre*. Un eros que se consuma en la muerte, bajo la luna "neutra luna de piedra sin semilla", la luna del Adán oscuro'.[25]

While the figure of the Moon presents itself as a prefiguring of heterosexual union in death, ultimately this paradigm is belied by the workings of the plot. The figure of the Moon therefore opens a liminal space for a discussion of the workings of desire within this play, as well as its entrenchment from myth into psychoanalysis and culture. The Moon is slippery, difficult to pin down – nothing more than a reflection in a puddle deep within the wood, or a ray of moonlight bouncing through the trees.

The androgyne, in its many incarnations, confounds the myth of the 'legible body' (Castle 1986: 57) by its suggestion that things may not be all that they seem. The pleasure associated with the androgyne consists in the playful scrambling of the signs. Confusion in gender, furthermore, seems to reach out and complicate the smooth face of binary oppositions per se. The androgyne, like the trickster-figure, is born and inhabits the liminal realm produced by difference. Our continued fascination with androgynes bears testament to our ongoing obsession with the limits of culture. The androgyne, in Lorca's work and elsewhere, goes some way to riddling the differences upon which culture is sustained.

---

[25] Angel Valente (1976: 200) writes that, 'el hilo central [de *Bodas de sangre*] va desde el clamor imperático de la ley antigua del eros genesíaco que sustenta la Madre, a la copulación imposible (la Novia queda intacta; no copula ni con el Novio ni con el amante) y la infracción total de la ley del eros germinativo que supone la lucha-orgasmo-muerte de los dos hombres solos en el punto climáctico de la tragedia'. Such a view is substantiated by Smith (1998b: 44–70) who writes persuasively that the lost object of *Bodas de sangre* is the desirable male body.

SECTION III

THE BODY IN PAIN:
COLLECTIVITY AND THE CARNIVALESQUE

V

THE BODY IN PAIN: ELEMENTS OF THE CARNIVALESQUE IN *EL PÚBLICO*

> Over the course of history there has been more
> or less anxiety, more or less philosophical, about
> the possibility that life might be a dream or all
> the world a stage. That has been the curious
> substance at the troubled heart of the drama, its
> essential distrust of the appearances of theater.
>
> Herbert Blau, *To All Appearances*, 1992

In the *Cuadro Quinto* of *El público*, four ladies, apparently members of the theatre audience, stand up in outrage and make to leave the theatre. As the commotion outside, which could be a student demonstration, a riot or a revolution, draws ever closer, the ladies find themselves trapped within the theatre: 'es horrible perderse en un teatro y no encontrar la salida' (*OC* II: 655),[1] cries the Dama 1°. 'Cuando amanezca nos guiaremos por las claraboyas' (*OC* II: 661), declares the Muchacho 1°. In the other plays examined in this study, the audience is led, through the trickster-function, into the liminal space which is theatre. In *El público*, the audience is confined within the liminal space, the fourth wall is broken down leaving no division between scenic action and spectating. The audience embark on a journey into the core of the drama. The trickster-function is thus complete.

In *El público* the liminal space of playful exploration finds full expression as the arena of the carnivalesque. Whether as the Saturnalia of Roman antiquity, the medieval Feast of Fools and charivari, similar festivals of misrule of the early modern period or the masquerades of the eighteenth century, the carnivalesque is the space where 'whirl is King, a world of dizzying transformation and intoxicating variety' (Castle 1986: 53). Like the masquerades, *El público* is 'a kind of chamber sublime – a condensed phantasmagoria, a bounded dreamscape of uncanny, disorientating power' (Castle 1986: 53). Hierarchies are inverted, spawning new combinations and playful new categories. The carnivalesque is the idyll of the trickster, a world of disguise

---

1   'Perderse', meaning literally to lose one's bearings, but also, to lose oneself in the plot, lose control, give way to emotions, identifications etc.

and inversion, where taboos can be indulged. Characters in *El público* are reminiscent of the carnivalesque, from the Caballos, Traje de Bailarina and the Prestidigitador who recall costumes from Corpus Christi and other carnival celebrations,[2] and the Harlequin figure, to the Pastor Bobo and Elena, who as George (1992: 107–33; 1995: 141–65) and de Ros (1996: 110–20) point out are also stock figures of carnival.[3] These carnivalesque figures introduce a paradigm by which, through the trickster-function, the audience can explore the playful and the taboo and take pleasure in the confusion of boundaries. But at the same time, the audience is trapped within the liminal space, assaulted by a text and a theatrical experience which offends, challenges and provokes. In this chapter I intend to explore *El público* in terms of the body and the collective space. I shall begin with a discussion of Bakhtin's notion of the grotesque body of carnival, a body which revels in the utopian possibilities of inversion and issue, and then move on to juxtapose Bakhtin's notion of the 'carnival of the night', and a ritual space for the exploration of provocation, fear and scape-goating, a space where the carnivalesque becomes 'interiorized and individualized, related to private terror, isolation and insanity rather than to robust, communal celebration' (White 1993: 171). A central image of the body as fragmentary, vulnerable and in pain emerges from this study, which I shall relate to the crisis of representation which is at the troubled heart of this drama. The performance of pain, then, will be seen to relate to and perhaps blur the distinctions between what Blau (1992: 38) refers to as the 'tautological impasse' – the dichotomy between life and art.

BODIES THAT MATTER

> If the skin were parchment and the blows you gave were ink. . . .
> William Shakespeare, *The Comedy of Errors*, III, i, 13–14.

Bakhtin's grotesque body of carnival, as depicted in his seminal work, *Rabelais and His World* (1965), is a collective made up of the thousands of people being born, dying and reborn in comedy, to be measured by the waste it produces. Unlike the Renaissance body, closed and individualised,

---

[2] The Caballos may be seen as reminiscent of Picasso's 1917 designs for Serge Diaghilev's *Parade* at the Ballet Russes. Kaplan (1992: 134–5) writes that these figures were in turn influenced by Corpus Christi parade animals. Picasso had arrived in Rome at Cocteau's invitation to undertake the designs during carnival time, shortly after attending carnival festivities in Barcelona. Kaplan notes that a Barcelona critic of the ballet noticed the similarities between Picasso's costumes for the ballet and the Chinese conjurer, a mannequin-like young American girl, two acrobats and horse costumes reminiscent of carnival.

[3] George (1992: 107–33; 1995: 141–65) explores Lorca's use of the figures of

Bakhtin's is the grotesque exaggeration of mouth, belly and genitals which, 'affirm the physical body as open to the world' (Morris: 1994: 226).[4] Perhaps the most obvious representation of the carnivalesque form in *El público* is the character of the Centurion's wife, who, we are told, 'pare por cuatro o cinco sitios a la vez y ronca al mediodía debajo de los árboles' (*OC* II: 618). This is a body which is full of orifices, grotesque and yet creative, in contrast to the closed beauty of a classical Renaissance subject:

> Hombre 1°:   ... los dos tenían ano y ninguno de los dos podía luchar con la belleza de los mármoles que brillaban conservando deseos íntimos defendidos por una superficie intachable ...
>
> (*OC* II: 622)

The juxtaposition of the metaphor of the body as open or closed provides a focus which rages at the body's thresholds and limitations.[5] *El público* is scattered with images of waste and excretions. These images constitute issue from the body, and signal an emphasis on the lower bodily stratum, as well as the body's orifices, both vital elements of the carnivalesque body. We find reference to 'sudor' (*OC* II: 600), 'escupir' (639), 'saliva' (600), 'mocos' (634), 'lágrimas' (600), 'orinar' (603), 'defecar' (622), 'gotas de sangre de mujer' (612), as well as references to scabs and wounds, and even, 'un recorte de tus uñas' (600). The metaphorical body which has spawned these scatological elements is firmly rooted in materiality. This body makes its presence felt in the play, providing a challenge to the Cartesian notion of the mind that can dissociate itself from the material body.

An article by Andrew Anderson provides a comprehensive pragmatic introduction to a discussion of the body in relation to *El público*. In ' "Un dificilísimo juego poético": Theme and Symbol in Lorca's *El público*', Anderson (1992a: 331–46) identifies, 'several important clusters or paradigms of imagery, the two most highly developed of which are based on the human body and on theatre'. In the first of these, 'the sequence of images moves, spatially and physically, from outside the body to deep within it'

Commedia dell'arte such as Pierrot and Harlequin in *El público* in relation to Bakhtin's conception of the carnivalesque, and discusses the mask as a symbol of rebirth and renewal. For an account of the roots of the figure of the *Pastor Bobo* in Spanish theatre, see Brotherton (1975).

4   The trickster often indulges in scatological pursuits. See for example, Hyde, 'Matter Out of Place' (1998: 173–99) and Makarius (1970 and 1974).

5   Bakhtin's non-grotesque, classical body is an 'entirely finished, completed, strictly limited body, which is shown from the outside as something individual [. . .] Then opaque surface and the body's "valleys" acquire an essential meaning as the border of a classical individuality that does not merge with other bodies in the world' (Bakhtin 1965: 320). 'The body that interests [Rabelais]', by contrast, 'is pregnant, delivers, defecates, is sick, dying and dismembered' (Bakhtin 1965: 179).

(Anderson 1992a: 332). This is the world 'inside-out' rather than 'upside-down'.[6] We begin with outfit, garb, dress, suit and different types of clothing from 'túnica' (*OC* II: 617) to 'vestido, abierto totalmente por delante [y los] muslos con apretada malla rosada' (608), 'traje blanca de ópera' (627) and 'traje de bailarina' (640). The notion of changing clothes is related to the huge, 'biombo' behind which the garb of various characters in the *Cuadro Primero* is transformed. From the clothes we pass on to the surface of the body, cosmetics ('lápiz para los labios' [*OC* II: 607]; 'carmín' [607]). Then there is reference to body hair: 'el peinado con la raya en medio' (606); 'el cabello blanco', 'cejas azules' (608); 'un bigote rubio' (608); 'barbas oscuras' (601) and finally, 'vello' (600). False hair is denoted by a 'peluca rubia' (601) and 'un bigote de tinta' (632). Bare skin is insinuated in 'los tatuajes' (607), 'cuero' (637) and 'senos' (636) as well as 'piel', but above all in the persistent metaphor of 'desnudar' (618). Under the skin lies 'carne' (607) and as Anderson (1992a: 332) writes, 'cutting the skin and piercing the flesh creates a wound – "herida" (*OC* II: 648), which in turn may take the form of a scab – "costra" ' (599). Countless references are also made to blood ('sangre' [637], 'sangriento' [621]), whether as a symbol of violence or a basic life-force, and then finally we reach the 'huesos' (627). The graphic image is 'desnudaré tu esqueleto' (639) – flesh is literally pared down to the bone.

If we add to Anderson's paradigmatic list the cluster of images of issue from the body, signalling its boundaries, we are presented with an impressively graphic configuration of the human body.

In the first place, these references to the body, scattered throughout the text, create a highly suggestive image of a body which is fragmented, broken and dismembered. The fetishisation of severed or disconnected limbs is characteristic of much avant-garde work of the period. The split eyeball of *Un chien andalou*, for example, is symptomatic of such startling, surrealist imagery.[7]

In addition, Anderson's collation of textual references to the body may remind us of Nancy's 'corpus', which is, 'a gleaned list, random in its order or in its degree of completion, a corpus of the body's *entries*: dictionary entries, entries into language, body registers, registers of bodies' (Nancy 1993: 17).

---

6 White (1993: 169) writes that 'whereas traditional carnival turned the world upside-down in a comic and communal inversion of the binary oppositions regulating society, Francis Bacon and modernism turn the world inside-out rather than upside-down'.

7 Dalí's painting, 'Thumb, Beach, Moon and Rotting Bird' (1928), for example, depicts a huge severed thumb lying on a sea-shore (from a private collection). Reproduced in exhibition catalogue, in Dawn Ades's article, 'Morphologising Desire' (Ades 1994: 134). Characteristic of most surrealist art of the period, however, was the dismemberment and objectification of the female body. Suleiman (1990: 24) points out that Surrealism, at its inception, involved, 'the imaginary faceless woman on which the Surrealist male artist

He continues:

> We need a passive recording, as by a seismograph with its impalpable and precise styluses, a seismograph of bodies, of sense, and again of the entries of these bodies: access, orifices, pores of all types of skin, and 'the portals of your body' (Apollinaire). We need to recite, to blazon, body after body, place after place, entry by entry.   (Nancy 1993: 17)

However, Nancy (1993: 17) writes that 'all this would be possible only if we had access to bodies, only if they were not impenetrable'. Nancy is concerned with the limits of both language, and bodies. For Nancy, bodies are inaccessible to language, literature and philosophy: 'only their impenetrability is penetrable. Words brought back to the mouth, or to the ink and the page: there is nothing here to discourse about, nothing to communicate. A community of bodies' (Nancy: 1993: 18). As he goes on to point out:

> We need a *corpus*: a simple nomenclature of bodies, of the places of the body, of its entry ways, a recitation enunciated from nowhere, and not even enunciated, but announced, recorded and repeated, as if one said: foot, belly, mouth, nail, wound, beating, sperm, breast, tattoo, eating, nerve, touching, knee, fatigue [. . .]
> Of course, failure is given at the outset, and intentionally so.
> (Nancy 1993: 18)

In the first place, then, I argue that, in this play, an enquiry is enunciated which is similar to the question posed by Nancy: 'how can one get hold of the body? I am already speechless' (Nancy 1993: 18). The insistence on nomenclature in *El público* can therefore be seen as an expression of the uneasy relationship between language and the body – an attempt to get hold of the body, to find a way to express the intangible living body, as well as the expression of an anxiety that this simply may not be possible. The suggestion of a journey into the centre of the body (posed by the X-ray windows and the 'biombo' which acts like a striptease) seems to show that the more one attempts to arrive at the truth, the more it recedes. The metaphorical body behind this text, then, is one situated at the limits of language and culture. *El*

---

could project his fantasies'. In *El público* it is the male body which is on display. Costumes such as the Roman tunics of the Centurión, the cloth around the torso of the Desnudo rojo, the playful nudity of the Figura de cascabeles and the Figura de pámpanos serve to highlight the male body as an object of spectacle. The first performance of *El público* by the Centro Dramático Nacional, directed by Lluís Pasqual at the Teatro Nacional María Guerrero, Madrid in 1986–87, designed costumes for the Caballos which featured jodhpurs with high boots, a mane of hair and leather bondage straps across the face of the male actors, suggesting reins.

público is concerned with how far an experience of the body can be communicated through language, philosophy and, above all (perhaps anticipating the failure of these two), through the theatrical medium.

The naming of body parts and the dialectic of surface and depth implied by the 'biombo' can be seen in terms of a search to find the centre or core of the human body. The question of locating a core has been discussed in relation to the self by Anderson (1992a) who suggests that:

> one might conclude that the 'correct' model for the self would not in this case be a palimpsest, but rather something more like an onion, a sum of the parts, an accretion of layers, but with no hidden core or centre.[8] (344 n. 14)

But these layers, I suggest, are not expressed as equal. The various body parts are implicated in differing paradigms and with different intensities.

The bodies in this text are infused and criss-crossed with meanings. The metaphorical body suggested by the words 'cáncer' (*OC* II: 605) and 'meningitis' (631) suggests both disease and contagion and the body operated on in the scene of the *Desnudo rojo*, is moribund and decaying. At the same time, in a vivid articulation of the blend of the spiritual and the corporeal which is at the heart of the Crucifixion scene,[9] the body of the Desnudo rojo is moribund, yet also blessed and beatified.

Frenck, Perriam and Thompson (1995: 68) have written of Lorca's *Poeta en Nueva York* that 'there is a tortured awareness of the body as poised hypersensitively on the edge of ecstasy and agony'. This, I suggest, is a valid description of the metaphorical body within the text of *El público*. Human relationships are portrayed as poised on this violent edge or cusp between pleasure and pain. For example, the theme of sexual violence and ambiva-

---

8   Anderson's (1992a) article also contains a review of certain critical positions with respect to the notion of a core to be discovered in this play. Early critics assumed that there was a core to be uncovered, writes Anderson. Those that differ from this view of subjectivity include Feal, who adopts a Sartrean view of the *être-pour-autrui*, in which the subject is partially constituted by its perception of the other; Mazzotti Pabello who proposes a reading based on existentialism, wherein personality and identity are similarly only created in the process of living; and Smith (1989) who proposes a Foucauldian account of self-referentiality and writes that '*El público* is structured around a constant metamorphosis which has no primary or originary term and a shimmering linguistic surface which conceals no hidden meanings or motives' (Smith 1989: 127).

9   Grosz (1994: 5) writes that 'Christ was a man whose soul, whose immortality is derived from God but whose body and mortality is human'. The Desnudo rojo is depicted as rooted to his moribund body, lying on an operating table. D. B. Morris (1991: 50) writes that the Crucifixion painting by Mattias Grünewald (1505–15) likewise emphasises the 'human-ness of Jesus'. Morris adds that such a depiction of Christ was also sought in Martin Scorsese's *The Last Temptation of Christ*, where the crucifixion scene is 'so bloody and shocking (the thick, heavy spikes pounded through bone and flesh) that the decorative crosses worn today like jewellery suddenly resemble nothing so much as little icons of forgetting and denial' (D. B. Morris 1991: 50–1).

lence towards the other is made explicit in the conversation between Elena, the Director and the Hombre 3°, in which she declares:

Elena:	yo te besaría los pies si tú me castigaras y te fueras con las otras mujeres. Pero tú me adoras demasiado a mí sola. Será necesario terminar de una vez.
Director:	¿Y yo? ¿No te acuerdas de mí? ¿No te acuerdas de mis uñas arrancadas? ¿Cómo no habría conocido a las otras mujeres y a ti no? ¿Por qué te he llamado, suplicio mio?
Elena:	Podrías seguir golpeando un siglo entero y no creería en ti. (*El Hombre 3° se dirige a Elena y le aprieta las muñecas*) Podrías seguir un siglo entero atenazando mis dedos y no lograrías hacerme escapar un solo gemido.
Hombre 3°:	¡Veremos quién puede más!
Elena:	Yo y siempre yo. (*OC* II: 608–9)

The term 'gemido' (like *le petit mort*), in this context, contains within it an expression of the ambiguous relationship between ecstasy and agony.

At the same time, the Director and the Hombre 1° run the risk of destroying one another in their game of mutual enslavement, in which incorporation threatens to become possession and then destruction. The Hombre 2° and Hombre 3° remark:

Hombre 3°:	Tendremos necesidad de separarlos.
Hombre 2°:	Para que no se devoren.
Hombre 3°:	Aunque yo encontraría mi libertad.
	(*El Director y el Hombre 1° luchan sordamente*)
Hombre 2°:	Pero yo encontraría mi muerte. (*OC* II: 626)

The Caballos, furthermore, show a sick devotion to the Director. In a radical subversion of the Victorian penchant for obtaining a lock of hair from the head of the beloved, the Caballos grasp at the issue from the body of the Director in an attempt to get closer to him, to attain some tangible part of him:

Los caballos:	[. . .] por trescientas pesetas, por doscientas pesetas, por un plato de sopa, por un frasco de perfume vacío, por tu saliva, por un recorte de tus uñas.
Director:	¡Fuera! ¡Fuera! ¡Fuera! (*Toca un timbre*).
Los caballos:	¡Por nada! Antes te olían los pies y nosotros teníamos tres años. Esperábamos en el retrete, esperábamos detrás de las puertas y luego te llenábamos la cama de lágrimas.
	(*OC* II: 600)

These are erotic bodies in that they appear as the agent as well as the object of desire. But in the scenes of domination that pervade the play, the body is the

vessel for domination and the infliction of pain. Sexual desire, love and
violence are easily collapsed into one:

Hombre 1°:	(*luchando*) Te amo.
Director:	(*luchando*) Te escupo.
Julieta:	¡Están luchando!
Caballo Negro:	Se aman. (*OC* II: 639)

The references to sadism are reinforced by the scattering through the text of
the terms 'látigo' (*OC* II: 614),[10] 'azotar' (614), 'castigar' (609), 'atormentar'
(612), 'golpear' (609), 'dominar' (613), 'obligar' (615), 'suplicio' (609),
'esclavo' (626), 'arrastrarme' (615), 'cadena' (616), 'clavos' (609), 'atenazar'
(609), 'punzones' (636), and 'me dolían las muñecas y los tobillos' (616).
This libertinarian Sadean landscape could be seen to reinforce the image of
El público as a carnivalesque romp, a ritual inversion, a journey of transgression. The body in question is erotic, yet also overlaid with meanings. The
enduring image we retain is that of a body caught and used as a vessel,
commodity, bartered, mutilated and enslaved.

The metaphorical body of this play can, I argue, be seen as an example of a
surface effect. For Nietzsche in *The Genealogy of Morals* (1887), civilisation
carves out its meanings on the body through cruelty and coercion – scarring,
tattooing, circumcising and remaking the body by surgical means are all
examples of ways in which civilisation exercises its power. This is an idea
which is reinforced by Foucault (1978), in *The History of Sexuality*, for whom
the increasing medicalisation of the body demonstrates a body pliable to
power, and for whom clothing and adornments mark the subject's body as
deeply as any surgical incision. Furthermore, for Nietzsche, as Grosz (1994:
34) writes, 'inscriptions mark the surface of the body, dividing it into zones
of intensified or de-intensified sensation, spreading a libidinal concentration
unevenly over the written and erotic surface', and Foucault (1978: 45) asserts
that bodies are caught in 'perpetual spirals of power and pleasure'. The notion
of the body as an example of surface effects seems apt for this play, in which
pain and pleasure are seen to erotically charge certain body parts with
libidinal intensity (for example, in the exchange between Elena and the
Director, feet are kissed and fingers mutilated as examples of devotion).
Furthermore, the textual references to surgery, wounds, scars and scabs, to
skin and tattoos clearly mark these bodies out as ones whose surfaces have
been culturally inscribed. For example the Director claims, 'te bordaré sobre
la carne':

---

10 For example, the ambivalence surrounding whipping (i.e. inflicting pain), or whipping with an orchid (a caress) in the speech of the Figura de pámpanos and the Figura de
cascabeles (*OC* II: 614).

Director
[to the *Hombre 1°*]:   Quiero escupirte y romperte el frac con unas tijeritas.
                          Dame seda y aguja. Quiero bordar. No me gustan los
                          tatuajes, pero te quiero bordar con sedas.   (*OC* II: 607)

The references within the text to adornments, from cosmetics ('lápiz para los
labios' [*OC* II: 607], 'carmín' [607]) and to prosthetics ('cejas azules' [608],
'un bigote de tinta' [632], 'peluca rubia' [601]) further attest to the notion of
a body as a surface text overlaid with meanings.[11]

Lingis's theories (developed in *Excesses: Eros and Culture* [1984])
compare the Western body with that of primitive societies and conclude that
the Western body is in every way as culturally marked as the adorned and
incised body of primitive societies. Incisions on the body, whether physical or
in the metaphorical sense function to increase the body's surface area,
making the whole body into a surface – these incisions are therefore an
attempt to create a body which is an expanse of different surfaces. In *El
público* the relation between surface and depth is dealt with interestingly
within the text:

Hombre 1°:   (*Al director*) Mi lucha ha sido con la máscara hasta
                       conseguir verte desnudo (*lo abraza*).
Caballo Blanco 1°:   (*Burlón*) Un lago es una superficie.
Hombre 1°:   ¡O un volumen!
Caballo Blanco 1°:   (*Riendo*) Un volumen son mil superficies.   (*OC* II: 638)

The layers of adornment and meanings which criss-cross like a grid over the
metaphorical body of *El público* serve, I argue, to extend its surface area, to
create it as a *surface effect*.

Lingis (1984) maintains that the function of this proliferation of the body's
surface area is to extend and intensify the body's erotogenic sensitivity. Grosz
(1994: 139) writes that 'welts, scars, cuts, tattoos, perforations, incisions,
inlays, function quite literally to increase the surface space of the body,
creating out of what may have been formless flesh a series of zones, loca-
tions, ridges, hollows, contours: places of special significance and libidinal
intensity'. These incisions and various body markings therefore create an
erotogenic surface with intensities which are unevenly distributed over the
body. Lingis argues that this:

---

11 Prosthetics (artificial supports for the human body) run throughout the work of
Goya, Dalí, Bosch and others. White (1993: 173) points out that these items are ontologi-
cally unstable, as they can be claimed neither by the body nor the world and hence violate
the coherence and integrity of the body-image.

... inscription is a working all over the skin, all surface effects. This cutting
in orifices and raising tumescences does not contrive new receptor organs
for a depth body [as for example, the prosthetic additions to the civilised
body do] [. . .] it extends an erotogenic surface [. . .] it is a multiplication of
mouths, of lips, of labia, anuses, these sweating and bleeding perforations
and puncturings [. . .] these warts raised all over the abdomen, around the
eyes.   (Lingis 1984: 34)

These puncturings and markings on the body do not simply displace
biological libidinal zones, but also, as Grosz writes, 'they constitute the
whole body in its entirety as erotic, and they privilege parts of the body as
self-constituted orifices' (Grosz 1994: 139). Furthermore, Lingis makes
possible the notion of an erotogenic orifice or rim.

The body of so-called primitive societies, Lingis claims, is not separated
from that of Western societies in terms of degrees of pain or cruelty – all civi-
lisations similarly have a history of barbarism. But Lingis contends that
where the Western world is mistaken is in its belief that surface hides some
depth or interiority:

We [in the Western world] find the ugliness of tattooed nakedness puerile
and shallow [. . .] The savage fixing his identity on his skin [. . .] Our identity is inward, it is our functional integrity as machines to produce certain
civilized, that is, coded types of action.   (Lingis 1984: 43)

Hence, as Grosz writes, 'Lingis refigures carnal desire in terms of the lateral
["horizontal"] contamination of one erotogenic zone or bodily surface by
another, rather than in terms of a "vertical relation" between [bodily] surface
and [psychical depth]'.

Lingis's theories of the erotogenic body seem relevant for the metaphorical
depiction of the body in this play in which the surface area of the body is
extended by the proliferation of cultural layers and the cutting of the skin to
create fresh surfaces and new orifices. The attempt to increase the surface
area of the body can be seen as the expression of the union of bodies: an
extension of the surface area of the body increases the possibility for sexual
pleasure.[12] The notion of skin-on-skin as the promotion of desire suggests the
desire to touch another body, or for auto-eroticism. Notably for the scenes of
sexual violence in this play, according to Lingis's theories, the various zones
of intensity are excited or intensified by pain as much as by caresses, and
'this may go some way to understanding the appeal of sado-masochism'
(Grosz 1994). Interestingly, we find this exchange in the *Cuadro Segundo*,
which likewise seems to confuse the codes between pain and pleasure:

[12] Naomi Segal applies Lingis's theories to a discussion of Jane Campion's film *The
Piano*, where pleasure is read as a drive to touch skin on skin. From a paper entitled,
'Skin', at *Sensual Reading*, a conference held at the University of Aberdeen, 1996.

Figura de cascabeles: Yo me convertiría en otro látigo. Un látigo hecho con
cuerdas de guitarra.
Figura de pámpanos: ¡No me azotes!
Figura de cascabeles: Un látigo hecho de maromas de barco.
Figura de pámpanos: ¡No me golpees el vientre!
Figura de cascabeles: Un látigo hecho con los estambres de una orquídea.

(*OC* II: 614)

Within and behind the body of this text, I argue, lies a suggestion of the body
as a profusion of orifices, erotogenic, carnal, libidinous, and polymorphous.
This body spreads its surfaces (valleys, contours and orifices) throughout the
text as it yearns to attain the feel of flesh upon flesh. If the threat of this body
lies in its carnality, then behind this there lies an even greater danger: if the
body is a socially inscribed surface then perhaps surface tension hides no
psychic (intellectual) interiority – perhaps the *surface effect* is all there is.

COLLECTIVE BODIES

Criado: ¡Señor!
Director: ¿Qué?
Criado: Ahí está el público.
Director: Que pase.

Federico García Lorca, *El público*.

There was nothing for the audience to do. They were silent. Their minds
and bodies were too close, yet not close enough. We aren't free, each of
them thought separately, to feel or to think separately, nor yet to fall asleep.
We're too close, but not close enough. So they fidgeted.

Virginia Woolf, *Between the Acts*.

Within the liminal space of *El público*, as in the carnivalesque, boundaries
are broken down, promoting the creation of hybrids, while prohibited practices are licensed, making the whole process into a collective experiment.
Bakhtin's grotesque body of carnival is a body which is open and unfinished,
thereby destroying the limits which separate individuals. Bakhtin writes of
the various bodily junctions – mouth, nose, anus, phallus – that 'within them
[. . .] the confines between bodies and between the body and the world are
overcome: there is an interchange and an interorientation' (Bakhtin 1965:
317). Hence we could view the focus on orifices and bodily functions in *El
público* as the expression of a removal of the margins which confine and
distinguish individuals. Carnival marked 'the suspension of all hierarchical
rank, privileges, norms and prohibitions', converting it into, the place for
working out, in a concretely sensuous, half-real, half-play-acted form, a new
mode of interrelationship between individuals, counterposed to the all-

powerful socio-hierarchical relationships of non-carnival life (Bakhtin 1965: 10, 7–11). The audience of the title of *El público* is seen to assume centre stage for this participatory journey into the liminal space. The emphasis on metamorphosis, disguise and flux could be seen as a way to reveal the arbitrary nature of cultural and semantic codes, symbols and hierarchies. Through the trickster-function, the audience can explore taboos and prohibitions and take pleasure in the flux revealed therein. As in the case of Turner's *communitas*,[13] the stress on the breaking down of limits and boundaries within the play (for example, the confines separating actor and spectator; the metaphorical union suggested by the commonality of issue from the body) could be seen as a way to emphasise the celebratory and rejuvenatory possibilities of the collective experience. This notion finds resonances within the play, such as the suggestion of ritual sacrifice and rebirth.[14] For example, the Hombre 1° must die to inaugurate the 'theatre beneath the sand': 'Hombre 1°: Tendré que darme un tiro para inaugurar el verdadero teatro bajo la arena', *OC* II: 604). By correlation, the collective experience can be seen to lead to a re-ordering of the world (e.g. the references to tearing down the walls of the theatre: 'es rompiendo todas las puertas el único modo que tiene el drama de justificarse' [*OC* II: 668] and the roars of the revolutionary crowd outside the walls: 'La primera bomba de la revolución barrió la cabeza del profesor de retórica' and: 'En este momento llega la revolución a la catedral') which may suggest the incorporation of theatre into social-praxis.

However, within the text of *El público*, the image of celebratory carnival is belied by the disturbing images conjured up for us by the Director:

> Yo vi una vez a un hombre devorado por la máscara. Los jóvenes más fuertes de la ciudad, con picas ensangrentadas, le hundían por el trasero grandes bolas de periódicos abandonados, y en América hubo una vez un muchacho a quien la máscara ahorcó colgado de sus propios intestinos.
>
> (*OC* II: 604)

The breaking down of boundaries can therefore also bring fears and anxieties. The notion of a body as a proliferation of orifices can create a body which is open, vulnerable to attack, to assault, penetration and even to emptying out. Fragmentation of the body can be related to an attack or

---

[13] In *From Ritual to Theatre*, Turner elucidates his theory of social drama, influenced by Van Gennep's notion of *Rites of Passage* (1908), to posit that theatre is a (potentially dangerous) liminal space where nothing is defined, and where the subject is between roles and social functions. For some theorists the liminal space may invert the established order but never subvert it. At the same time, this is a space removed from daily activity for members of a community to 'think about how they think in propositions that are not *in* cultural codes but *about* them' (Turner 1969).

[14] For Bakhtin, death is never an isolated event, but always a process which includes birth.

assault on the symbolic or physical integrity of the human body. In addition, orifices can be the locus for danger and threat. This is a notion explored by Kristeva (1980) for whom issue from the body (what she terms the *abject*) signifies a potential danger which hovers at the body's entrances.[15] In *Powers of Horror*, she describes the abject as what is 'thrust aside in order to live'. Drawing on Mary Douglas' *Purity and Danger* (1966), she notes that dirt is relative to the construction of a social body. For Kristeva, the abject is thrust aside as the subject moves from the pre-Oedipal to its constitution as a social body. The abject is threatening to the subject in that it demonstrates that this expulsion can never be complete. Furthermore, the abject is linked, for Kristeva, to a fear of death – identity is threatened by the abject: 'it is thus not lack of cleanliness that causes abjection, but what disturbs identity, system, order. What does not respect borders, positions, rules. The in-between, the ambiguous, the composite' (Kristeva 1980: 4). I argue that this focus on abjection in *El público* is a clearly provocative tack, forcing attention on an aspect of human life that is normally wilfully ignored. In terms of the theatrical experience, we could term this focus an *attack* on the audience. Abjection describes the fear and disgust (tinged with desire) that we feel for the 'abominable and filthy' things with which we are unable to cope. It describes the 'panicky, twisting aside and away from those "things" which burn and mutilate our self-possession' (White 1993: 166). It is reactive, almost reflexive rejection, which is, 'violent, jolting and immediate in its carnivorous assault on the body' (White 1993: 166). The subject thus feels 'split between a self and internalized otherness which s/he attempts to expel. This split or *Ich-spaltung* (Freud) destroys the fundamental subject–object boundary which both preserves subjective identity as such and keeps the world at bay' (White 1993: 166). A collective focus on the abject, I suggest, relates to the boundaries separating individuals and comes to signify a drive towards individuality, and the associated fear of loss of control – a fear that the social will be eroded into the mass, an amorphous, material conglomeration which is not so very far removed from the terrifying decaying matter which is the corpse.

In *El público* the audience is metaphorically trapped within the liminal space. In the *Cuadro Quinto*, several ladies leave their theatre-box and try to leave the theatre. But their passage is blocked by the revolution: 'Dama 3°: Cuando subíamos por el monte de la ruina, creímos ver la luz de la aurora, pero tropezamos con los telones y traigo mis zapatos de tisú manchados de petróleo'. This sense of containment is reinforced by references to the blocking of entrances and exits of the theatre, 'la callejuela está llena de gente armada y es difícil huir por allí' (*OC* II: 649), and the Director cries:

---

[15] For comparisons between Bakhtin's grotesque and Kristeva's abject, see Vice (1997: 160–74); Stallybrass and White (1986: 175); Russo (1986: 10); and White (1993: 168).

'Todo el teatro sale de las humedades confinadas' (*OC* II: 665). Within this confined, humid space, images of contagion abound: 'yo envenenaría el aire libre' (*OC* II: 599), and 'meningitis', which seems to recall the nineteenth century European theatre audience's concerns with hygiene and the containment of disease. For example, Read (1993) writes that fears circulated surrounding air pollution which could 'poison women of delicate constitution', and the blocking of doors and exits in the theatre could cause mass hysteria, following the experience of previous disasters. The references to fire in the auditorium in *El público* contribute to the air of claustrophobia and fear of contagion. The audience is thus confined within the liminal space, and forced to react, to participate (perhaps through reactive fear and revulsion) in this provocative assault on the senses and sensibilities: 'Director: ¿Y la moral? ¿Y el estómago de los espectadores? Hombre 1°: Hay personas que vomitan cuando se vuelve un pulpo al revés y otras que se ponen pálidas si oyen pronunciar con la debida intención la palabra cáncer' (*OC* II: 605).[16] The audience reacts angrily to distasteful topics, preferring the theatre of entertainment, the 'theatre of the open air'.[17] Thus while the 'humedades confinadas' which is the preferred theatrical space of the Director may seem to recall Rousseau's 'gloomy cavern' which is the theatre of entertainment where the melancholy spectators sit, cut off from the open air, a 'fearful and immobile' mass, – gazing, perhaps, but silent, barely listening, with no capacity for action',[18] here the liminal space involves the audience in a process

---

16 Lorca wanted to shock the theatre-goers, to *pour épater le bourgeois*. The phrase, '¿Cómo orinaba Romeo, señor Director? ¿Es que no es bonito ver orinar a Romeo?', can be seen as part of this provocative tack. Lorca first read the play at the home of the Loynaz family in Havana: 'Dulce María Loynaz, poetisa, es hoy una señora reticente, salvo cuando habla de esta obra: "Un horror" – dice-; "absurda y escandalosa. Federico me regaló el manuscrito y yo lo rompí y tiré al cesto de los papeles' (Amorós 1986: 172). On another occasion, at the Morla Lynch household in Madrid, the play was described as 'estupendo, pero irrepresentable' and 'yo la verdad no he entendido nada' (Amorós 1986: 171). Lorca famously noted to Nadal that the play was 'muy difícil, y por el momento irrepresentable. Pero dentro de diez años será un exitazo; ya lo verás' (Martínez Nadal 1970: 17). Fifty years later, at the *estreno* of the play at the Piccolo Teatro Studio, Milan, Lluís Pasqual (director of this production) described the play as 'un gran insulto', 'una enorme provocación', 'una gran blasfemia' and 'un gran vómito' (Armiño 1986). But it was also regarded as a huge success, attended by Isabel García Lorca and greeted with 'calurosas y prolongados aplausos y gritos de ¡bravo! Fue lo que se dice un triunfo' (Sagarra 1986). One dissenting voice was that of Vizcaíno Casas (1987) who wrote: 'he leído todas las críticas, sin conseguir de saber si es buena, regular o mala. Hacen garabos, se marchan por los ramos, rizan el rizo, con tal de no pronunciarse en contra. La sensación que dan esas críticas es de que [. . .] *El público* no le gustó al ídem'.

17 Woods (1998: 268) makes the point that the audience regards the love between men as a distasteful topic and they react angrily. I am grateful to Michael Ward for drawing my attention to this work.

18 Jean-Jacques Rousseau, *Politics and the Arts: Letter to M. D'Alembert on the*

of provocation and attack intended to unnerve and enliven even as they sit immobile.

I argue that the images of contagion and fire within the auditorium address the fear that is to be experienced by people who form crowds. When somebody shouts 'Fire!' in the auditorium, the audience turn into a crowd, perhaps even a mob. Crowds are a common feature of life, and participating in a theatre audience is just one example of the many reasons we find to group together. 'Man petrifies and darkens', wrote Elias Canetti, 'in the distances he has created'. This is the lure of the crowd, the 'blessed moment', 'that density, where there is scarcely any space between, and body presses against body' (Canetti 1960: 19). But John Ashberry notes that, 'we never knew, never knew what joined us together. Perhaps only the congealing of a closeness, deserving of no special notice'.[19] The removal of the distance separating individuals, that ruthless discharge, can lead to the enactment of collective acts and atrocities. *El público*, I suggest, is rife with references to scapegoating, witch-hunts and collective murders, the darker sides of human communal acts. The angry lynch-mob ('los jóvenes más fuertes de la ciudad') responsible for the assault on the man metaphorically devoured by the social mask ('con picas ensangrentadas, le hundían por el trasero grandes bolas de periódicos abandonados') and the case in America, where a man was murdered by hanging him by his intestines, are both examples of gang assault. Outside the walls of the theatre, the crowd advances, shouting, 'piden la muerte del Director de escena', while inside, a sub-group has set upon and murdered Juliet: 'y que hayan asesinado también a la verdadera Julieta que estaba debajo de las butacas'. This is a nightmare world of assassination plots, murderous intent, and bloodlust. There are crowds metaphorically roaming all over this dangerous, unlicensed realm. But who are these angry murderers? It soon becomes clear that they are none other than members of the audience:

Director: ¿Qué hago con el público si quito las barandas al puente? Vendría la máscara a devorarme. Yo vi una vez a un hombre devorado por la máscara [. . .] Los jóvenes más fuertes de la ciudad, con picas ensangrentadas, le hundían por el trasero. . .
(*OC* II: 604)

If the handrails are removed, the audience will spill up and over, seeping and flooding, an uncontrollable mass, like a rendering of Sartre's *viscosity* of fear. The spectators have become the mob, *canaille*, crowd, *plebs*, *demos* – in revolutionary terms they are supporters, rebels, anarchists, open to

Theater, trans. Allen Bloom (Ithaca: Cornell University Press, 1960), p. 125, cited in Blau (1990: 131).

19 John Ashberry, *Three Poems* (New York: Harvest-Harcourt, Brace 1969: 188), cited in Blau (1990: 1–2).

120 SARAH WRIGHT

manipulation by skilful political leadership, leaving individual responsibilities aside, and going along with the will of mob-rule:

Estudiante 4: Romeo era un hombre de treinta años y Julieta un muchacho de quince. La denuncia del público fue eficaz. (*OC* II: 657)

Estudiante 2: El Director de escena evitó de manera genial que la masa de los espectadores se enterase de esto, pero los caballos y la revolución han destruido sus planes.

Estudiante 4: Lo que es inadmisible es que los hayan asesinado.

Estudiante 1: Y que hayan asesinado a la verdadera Julieta que gemía debajo de las butacas. (*OC* II: 658)

The audience has become swept up by the revolutionary fervour raging outside, whipped into a frenzy of hatred used for their own ends.

In a final correlation, in the scene of the crucifixion of the Hombre 1°/Desnudo rojo, the audience has switched from church congregation, to voyeuristic spectators of a surgical operation, to a violent group responsible for a ritual scape-goating and martyrdom (the correlation of the Desnudo rojo with the figure of Christ/St. Sebastian) or an angry mob fearful of difference and otherness (the death of the Hombre 1° and the references to homosexuality).

Within this liminal space, then, the crowd is forced metaphorically to assume different roles in the drama, from the relative innocence of the spectator to lynch-mob responsible for murder. These are people who are frightened of alterity,[20] fearful of being touched by an unknown quantity in the darkness: 'In the dark, the fear of an unexpected touch can mount to panic. Even clothes give insufficient security: it is easy to tear them and pierce through to the naked, smooth, defenceless flesh of the victim' (Canetti 1960: 15). These spectators are hypochondriacs, frightened of contagion, phobic, even hysterical.[21] The limitless terror of otherness, of marginality, thus engendered, is seen to be at the root of violence and murder, while the emphasis on bodily discharge is seen, paradoxically, to be what links all of the cast of this nightmarish circus, actors and spectators alike, regardless of difference. Edwards (1980: 63–4) draws links between *El público* and Bosch's *The Garden of Earthly Delights* as well as Goya's *Disasters of War* and *Caprichos* – *El público* likewise manifests, he says, 'uncompromising images of man's inhumanity to man'. The celebratory communion of the carnivalesque, seen through the distorting fairground mirror now becomes

[20] See Girard (1982: 22) for whom 'persecutors are never obsessed by difference but rather its unutterable contrary, the lack of difference'. Perhaps the notion of guilty pleasures lies behind the scenes of persecution in the play – it is not fear of difference which motivates the attacks, but rather, a fear of sameness.

[21] In 1928, Breton and Aragon declared hysteria to be 'the greatest poetical discovery of the twentieth-century' (White 1993: 176).

Bakhtin's darker nightmarish side of carnival, the 'carnival of the night', where 'the carnivalesque becomes interiorized and individualized, related to private terror, isolation and insanity rather than to robust, communal celebration' (White 1993: 171).

THE SPECTACLE OF PAIN

> Without cruelty, there is no festival.
> Friedrich Nietzsche, *On the Genealogy of Morals.*

Among the fragments and shards of the metaphorical body within the text of *El público*, there emerges a profound sense of bodies which are flayed, visceral and physical: this, I suggest, builds up a highly suggestive image that can best be described as a body in pain. The imagery of mutilations, inscriptions on flesh, wounds, scars, decay and disease reaches a climax in the figure of the Desnudo rojo, which is a violent transposition of the scene of the Crucifixion onto the more mundane but even more vivid setting of the operating theatre. The Desnudo rojo/Hombre 1°/Gonzalo revels in bodiliness. He is 'coronado de espinas' (*OC* II: 647) and is lying on a hospital bed perpendicular to the floor which has been painted 'como por un primitivo'. He establishes his credentials as a Christ-figure, '¿Cuánto falta para Jerusalén?' (*OC* II: 648), and says: 'Padre mío, aparta de mí este cáliz de amargura' (*OC* II: 648). But the male nurse scolds him: 'Cállate. Ya es éste el tercer termómetro que rompes' (*OC* II: 649) (a play on the three stages of betrayal before the Crucifixion) and deepens his wounds:

Desnudo: Yo deseo morir ¿Cuántos vasos de sangre me habéis sacado?
Enfermero: Cincuenta. Ahora te daré la hiel, y luego, a las ocho, vendré con el bisturí para ahondarte la herida del costado.

(OC II: 648)

This Christ-figure presents a blend of the human and divine (we might even describe him as a trickster-figure, with one foot on earth and the other in Heaven, 'Padre, en tus manos encomiendo mi espíritu' [*OC* II:656]), but here the Desnudo rojo is rooted to his moribund, material corpse.

From the pain of the religious ascetic, the erotic pleasure/pain of sadism, the suffering of the torture victim, the pain of hysterical fear to the pain of the moribund, diseased body, *El público* shows the different sources of pain, and the way that pain can be overlaid with cultural significations.

The emphasis on depictions of pain in *El público* is related to the search for authenticity in the theatre, an attempt to sift through the debris of the masks and artificiality of carnival and arrive at some force which is unmediated by language and representation. Thus pain can be seen to be related to the divisions of the Apolline and Dionysiac referred to in the introduction to this study. The Apolline represents the layers of artifice, cultural inscriptions laid one upon the other while the Dionysiac represents those aspects of cultural experience (e.g. pain, death) which lie outside the limits of culture. Pain shatters or breaks up language as Scarry (1985: 4) writes. Pain is indescribable in linguistic terms – we must resort to analogies, or to animal-like shrieks in an attempt to communicate the depth of our pain to others. At the darkest root of the scream, 'la oscura raíz del grito' (*OC* II: 799), there are no words, there is no communication, just a reeling silence: 'whatever pain achieves, it achieves in part through its unsharability, and it ensures this unsharability through its resistance to language' (Scarry 1985: 4). Pain is universal, the great leveller, understood by all, but it is also a solitary experience.

The focus on images of pain in *El publico* can be seen as part of the provocation launched on the audience, a technique similar to Artaud's 'sudden shocks', which aim to enliven and unnerve the spectators.[22] Artaud's *Theatre of Cruelty* involved 'physical, objective elements perceptible to all' (Artaud 1993: 72). He writes that, 'there can be no spectacle without an element of cruelty at the basis of every show. In our present degenerative state, metaphysics must be made to enter the mind through the body' (1993: 72). Artaud's theatre 'wakes up the heart and the nerves', demanding a 'hyper--consciousness' on the part of the spectators. Hence, there will be no division separating actors and spectators, and furthermore, cruelty will make theatre into 'the equal of life – not an individual life, that individual aspect of life in which *characters* triumph, but the sort of liberated life which sweeps away human individuality and in which man is only a reflection' (Artaud 1993: 116). As Derrida writes, 'Artaud wants to have done with the *imitative* concept of art, with the Aristotelian aesthetics in which the metaphysics of Western art comes into its own: "Art is not the imitation of life, but life is the imitation of a transcendental principle which art puts us into communication with once again" ' (Derrida 1978: 234). Cruelty, like pain, attempts to break through mimesis to an unrepresentable heart under the carnage of layer upon layer of representation.

But in *El público*, despite the emphasis on the breaking down of boundaries between actor and spectator, the carnival without footlights, it is clear that what the audience is faced with, particularly in the Crucifixion scene, is the spectacle of pain. Pain is thus aestheticised, represented, mediated. Furthermore, despite the rendering more acute of the pain of the Desnudo

---

[22] De Ros (1996: 114–15) also compares *El público* to the work of Artaud. She writes that Lorca may well have been acquainted with Artaud's ideas through his sojourn at the Residencia de Estudiantes in Madrid. Artaud's article 'Cinema and Reality' accompanied his film scenario *La coquille et le clergyman*, which was shown at the Residencia in a session organised by Buñuel.

rojo, at the same time the scene is highly stylised, a 'primitivo', a piece of naive art. The divisions separating individuals are also re-inscribed as the audience switches from religious devotee, to sadist, to voyeur. The liminal space, that contained arena implied by the 'teatro bajo la arena' comes to suggest the original pain of ancient ritual sacrifice,[23] but at the same time, that ritual arena resonates with the historical and mythical past – past rituals and past audiences. Tragedy, writes Northrop Frye, is a 'mimesis of sacrifice', in which the audience participate as communicants, sharing symbolically the sacred body (Frye 1957: 214). This recalls the Eucharist where the bread and the wine are eaten and drunk 'in remembrance of me' (Luke 22: 17–20 and 1 Corinthians 11: 23–5) at Jesus' command. In transubstantiation the wine and bread is wholly transformed into the body of Christ, but even here the call for 'remembrance' reflects the memory of centuries of other worshippers who ate, drank and remembered. This ritual space in *El público*, which might be a sacrificial arena (suggested by the play on 'arena/sand') or an operating theatre (for the bodies of the audience to receive 'sudden shocks') therefore resonates with original, primeval pain, but also contains the ghosts of a pain and a suffering which has been resurrected in remembrance.

The transposition of the ritual arena to the operating theatre does, however, serve to make the scene more immediate, more physical, more real. *El público* is obsessed with the notion of representation, of repetition. How to move away from the staging of representation upon representation, encapsulated in the image of the 'teatro del aire libre' and its master-of-ceremonies the Prestidigitador. Romeo and Juliet are caught within this repetition of repetition, like a tapeloop which endlessly repeats:

Hombre 2°:   ¿Cómo orinaba Romeo, señor Director? ¿Es que no es bonito ver orinar a Romeo? ¿Cuántas veces fingió tirarse de la torre para ser apresado en la comedia de su sufrimiento? ¿Qué pasaba, señor Director, cuando no pasaba?   (*OC* II: 603)

Juliet, likewise, has never seen the perfection of a whole night, doomed endlessly to sleep before dawn breaks. Romeo and Juliet are eternally young, each night they try to recreate the joy of their first kiss: 'la repetición del acto ha sido maravilloso porque indudablemente se amaban con un amor incalcu-

---

[23] Anderson (1992a: 336) writes that 'the basic meaning of "arena" in Spanish is sand, but it can also by extension denote an arena, or, if you like, an amphitheatre, leading us back to the "teatro bajo la arena". Subsequently, the Director asserts that "el verdadero drama es un circo de arcos", bringing to mind not the modern tented circus but rather the permanent Roman one, the arena for gladiatorial combat. Taking the sense of (Roman) arena, amphitheatre or circus, this in turn could suggest the "ruina romana" of the "Cuadro Segundo", a "ruina" filled with "columnas", "capiteles", and sand – "arena", and which is precisely the scene of the "lucha" or "festín sangriento" '.

lable' (*OC* II: 658). These images contain the anxiety of the *theatrum mundi*, that all the world might be a stage, and that we are doomed endlessly to repeat the past. Where does the audience go, when they leave the theatre? In this play the suggestion (with the shouts of imaginary revolution outside the walls) is that they merely enter more spirals of chaos, caught up in the whirl-wind of other dream-worlds.

The Director cries 'Pero, ¿qué es lo que quiere de mí? ¿Trae usted una obra nueva?' (*OC* II: 605). The Hombre 1°, in Pirandellian style, replies, '¿Le parece a usted obra más nueva que nosotros con nuestras barbas [. . .] y usted?' The Director will inaugurate a new theatrical space – the 'teatro bajo la arena'. The Prestidigitador accuses him of recycling stale drama ('¿por qué eligieron ustedes una tragedia manida y no hicieron un drama original?' [*OC* II: 664]). But the Director is adamant:

> . . . Para expresar lo que pasa todos los días en todas las grandes ciudades y en los campos por medio de un ejemplo que, admitido por todos a pesar de su originalidad, ocurrió sólo una vez. Pude haber elegido el *Edipo* o *Otelo*. En cambio, si hubiera levantado el telón con la verdad original, se hubieran manchado de sangre las butacas desde las primeras escenas.   (*OC* II: 664)

In this drama, characters do not pretend to die, but rather 'queman la cortina y mueren de verdad en presencia de los espectadores' (*OC* II: 666). This is a drama which 'ha sostenido un verdadero combate que ha costado la vida a todos los intérpretes' (*OC* II: 668).

This new theatre is like the non-theological stage of Artaud's theatre of cruelty. As Derrida writes, 'theatrical art should be the primordial and privi-leged site of this destruction of imitation: more than any other art, it has been marked by the labor of total representation in which the affirmation of life lets itself be doubled and emptied by negation' (Derrida 1978: 234). For Derrida, 'the theater of cruelty is not a *representation*. It is life itself, in the extent to which life is non-representable. Life is the non-representable origin of representation' (Derrida 1978: 234). This new theatrical space will no longer privilege the visual, nor the word, dictating from afar, but rather, 'the-ater space will be utilized not only in its dimensions and volume but, so to speak, in its undersides' (Derrida 1978: 238). Just as the Director stresses the great dramas, such as Oedipus and Othello as the origins of drama which occurred just a single time, so Derrida writes of Artaud that 'he kept himself as close as possible to the limit: the possibility and impossibility of pure theatre. Presence, in order to be presence and self-presence, has already begun to represent itself, has always already been penetrated. Affirmation itself must be penetrated in repeating itself. Which means that the murder of the father which opens the history of representation and the space of tragedy, the murder of the father that Artaud, in sum, wants to repeat at the greatest proximity to its origin but *only a single time* – this murder is endless and repeated indefinitely'. For Derrida then, the 'closure of representation' is the 'circular limit within which difference infinitely repeats itself' (1978: 250). Lorca, I argue, like Artaud, attempts to get close to this original representation – the closest we can ever get to the limit of representation. The end of *El público* begins as it ends, with the audience's arrival, but this time the performance begins in another time and another space (off-stage):

Criado:	¡Señor!
Director:	¿Qué?
Criado:	(*Cayendo de rodillas*) Ahí está el público.
Director:	(*Cayendo de bruces sobre la mesa*)
	¡Que pase! [. . .]
Voz:	(*Fuera*) Señor.
Voz:	(*Fuera*) Qué.
Voz:	(*Fuera*) El público.
Voz:	(*Fuera*) Que pase. (*OC* II: 671–2)

I suggest that pain reflects a fundamental crisis at the heart of *El público* – that history is a series of repetitions, and that there is nothing which is unmediated. Pain seems to hint at the possibility of an unmediated origin of representation. Ultimately, pain enables humanity to foresee its own death: a space beyond representation, beyond words. But this is for the present time unknowable: while we may reflect on our own deaths, it is always presently represented: 'there is no knowing death, no experiencing it and then returning to write about it' (Goodwin and Bronfen 1993: 4). Death, like pain, is the common denominator of humanity. It is what binds us all together – our lurch towards that silent space. But at the same time, it is what separates us. Death, like pain, is a profoundly solitary experience. The guilty pleasure of theatre, I suggest, is the possibility for the audience to vicariously experience pain and death through a liminal realm. The power of Lorca's theatre is that once the lights go up after the performance, the audience is left sitting profoundly aware of the solitary nature of human existence: the audience is caught up in nothing more substantial than a collective solipsism.

CONCLUSION: OFF LIMITS

> Pasa la farsa de inquietudes
> Del carnaval
> Federico García Lorca, *Carnaval, 1918*

In the preceding chapters, various (often non-naturalistic) trickster-figures lead the audience into liminal space of the theatre. They offer an invitation to revel in the festive aspects of literature: the carnivalesque, the playful, the taboo. Theatre becomes, like carnival, 'an interstitial, transgressive moment' (Pérez Firmat 1986: xv) in which to probe the limits of gender, and to explore time, the visual and the physical body at the margins. From an investigation of the instability of visuals, to time-shifting and gender transformations, the impression we retain of Lorca's theatre is that of restless movement, an endless search to discover the limits of the world in which we live. A study of the margins of Lorca's theatre focuses attention not just on what lies beyond the limits of culture but also on the boundaries themselves. It is the strictness of the delimitations within culture that permits such playful (and taboo) excursions, strict limits held together by rigid codes hiding fear and prejudice. Long after it was first written, García Lorca's theatre offers us a safe arena, a liminal space, from which to explore the codes of our society, to test its limits and to investigate its fears. Repeatedly, however, in the preceding chapters, the playful 'margins of mess' (Babcock-Adams 1975) reveal a preoccupation with another, more serious, concern: the playful antics of the figures of the carnivalesque merely serve to hide the absence which is death. Life is presented as a series of glittering masks, nothing more than red herrings designed to ward off our lurch towards death. If the trickster deals in the anomaly, that which lies outside culture, beyond the limits, then repeatedly, Lorca's theatre shows that the ultimate anomaly is death.

Death lies outside system and order, destroying any illusions we may have of control or understanding of it: the poker game in the closing moments of *Así que pasen cinco años* is a perfect example of the arbitrariness of this cruel game of chance.

Death fascinates us and we continually find ways to experience it vicariously. Theatre therefore provides an opportunity to make the world manageable (a microcosmic vision), to attempt to impose limits on it, a structure and a sense of control. It is thus similar to Freud's claims (in his article,

'Humour') of the father who laughs at his child's seriousness: 'Look! Here is the world, which seems so dangerous! It is nothing more than a game for children – just worth making a jest about!' (Freud 1927: 166). As Borch-Jacobsen (1982: 147) writes, 'let's act, in other words, as *if* we could raise ourselves above our precious self, as if we could, just for the time of an improbable grace period, make fun of its shabby finitude'.[1] If life is a mere grace period before death, 'nothing more than an unspeakable farce, an improbable gag lost in the immensity of the universe' (Borch-Jacobsen 1982: 147), then theatre provides an improbable grace period from which to explore death. Theatre is a spectacle which imposes a limit between those tricky areas of culture which lie beyond boundaries, and ourselves as decoders, solvers of riddles. The spectacle of death is an attempt to distinguish ourselves from the dying man. Theatre allows us to experience the thrill and dread of death, without the danger – turning it into a kind of collective disavowal. But Borch-Jacobsen suggests (1982: 164) that, when we *laugh* at the dead man, 'at one with his fall, and identifying with him, we *are* dead. We are, like him, other than ourselves, senseless'. Through laughter, 'the dead man drags us with him into a vertigo where we *are* finally – *other*: being at the same time not being, laughing and at the same time being dead, laughing at being already dead. Laughing at being' (Borch-Jacobsen 1982: 154). The liminal space of theatre can be seen, like Borch-Jacobsen's theory of laughter, as a non-being, a rendering of ourselves as *other* which relates us to the stasis and inertia, a 'single decomposing throng', of death. Through theatre we may laugh at death, but the laugh is ultimately on us. It is a 'roar of irreconciliation' (Borch-Jacobsen 1982: 148), for death respects no boundaries and may be deferred, but not indefinitely, and may unite, but then separates. Theatre, is an example of *serio ludere*, a concept often associated with the trickster. The power of García Lorca's theatre, ultimately, is its willingness to engage playfully with the serious game of death.

A discovery of an awareness of ever-present death as the basis for García Lorca's work is not a new concept (a product, in part, of the terrible circumstances of Lorca's own death, which have tended to inflect many subsequent readings of the plays and poetry). Yet the recuperation of the margins of Lorca's theatre (both in terms of the texts chosen and the themes addressed) has also given way to a shift in emphasis which interrogates the thematic strains which traditionally emerge from Lorca's work. This has been a study of the trickster and the carnivalesque, but it has yielded a view of García Lorca's work which accents male fantasy, masochism, androgyny and scatology. These are fresh perspectives offered in the spirit of a reappraisal of García Lorca's theatre. It is in the shifting of perspectives of Lorca's theatre

[1]   I am grateful to Tracey Jermyn for drawing my attention to this article.

that its power lies: Lorca's work is subject to constant challenges and reinventions through time. Rather than offering conclusions to Lorca's work, my readings of the plays aim to open them up for further discussion, widening the sources of themes and ideas normally applied to his work, to make way for future scrutiny. Over one hundred years after his birth, Lorca remains a testing ground for new ideas and a space for the powerful exploration of the most profound concerns of our culture.

BIBLIOGRAPHY

Ades, D. 1994. 'Morphologies of Desire', in M. Raeburn (ed.) *Salvador Dalí: The Early Years*, pp. 129–60. London: South Bank Centre.

Adlam, C., Falconer, R., Maklin, V. and Renfrew, A. (eds) 1997. *Face to Face: Bakhtin in Russia and the West*. Sheffield: Sheffield Academic Press.

Allen, R. C. 1974. *Psyche and Symbol in the Theater of Federico García Lorca: Perlimplín, Yerma, Blood Wedding*. Austin, TX, and London: University of Texas Press.

Allen, V. 1983. *The Femme Fatale: Erotic Icon*. New York: The Whitson Publishing Co.

Amorós, A. (ed.) 1986. *Cuadernos: Centro Dramático Nacional*. Madrid: Ministerio de Cultura.

Anderson, A. A. 1982. '¿De qué trata *Bodas de sangre*?', *Hommage à Federico García Lorca* XX, series A, 53–64.

———— 1983. 'The Evolution of Federico García Lorca's Poetic Projects 1929–36 and the Textual Status of *Poeta en Nueva York*', *BHS* 60, 221–46.

———— 1985. 'Some Shakespearean Reminiscences in Federico García Lorca's Drama', *Comparative Literature Studies* 22, 187–210.

———— 1986a. 'The Strategy of Federico García Lorca's Dramatic Composition 1930–36', *RQ* 33, 211–29.

———— 1986b. 'El último Lorca: unas aclaraciones a *La casa de Bernarda Alba*, *Sonetos*, y *Drama sin título*', in A. Soria Olmedo (ed.), *Lecciones sobre Federico García Lorca*, pp. 131–45. Granada: Comisión Nacional del Cinquentenario.

———— 1990. *Lorca's Late Poetry: A Critical Study*. Leeds: Francis Cairns.

———— 1991a. 'Lorca at the Crossroads: "Imaginación, Inspiración, Evasión" and the *novísimas estéticas*', *ALEC* 16, 149–73.

———— 1991b. *Critical Guides to Spanish Texts: La zapatera prodigiosa*. London: Grant & Cutler Ltd.

———— 1991c. 'Bewitched, Bothered and Bewildered: Spanish Dramatists and Surrealism, 1924–1936', in C. B. Morris (ed.), *The Surrealist Adventure in Spain*, pp. 240–81. Ottawa: Ottawa Hispanic Studies.

———— 1992a. 'Un dificilísimo juego poético: Theme and Symbol in Lorca's *El público*', *RQ* 39, 331–46.

———— 1992b. '*El público, Así que pasen cinco años* y *El sueño de la vida*: tres dramas expresionistas de García Lorca', in D. Dougherty and M. F. Vilches de Frutos (eds) *El teatro en España: entre la tradición y la vanguardia 1918–1939*, pp. 215–26. Madrid: CSIC/ Fundación FGL/ Tabacalera.

———— 1993. 'On Broadway, Off Broadway: García Lorca and the New York Theatre, 1929–30', *Gestos* VIII(16), 135–48.

Anderson, A., and Maurer, C. (eds) 1997. *Federico García Lorca: epistolario completo*. Madrid: Cátedra.

Anderson, R. 1984. *Federico García Lorca*. London: Macmillan.

———— 1988. 'Prólogos and Advertencias: Lorca's Beginnnings', in C. B. Morris (ed.), *'Cuando yo me muera': Essays in Memory of Federico García Lorca*, pp. 209–31. Lanham and London: University Press of America.

Anon. 1935. 'Después del estreno de *Yerma*', *El Sol* (Madrid), 1 January 1935, *OC* III, 619.

Armiño, M. 1986. '*El público* de García Lorca', *Cambio 16*, 29 December 1986, Madrid.

Artaud, A. 1993. *The Theatre and Its Double*. London: Calder.

Ashberry, J. 1969. *Three Poems*. New York: Harvest-Harcourt Brace.

Babcock-Adams, B. 1975. ' "A Tolerated Margin of Mess": The Trickster and His Tales Reconsidered', *Journal of the Folklore Institute* XI(3), 147–86.

———— 1978. *The Reversible World: Symbolic Inversion in Art and Society*. Ithaca, NY: Cornell University Press.

Bacarisse, P. 1992. 'Perlimplín's Tragedy', in R. Havard (ed.), *Lorca: Poet and Playwright*, pp. 71–92. Cardiff: University of Wales Press.

Baker, G. 1996. 'Photography Between Narrativity and Stasis: August Sander, Degeneration, and the Decay of the Portrait', *October* 76 (Spring), 73–113.

Bakhtin, M. [1929]. *Problems of Dostoevsky's Poetics*, trans. and ed. C. Emerson. Minneapolis, Minnesota: University of Minnesota Press (1984).

———— [1934–5]. 'Discourse in the Novel', in C. Emerson (trans.) and M. Holquist (ed.) *The Dialogic Imagination: Four Essays*. Austin, TX: University of Texas Press (1981).

Bakhtin, M. 1965. *Rabelais and His World*. Bloomington: Indiana University Press (1984).

Bal, M. 1988. 'Tricky Thematics', *Semeia* 42, 133–55.

Balboa Echevarría, M. 1982. 'The Inner Space in *The Love of Don Perlimplín and Belisa in his Garden*', *Romanic Review* LXXII(1), 98–109.

———— 1986. 'Espacio teatral y escenario interior. *Amor de Don Perlimplín con Belisa en su jardía*', in *Lorca: el espacio de la representación: reflexiones sobre surrealismo y teatro*, pp. 85–102. Barcelona: Éditions del Mall.

Banfield, A. 1982. 'Narration and Representation: The Knowledge of the Clock and the Lens', in *Unspeakable Sentences: Narration and Representation in the Language of Fiction*. Boston and London: Routledge & Kegan Paul.

Barthes, R. 1971. *Sade, Fourier, Loyola*. Paris: Edicions du Seuil.

———— 1977. 'The Death of the Author', in S. Heath (ed.) *Image-Music-Text*, pp. 142–8. London: Harper Collins.

———— 1980. *Camera Lucida*, trans. R. Howard. London: Vintage Books (1993).

———— 1985. *The Responsibility of Forms*. New York: Hill & Wang.

Basso, E. B. 1987. *In Favour of Deceit: A Study of Tricksters in an Amazonian Society*. Tucson: University of Arizona Press.

Bataille, G. 1962. *Eroticism*, trans. M. Dalywood. London: Boyars (1987).

Bauer, C. 1983. *The Public and Play Without a Title: Two Posthumous Plays by Federico García Lorca*. New York: New Directions Books.

Bazin, A. 1967. *What Is Cinema?* Berkeley and Los Angeles: University of California Press.

Beckett, S. 1952. *En attendant Godot.* Paris: Minuit.

Benjamin, W. 1982. *Das Passagen-Werk*, vol. V, ed. R. Tiedeman. Frankfurt Am Main: Suhrkamp Verlag.

Berger, J. 1972. *Ways of Seeing.* London: BBC and Penguin Books.

Bergson, H. 1903. 'Introduction à la métaphysique', in *La Penseé et le Mouvant: essais et conférences.* Paris: PUF (1985).

Berkeley, G. 1975. *Philosophical Works: Including the Works on Vision*, trans. M. R. Ayers. London: J. M. Dent & Sons Ltd (1992).

Bhabha, H. 1983. 'The Other Question: Difference, Discrimination and the Discourse of Colonialism', in R. Fergusson, M. Gever, T. Minh-ha and C. West (eds) *Out There: Marginalization and Contemporary Cultures*, pp. 71–88. Cambridge, Mass.: MIT Press (1990).

Binding, P. 1985. *Federico García Lorca: The Gay Imagination.* London: GMP Publishers.

Blau, H. 1990. *The Audience.* Baltimore and London: The Johns Hopkins University Press.

———— 1992. *To All Appearances: Ideology and Performance.* New York and London: Routledge.

Boas, F. 1898. 'Introduction', in J. Teit, *Traditions of the Thompson River Indians in British Columbia.* Boston, Mass.: Houghton Mifflin.

Borch-Jacobsen, M. 1982. 'The Laughter of Being', *MLN* 102, 737–60.

Bordo, S. 1990. 'Feminism, Postmodernism and Gender-Scepticism', in L. J. Nicholson (ed.), *Feminism/Postmodernism*, pp. 133–56. London and New York: Routledge.

Bordwell, D., and Thompson, K. 1980. *Film Art: An Introduction.* Reading, Mass.: Addison-Wesley Publishing Co.

Breitenberg, M. 1996. *Anxious Masculinity in Early Modern England.* Cambridge: Cambridge University Press.

Brewer, J. 1997. *The Pleasures of the Imagination: English Culture in the Eighteenth Century.* London: Harper Collins Publishers.

Brooks, P. 1993. *Body Work: Objects of Desire in Modern Narrative.* Cambridge, Mass.: Harvard University Press.

Brotherton, J. 1975. *The* Pastor Bobo *in the Spanish Theatre Before the Time of Lope de Vega.* London: Tamesis.

Brown, G. G. 1972. *A Literary History of Spain: Twentieth Century.* London: Ernest Benn Ltd.

Brown, N. O. 1947. *Hermes The Thief.* New York: Random Books (1969).

Brunel, P. 1992. *Companion to Literary Myths, Heroes and Archetypes.* London and New York: Routledge.

Buchbinder, D. 1994. *Masculinities and Identities.* Victoria: Melbourne University Press.

Buci-Glucksman, C. 1994. *Baroque Reason: The Aesthetics of Modernity.* London: Sage Publications.

Buck-Morss, S. 1995. 'The City as Dreamworld and Catastrophe', *October* 73, 4–26.

Buñuel, L. 1982. *Mi último suspiro.* Barcelona: Plaza y Janés.

Burgin, V., Donald, J., and Kaplan, C. 1986. *Formations of Fantasy*. London and New York: Routledge.

Burton, J. 1983. 'The Greatest Punishment: Female and Male in Lorca's Trage-dies', in B. Miller (ed.) *Women in Hispanic Literature: Icons and Fallen Idols*, pp. 259–79. Berkeley, CA: University of California Press.

Busst, A. J. L. 1967. 'The Image of the Androgyne in the Nineteenth Century', in I. Fletcher (ed.), *Romantic Mythologies*, pp. 1–95. London: Routledge & Kegan Paul Ltd.

Butler, J. 1990. *Gender Trouble: Feminism and the Subversion of Identity*. New York: Routledge.

————— 1993. *Bodies That Matter: On the Discursive Limits of 'Sex'*. New York and London: Routledge.

Canetti, E. 1960. *Crowds and Power*, trans. C. Stewart. London: Penguin (1992).

Cardwell, R. 1995. ' "Mi sed inquieta": expresionismo y vanguardia en el drama lorquiana', in García C. Cuevas and E. Baena (eds) *El teatro de Lorca: tragedia, drama y farsa*, pp. 100–26. Málaga: Publicaciones del Congreso de Literatura Española Contemporánea.

Cao, A. F. 1984. *Federico García Lorca y las vanguardias: hacia el teatro*. London: Tamesis.

Carpenter, E. 1908. 'The Intermediate Sex: A Study of Some Transitional Types of Men and Women', in D. W. Cory (ed.) *Homosexuality: A Cross Cultural Approach*, pp. 139–204. New York: The Julian Press (1956).

Castle, T. 1986. *Masquerade and Civilization: The Carnivalesque in Eighteenth-Century English Culture and Fiction*. Stanford, CA: Stanford University Press.

Chabas, J. 1934. 'Federico García Lorca y la tragedia', *OC* III, 604–6.

Chambers, R. 1988. 'Narratorial Authority and "The Purloined Letter" ', in J. P. Muller and W. J. Richardson (eds), *The Purloined Poe: Lacan, Derrida and Psychoanalytic Reading*, pp. 285–306. Baltimore and London: The Johns Hopkins University Press.

Cohan, S., and Hark, I. R. 1993. *Screening the Male: Exploring Masculinities in Hollywood Cinema*. London: Routledge.

Collier, P., and Davies, J. 1990. *Modernism and the European Unconscious*. Cambridge: Polity Press.

Cory, D. W. (ed.) 1956. *Homosexuality: A Cross Cultural Approach*. New York: The Julian Press.

Cottingham, J. G., Stoothoff, R. and Murdoch, D. (eds) 1985. *The Philosophical Writings of Descartes*, 2 vols. Cambridge: Cambridge University Press.

Crary, J. 1990. *Techniques of the Observer: On Vision and Modernity in the Nine-teenth Century*. Cambridge, Mass. and London: MIT Press.

Crommelynck, F. 1987. *Le cocu magnifique*, J. Duviguard. Bruxelles: Labor.

Cueto, R. 1991. 'Lorca's Don Perlimplín. The Paradoxical Apotheosis of a Great Lover', *Leeds Papers on Hispanic Drama*, ed. Margaret A. Rees, pp. 93–124. Leeds: Trinity and All Saints College.

Cuevas García, C., and Baena, E. (eds) 1995. *El teatro de Lorca: tragedia, drama y farsa*. Málaga: Publicaciones del Congreso de Literatura Española Contemporánea.

Cunliffe, R. 1997. 'Bakhtin and Derrida: Drama and the Phoneyness of the

Phonè', in C. Adlam, R. Falconer, V. Maklin and A. Renfrew (eds) *Face to Face: Bakhtin in Russia and the West*, pp. 347–65. Sheffield: Sheffield Academic Press.

Curry, W. C. 1935. 'Sacerdotal Science in Shakespeare's *The Tempest*', *Archiv* 90, 25–36, 185–6.

De Lauretis, T. 1986. *Feminist Studies/Critical Studies*. Bloomington: Indiana University Press.

De Paepe, C. (ed.) 1994. *Federico García Lorca: poesía inédita de juventud*. Madrid: Cátedra.

———— 1995. *Catálogo general de los fondos documentales de la Fundación Federico García Lorca*. Madrid: Ministerio de Cultura.

De Ros, X. 1996. 'Lorca's *El público*: An Invitation to the Carnival of Film', in D. Harris, *Changing Times in Hispanic Culture*, pp. 110–20. Aberdeen: University of Aberdeen Press.

Delcourt, M. 1958. *Hermaphrodite: Myths and Rites of the Bisexual Figure in Classical Antiquity*, trans. J. Nicholson. London: Studio Books.

Deleuze, G. 1989. *Masochism: An Interpretation of Coldness and Cruelty*. New York: Zone Books.

Delgado, M. 1998. 'Enrique Rambal: The Forgotten *Auteur* of Spanish Popular Theatre', *Contemporary Theatre Review* 7(3), 67–91.

Dent, R. W. 1965. 'Imagination in *A Midsummer Night's Dream*', *Shakespeare Quarterly* 15, 115–29.

Derrida, J. 1975. 'The Purveyor of Truth', trans. Alan Bass, in J. P. Muller and W. J. Richardson (eds), *The Purloined Poe: Lacan, Derrida and Psychoanalytic Reading*, pp. 173–212. Baltimore and London: The Johns Hopkins University Press (1988).

———— 1978. 'The Theater of Cruelty and the Closure of Representation', in A. Bass (trans.) *Writing and Difference*, pp. 232–50. London: Routledge (1990).

———— 1979. *Spurs: Nietzsche's Styles*, trans. Barbara Harlow. Chicago: University of Chicago Press.

———— 1981. *Dissemination*, trans. B. Johnson. London: The Athlone Press.

Didier, B. 1981. 'Sade et Don Juan', in *Obliques: Don Juan* 2, 67–71.

Díez de Revenga, J. and de Paco, M. (eds) 1999. *Tres poetas, tres amigos: estudios sobre Vicente Aleixandre, Federico García Lorca y Dámaso Alonso*. Murcia: Caja Murcia.

Doane, M. A. 1991. *Femmes Fatales: Feminism, Film Theory, Psychoanalysis*. New York: Routledge.

Dorje, R. 1975. *Tales of Uncle Tompa: The Legendary Rascal of Tibet*. San Rafael: Dorje Ling.

Doty, W. 1993. 'A Life-Time of Trouble-Making: Hermes as Trickster', in W. J. Hynes and W. G. Doty (eds), *Mythical Trickster Figures*, pp. 49–65. Tuscaloosa and London: The University of Alabama Press.

Doueihi, A. 1993. 'Inhabiting the Space Between Discourse and Story in Trickster Narratives', in W. J. Hynes and W. G. Doty (eds), *Mythical Trickster Figures*, pp. 193–201. Tuscaloosa and London: The University of Alabama Press.

Dougherty, D. and Vilches de Frutos, M. F. (eds) 1992. *El teatro en España: entre la tradición y la vanguardia 1918–1939*. Madrid: CSIC/ Fundación FGL/ Tabacalera.

Douglas, M. 1966. *Purity and Danger: An Analysis of the Concepts of Pollution and Taboo*. London: Ark.

Duchamp, M. 1923. *The Bride Stripped Bare By Her Bachelors, Even: A Typographic Version by Richard Hamilton of Marcel Duchamp's Green Box*, trans. G. H. Hamilton. Stuttgart: Edition Hansjörg Mayer (1976).

Edwards, G. 1980. *Lorca: The Theatre Beneath the Sand*. London: Marion Boyars.

―――― 1981. 'Lorca and Buñuel: *Así que pasen cinco años* and *Un chien andalou*', *García Lorca Review* IX(2), 128–41.

Eliot, T. S. 1922. *The Waste Land*, ed. T. Davies and N. Wood. Buckingham: Open University Press.

Epstein, J. and Straub, K. 1991. *Body Guards: The Cultural Politics of Gender Ambiguity*. New York and London: Routledge.

Espinosa, A. M. 1946. 'El oricuerno', *Cuentos populares españoles recogidos de la tradición española*, pp. 378–80. Madrid: Espinosa.

Evans, D. 1996. *An Introductory Dictionary of Lacanian Psychoanalysis*. London: Routledge.

Feal Deibe, C. 1970. 'Crommelynck y Lorca: Variaciones sobre un mismo tema', *Revue de Littérature Comparée* 44, 403–9.

―――― 1989. *Lorca: tragedia y mito*, Ottawa Hispanic Studies 4. Ottawa: Dovehouse Editions.

Felman, S. 1980. *The Literary Speech Act: Don Juan With J. L. Austin, or Seduction in Two Languages*, trans. C. Porter. Ithaca, NY: Cornell University Press (1983).

Fenichel, O. 1949. 'The Symbolic Equation: Girl = Phallus', *Psychoanalytic Quarterly* XVIII(3), 303–21.

Fergusson, F. 1957. *The Human Image in Dramatic Literature*. New York: Doubleday.

Fergusson, R., Gever, M., Minh-ha, T. and West, C. (eds) 1990. *Out There: Marginalization and Contemporary Cultures*. Cambridge, Mass.: MIT Press.

Fernández Cifuentes, L. 1986. *García Lorca en el teatro: la norma y la diferencia*. Zaragoza: Prensas Universitarias de Zaragoza.

Fiore, R. 1984. *Lazarillo and El Buscón*, trans. R. Fiore. Boston: Twayne.

Fletcher, I. 1967. *Romantic Mythologies*. London: Routledge & Kegan Paul Ltd.

Flores, A. (ed.) 1930. *T. S. Eliot: la tierra baldía*, trans. A. Flores. Barcelona: Cervantes.

Flower MacCannell, J. and Zakarin, L. 1994. *Thinking Bodies*. Stanford, CA: Stanford University Press.

Flügel, J. C. 1953. 'Death Instinct, Homeostasis and Allied Concepts', *International Journal of Psychoanalysis* 34, 43–74.

Foucault, M. 1970. 'Las Meninas', in *The Order Of Things*, pp. 3–16. London: Routledge.

―――― 1977. 'A Preface to Transgression', in D. Bouchard (ed.), *Language, Counter-Memory, Practice*, pp. 29–52. Oxford: Basil Blackwell.

―――― 1978. *The History of Sexuality*, trans. R. Hurley. Harmondsworth: Penguin (1981).

———— 1980. *Herculine Barbin: Being the Recently Discovered Memoirs of a Nineteenth Century French Hermaphrodite*. Brighton: Harvester.

———— 1983. *Ceci n'est pas une pipe*, trans. James Harkness. Berkeley and London: University of California Press.

Freud, S. 1900. *The Interpretation of Dreams*, in *SE*, vols IV and V, 1–714.

———— 1905a. *Three Essays on the Theory of Sexuality*, in *SE*, vol. VII, 1–307.

———— 1905b. *Jokes and Their Relation to the Unconscious*, in *SE*, vol. VIII, 3–250.

———— 1908. 'On the Sexual Theories of Children', in *SE*, vol. IX, 205–26.

———— 1913. *Totem and Taboo*, in *SE*, vol. XIII, 1–242.

———— 1915a. 'Instincts and Their Vicissitudes', in *SE*, vol. XIV, 117–40.

———— 1915b. 'Our Attitude Towards Death', in *SE*, vol. XIV, 289–300.

———— 1919a. ' "A Child is Being Beaten": A Contribution to the Study of the Origin of Perversions', in *SE*, vol. XVII, 175–204.

———— 1919b. 'The Uncanny', in *SE*, vol. XVII, 217–52.

———— 1920. *Beyond the Pleasure Principle*, in *SE*, vol. XVIII, 1–64.

———— 1922. 'Medusa's Head', in *SE*, vol. XVIII, 273–4.

———— 1924. 'The Economic Problem of Masochism', in P. Rieff (ed.) *General Psychological Theory: Papers on Metapsychology*, pp. 190–210. New York: Macmillan/Collier Books (1963).

———— 1927. 'Humour', in *SE*, vol. XXI, 159–66.

———— 1974. *The Standard Edition of the Complete Psychological Works of Sigmund Freud*, trans. and ed. J. Strachey, 23 vols. London: The Hogarth Press and the Institute of Psychoanalysis.

Frenck, S., Perriam, C. and Thomson M. 1995. 'The Literary Avant–Garde: A Contradictory Modernity', in H. Graham and J. Labanyi (eds) *Spanish Cultural Studies: An Introduction. The Struggle for Modernity*, pp. 63–70. Oxford: Oxford University Press.

Frutos Cortés, E. 1983. *El gran teatro del mundo/ el gran mercado del mundo*. Pedro Calderón de la Barca, Madrid: Cátedra.

Frye, N. 1957. *The Anatomy of Criticism*. Princeton, NJ: Princeton University Press.

Gaines, J. and Herzog, C. (eds) 1990. *Fabrications: Costume and the Female Body*. London and New York: Routledge.

Garber, M. 1995. *Vice Versa: Bisexuality and the Eroticism of Everyday Life*. London: Penguin.

García Lorca, Federico 1986. *Obras completas*, Arturo del Hoyo, ed., pról de Vicente Aleixandre. Madrid: Aguilar.

García Lorca, Francisco 1980. *Federico y su mundo*. Madrid: Alianza Editorial.

Gasner, J. 1954. *Masters of Modern Drama*. New York: Dover Publications.

Gediman, H. K. 1995. *Fantasies of Love and Death in Life and Art: A Psychoanalytic Study of the Normal and the Pathological*. New York and London: New York University Press.

George, David. 1983. 'Harlequin comes to Court: Valle-Inclán's *La Marquesa Rosalinda*', *Forum for Modern Language Studies* XIX(4), 364–74.

———— 1992. 'Lorca and the *Commedia dell'arte*', in R. Havard (ed.), *Lorca: Poet and Playwright*, pp. 107–33. Cardiff: University of Wales Press.

————1995. *The History of the Commedia dell'Arte in Modern Hispanic Litera-*

ture with Special Attention to the Work of García Lorca. Lewiston, Queenston and Lampeter: The Edwin Mellen Press.

Gibson, I. 1974. *The Death of Lorca*. St Albans: Paladin.

—— 1999. 'Federico García Lorca y el amor imposible', in J. Díez de Revenga and M. de Paco (eds) *Tres poetas, tres amigos: estudios sobre Vicente Aleixandre, Federico García Lorca y Dámaso Alonso*, pp. 135–60. Murcia: Caja Murcia.

Gifford, D. J. 1979. 'Iconographical notes towards a definition of the medieval fool', in P. Williams (ed.), *The Fool and the Trickster: Studies in Honour of Enid Welsford*, pp. 18–35. Cambridge: D. S. Brewer.

Gil Benumeya, R. 1931. 'Estampa de García Lorca', *La Gaceta Literaria*, Madrid, 15 January 1931, in *OC* III, 502–5.

Gilbert, H. (ed.) 1993. *The Sexual Imagination: From Acker to Zola: A Feminist Companion*. London: Jonathan Cape Ltd.

Girard, R. 1961. *Deceit, Desire and the Novel: Self and Other in Literary Structure*, trans. Y. Freccero. Baltimore, Maryland: The Johns Hopkins University Press, 1965.

—— 1982. *The Scapegoat*, trans. Y. Freccero. Baltimore: The Johns Hopkins University Press.

Goodwin, S. W. and Bronfen, E. (eds) 1993. *Death and Representation*. Baltimore and London: The Johns Hopkins University Press.

Goody, J. 1997. *Representations and Contradictions: Ambivalence Towards Images, Theatre, Fiction, Relics and Sexuality*. Oxford: Blackwell.

Graham, H. and Labanyi, J. (eds) 1995. *Spanish Cultural Studies: An Introduction. The Struggle for Modernity*. Oxford: Oxford University Press.

Grant, H. 1964. 'Una aleluya erótica de Federico García Lorca y las aleluyas populares del siglo XIX', *Actas del Primer Congreso de Hispanistas*, pp. 307–14. Oxford: Dolphin Book Co.

Gregg, J. 1994. *Maurice Blanchot and the Literature of Transgression*. Princeton, NJ: Princeton University Press.

Grosz, E. 1994. *Volatile Bodies: Toward a Corporeal Feminism*. Bloomington and Indianapolis: Indiana University Press.

Grotowski, C. and Fox-Keller, E. 1983. 'The Mind's Eye', in S. Harding and M. Hintikka, *Discovering Reality*, pp. 207–24. Dordrecht: Kluwer Academic Publishing.

Halley des Fontaines, J. C. L. 1938. *Contributions à l'étude de l'androgynie. La notion d'androgynie dans quelques mythes et quelques rites*, Paris.

Hammond, P. 1974. *Marvellous Méliès*. London: Gordon Fraser.

Harding, S. and Hintikka, M. (eds) 1983. *Discovering Reality*. Dordrecht: Kluwer Academic Publishing.

Harris, D. (ed.) 1995. *The Spanish Avant-garde*. Manchester: Manchester University Press.

—— 1996. *Changing Times in Hispanic Culture*. Aberdeen: University of Aberdeen Press.

Harris Smith, S. V. 1984. *Masks in Modern Drama*. Berkeley and Los Angeles, CA: University of California Press.

Havard, R. (ed.) 1992. *Lorca: Poet and Playwright*. Cardiff: University of Wales Press.

Heilbrun, C. G. 1973. *Towards Androgyny: Aspects of Male and Female in Literature*. London: Victor Gollancz Ltd.

Hernández, M. 1982. *La zapatera prodigiosa: farsa violenta con bailes y canciones populares de los siglos XVIII y XIX en dos partes, con un solo intervalo*. Madrid: Alianza Editorial.

—— 1986. *Federico García Lorca: dibujos*. Barcelona: Caixa de Barcelona.

—— 1990. *Libro de los dibujos de Federico García Lorca*. Madrid: Tabapress/ Fundación Federico García Lorca.

Holmlund, C. 1993. 'Masculinity as Multiple Masquerade', in S. Cohan and I. R. Hark (eds), *Screening the Male: Exploring Masculinities in Hollywood Cinema*, pp. 213–29. London: Routledge.

Honderich, T. 1995. *The Oxford Companion to Philosophy*. Oxford: Oxford University Press.

Honig, E. 1944. *García Lorca*. Norfolk, Conn: New Directions.

Huélamo Kosma, J. 1989. 'La influencia de Freud en Federico García Lorca', *Boletín de la Fundación Federico García Lorca* 6, 59–83.

Hutcheon, L. 1985. *A Theory of Parody: The Teachings of Twentieth-Century Art Forms*. New York: Routledge.

Hyde, L. 1998. *Trickster Makes This World: Mischief, Myth and Art*. New York: Farrar, Straus, Giroux.

Hynes, W. J. 1993a. 'Mapping the Characteristics of Mythic Tricksters: A Heuristic Guide', in W. J. Hynes and W. G. Doty (eds), *Mythical Trickster Figures*, pp. 33–45. Tuscaloosa and London: The University of Alabama Press.

Hynes, W. J. 1993b. 'Inconclusive Conclusions: Tricksters – Metaplayers and Revealers', in W. J. Hynes and W. G. Doty, *Mythical Trickster Figures*, pp. 202–18. Tuscaloosa and London: The University of Alabama Press.

Hynes, W. J. and Doty, W. G. (eds) 1993. *Mythical Trickster Figures*. Tuscaloosa and London: The University of Alabama Press.

Irigaray, L. 1983. 'Veiled Lips', trans. Sara Speidel, *Mississippi Review* 11(3), 96–120.

Irizarry, E. 1987. 'The Ubiquitous Trickster Archetype in the Narrative of Francisco Ayala', *Hispania* 70(2), 222–30.

Jenkins, S. 1981. *Fritz Lang: The Image and the Look*. London: BFI Publishers.

Johnston, D. 1998. *Outlines: Federico García Lorca*. Bath: Absolute Press.

Jones, A. R. and Stallybrass, P. 1991. 'Fetishizing Gender: Constructing the Hermaphrodite in Renaissance Europe', in J. Epstein and K. Straub (eds), *Body Guards: The Cultural Politics of Gender Ambiguity*, pp. 80–111. New York and London: Routledge.

Jung, C. G. 1921a. *Psychological Types*, in *CW*, vol. VI, 1–398.

—— 1921b. 'The Apollinian and the Dionysian', in *CW*, vol. VI, 136–46.

—— 1921c. 'General Description of the Types', in *CW*, vol. VI, 30–370.

—— 1934. *Archetypes and the Collective Unconscious*, in *CW*, vol. IX, part 1, 3–451.

—— 1943–48. 'The Spirit Mercurius', in *CW*, vol. XIII.

—— 1954. 'On the Psychology of the Trickster Figure', in *CW*, vol. IX, part 1, 255–72.

———— 1959. *The Collected Works of Carl Gustav Jung*, trans. R. F. C. Hull. London: Routledge & Kegan Paul (1980).

Kaplan, E. A. 1981. *Women In Film Noir*. London: BFI Publishers.

Kaplan, T. 1992. *Red City, Blue Period: Social Movements in Picasso's Barcelona*. Berkeley, Los Angeles: University of California Press.

Kappeler, S. 1986. *The Pornography of Representation*. Minneapolis: University of Minnesota Press.

Kernan, A. B. 1979. *The Playwright as Magician: Shakespeare's Image of the Poet in the English Public Theater*. New Haven: Yale University Press.

Kinney, A. F. 1974. *Markets of Bawdrie: The Dramatic Criticism of Stephen Gosson*. Salzburg: Institut für Englische Sprache und Literatur.

Kosofsky Sedgwick, E. 1990. *Epistemology of the Closet*. London: Penguin (1994).

Kossovitch, E. A. 1988. 'Don Juan e Sade', in R. J. Ribeiro (ed.), *A Seduçcao e suas Máscaras*, pp. 77–82. São Paolo: Companhia das Letras.

Krafft-Ebing, R. von 1886. *Psychopathia Sexualis*, trans. F. J. Rebman. New York: Special Books (1965).

Kristeva, J. 1980. *Powers of Horror: An Essay on Abjection*. New York: Columbia University Press (1982).

Lacan, J. 1954. *The Seminar, Book II, The Ego in Freud's Theory and in the Technique of Psychoanalysis, 1954–55*, trans. S. Tomaselli. Cambridge: Cambridge University Press (1988).

———— 1955. *The Seminar. Book III. The Psychoses, 1955–6*, trans. Russell Grigg. London: Routledge (1993).

———— 1956. *Le Séminaire, Livre IV, La relation d'objet, 1956–7*, ed. J.-A. Miller. Paris: Seuil (1994).

———— 1957. 'L'instance de la lettre dans l'inconscient ou la raison depuis Freud', in Lacan, *Écrits*, pp. 493–528. Paris: Seuil (1966) [for English translation see Lacan 1977 below].

———— 1958. 'The Meaning of the Phallus', in Mitchell and Rose 1982: 74–85.

———— 1964. 'Guiding Remarks for a Congress on Female Sexuality', in J. Mitchell and J. Rose (eds) *Feminine Sexuality: Jacques Lacan and the école freudienne*, pp. 86–98. London: Macmillan (1982).

———— 1972. 'Seminar on "The Purloined Letter"', trans. J. Mehlman in J. P. Muller and W. J. Richardson (eds), *The Purloined Poe: Lacan, Derrida and Psychoanalytic Reading*, pp. 28–54. Baltimore and London: The Johns Hopkins University Press (1988) [first published in *French Freud: Structural Studies in Psychoanalyisis. Yale French Studies* 48 (1972), 38–72].

———— 1973. *Télévision*. Paris: Seuill.

———— 1977. 'The agency of the letter in the unconscious or reason since Freud', trans. Alan Sheridan in Lacan, *Écrits: A Selection*, pp. 146–78. London: Tavistock.

———— 1979. *Four Fundamental Concepts of Psychoanalysis*, ed. Jacques-Alain Miller, trans. Alan Sheridan. Harmondsworth: Penguin.

Laplanche, J and Pontalis, J-B. 1988. *The Language of Psychoanalysis*. London: The Institute of Psychoanalysis and Karnac Books.

Lemaire, A. 1970. *Jacques Lacan*. London: Routledge (1994).

Leprince de Beaumont, J-M. 1949. *Belle et la Bête*, trans. P. H. Muir. New York: Limited Editions Club.

Lévi-Strauss, C. 1966. *The Savage Mind*, trans. G. Weidenfeld. Chicago: University of Chicago Press.

———— 1967. *Structural Anthropology*, trans. C. Jacobson and B. Grundfoot. New York: Doubleday and Co.

Levine, L. 1994. *Men in Women's Clothing: Anti-theatricality and Effeminization 1579–1642*. Cambridge: Cambridge University Press.

Lévy, A. D. 1992. 'Isis', in P. Brunel, *Companion to Literary Myths, Heroes and Archetypes*, pp. 611–18. London and New York: Routledge.

Lewis, A. 1971. *The Contemporary Theatre*. New York: Crown Publishers.

Lima, R. 1963. *The Theatre of García Lorca*. New York: Las Américas.

Lingis, A. 1984. *Excesses: Eros and Culture*. New York: State University of New York.

Llafranque, M. 1982. 'Equivocar el camino, Regards sur un scenario de Federico García Lorca', *Hommage à Federico García Lorca*, pp. 24–30. Toulouse: Université de Toulouse-le-Mirail.

———— 1987 *Teatro inconcluso: fragmentos y proyectos inacabados*. Granada: Universidad de Granada.

London, J. 1996. *The Unknown Federico García Lorca*. London: Atlas Press.

Lowie, R. H. 1909. 'The Hero-Trickster Discussion', *Journal of American Folklore* 22, 431–3.

MacRitchie, L. 1996. 'Rose English: A Perilous Profession', *Performance Research*, 1(3), 58–70.

Makarius, L. 1970. 'Ritual Clowns and Symbolic Behaviour', *Diogenes* 69, 44–73.

———— 1974. 'The Magic of Transgression', *Anthropos* 69, 537–52.

Malinowski, B. 1926. *Myth in Primitive Psyhchology*. New York:

Mallarmé, S. [1897]. 'Mimique', in J. Derrida, *Dissemination*, trans. B. Johnson, pp. 175–6. London: The Athlone Press (1981).

Mandrell, J. 1992. *Don Juan and the Point of Honour: Seduction, Patriarchal Society and Literary Tradition*. Pennsylvania: The Pennsylvania State University Press.

Mann, T. 1929. *Mario and the Magician: and Other Stories*, trans. H. T. Lowe-Porter. London: Minerva.

Martín, E. 1986. *Federico García Lorca: heterodox y mártir: análisis y proyección de la obra juvenil inédita*. Madrid: Siglo XXI Editores.

Martínez Nadal, R. 1970. *El público: amor y muerte en la obra de Federico García Lorca*. Madrid: Ediciones Hiperión.

———— 1974. *Lorca's "The Public": A Study of His Unfinished Play ("El Público") and of Love and Death in the Work of Federico García Lorca*. London: Calder and Boyars.

———— (ed.) 1976. *Federico García Lorca: Autógrafos: II: El Público*. Oxford: Dolphin Book Co.

Mast, G., Cohen, M. and Braudy, L. 1992. *Film Theory and Criticism: Introductory Readings*, 4th edn. Oxford and New York: Oxford University Press.

Maurer, C. 1979. 'Five Uncollected Interviews', *García Lorca Review* 7, 102–3.

———— (ed.) 1986. 'Federico García Lorca escribe a su familia desde Nueva York y La Habana 1929–30', *Poesía* (journal), vols 23–24, 55–70.

———— (ed.) 1988. 'Introduction' to *Poet in New York* by Federico García Lorca. London: Penguin Books.

———— (ed.) 1994. *Federico García Lorca: prosa inédita de juventud*. Madrid: Cátedra.

McDermott, P. 1995. 'Subversions of the Sacred: The Sign of the Fish', in D. Harris (ed.) *The Spanish Avant-garde*, pp. 204–17. Manchester: Manchester University Press.

———— 1996. 'Lorca's *Viaje a la luna*: The Cinema as Sacrilegious Act', in D. Harris (ed.), *Changing Times in Hispanic Culture*, pp. 121–32. Aberdeen: University of Aberdeen Press.

McKendrick, M. 1992. *El mágico prodigioso*, Pedro Calderón de la Barca. Oxford: Clarendon Press.

Miller, B. (ed.) 1983. *Women in Hispanic Literature: Icons and Fallen Idols*. Berkeley: University of California Press.

Mitchell, J. 1990. 'El mito de don Juan', *Mitos*, vol. 3. Sociedad Peruana de Psicoanálisis, 77–84.

Mitchell, J. and Rose, J. (eds) 1982. *Feminine Sexuality: Jacques Lacan and the école freudienne*. London: Macmillan.

Monegal, A. 1994a. *Viaje a la luna*. Valencia: Pretextos.

Monegal, A. 1994b. 'Unmasking the Maskuline: Transvestism and Tragedy in García Lorca's *El público*', *MLN* 109, 204–16.

Morales, F. 1936. 'Conversaciones literarias. Al habla con Federico Garcia Lorca', *La Voz* (Madrid), 7 April 1936, in *OC* III, 671–6.

Morris, C. B. 1988. '*Cuando yo me muera*': *Essays in Memory of Federico García Lorca*. Lanham and London: University Press of America.

———— 1991. *The Surrealist Adventure in Spain*. Ottawa: Dovehouse.

———— 1997. *Son of Andalusia: The Lyrical Landscapes of Federico García Lorca*. Nashville, Tennessee: Vanderbilt University Press.

Morris, D. B. 1991. *The Culture of Pain*. Berkeley, CA: University of California Press.

Morris, P. (ed.) 1994. *The Bakhtin Reader: Selected Writings of Bakhtin, Medvedev, Voloshinov*. London: Edward Arnold Publishers Ltd.

Mortenson, P. 1972. 'Friar Bacon and Friar Bungay: Festive Comedy and the Three Form'd Luna', *English Literary Renaissance* 2, 194–207.

Mowat, B. A. 1981. 'Prospero, Agrippa, and Hocus Pocus', *English Literary Renaissance* 2, 281–303.

Mullaney, S. 1988. *The Place of the Stage: License, Play and Power in Renaissance England*. Chicago and London: University of Chicago Press.

Muller J. P. and Richardson, W. J. 1988. *The Purloined Poe: Lacan, Derrida and Psychoanalytic Reading*. Baltimore and London: The Johns Hopkins University Press.

Mulvey, L. 1975. *Visual And Other Images*, pp. 14–26. London: Macmillan Press (1989).

Murray, T. (ed.) 1997. *Mimesis, Masochism and Mime: The Politics of Theatricality in Contemporary French Thought*. Ann Arbor: University of Michigan Press.

Nancy, J-L. 1993. 'Corpus', trans. C. Sartillot, in J. Flower MacCannell and L. Zakarin (eds), *Thinking Bodies*, pp. 17–31. Stanford, CA: Stanford University Press (1994).

Newberry, W. 1973. *The Pirandellian Mode in Spanish Literature from Cervantes to Sastre*. New York: State of New York Press.

Nicholson, L. J. 1990. *Feminism/Postmodernism*. London and New York: Routledge.

Nietzsche, F. 1871. *The Birth of Tragedy*. London: Penguin, 1993.

—— 1882. *The Gay Science*, trans. Walter Kaufmann. New York: Vintage Books (1974).

—— 1887. *On The Genealogy of Morals*, trans. by D. Smith. Oxford: Oxford University Press (1996).

Oppenheimer, H. 1986. *Lorca: The Drawings*. London: The Herbert Press.

Ortega y Gasset, J. 1923. *El tema de nuestro tiempo*. Madrid: Calpe.

Ovid. 1994. *Metamorphoses*, trans. D. R. Stavitt. London and Baltimore: The Johns Hopkins University Press.

Pacteau, F. 1986. 'The Impossible Referent: Representations of the Androgyne', in V. Burgin, J. Donald and C. Kaplan (eds), *Formations of Fantasy*, pp. 62–84. London and New York: Routledge.

Pelton, R. D. 1980. *The Trickster in West Africa: A Study of Mythic Irony and Sacred Delight*. Los Angeles and London: University of California Press.

Pérez Firmat, G. 1986. *Literature and Liminality: Festive Readings in the Hispanic Tradition*. Durham: Duke University Press.

Pielmuter Pérez, R. 1976. 'The Rogue as Trickster in *Guzmán de Alfarache*', *Hispania* 59, 820–6.

Place, J. 1978. 'Women in Film Noir', in E. A. Kaplan, *Women In Film Noir*, pp. 35–54. London: BFI Publishers (1981).

Plato 1994. *The Republic*, trans. R. Waterfield. Oxford: Oxford University Press.

—— 1994. *The Symposium*, trans. R. Waterfield. Oxford and New York: Oxford University Press.

—— 1997. *The Complete Works*, ed. John Cooper. Indianapolis: Hackett Publishers.

Pontalis, J. B. 1973. 'L'insaississable entre-deux', in *Nouvelle Revue de Psychanalyse* 7, 13–26.

Pope, A. 1721. *The Rape of the Lock: An Anti-Heroi-comical Poem*. New Rochell, NY: C. Cornwell at the Elston Press (1902).

Prats, A. 1934. 'Los artistas en el ambiente de nuestro tiempo', *OC* III, 610–15.

Prévost, A. 1731. *Manon Lescaut*, trans. Leonard Tavistock. London: Penguin (1991).

Radin, P. 1954. *The Trickster: A Study in American Indian Mythology*. New York: Greenwood Press, 1969.

Raeburn, M. (ed.) 1994. *Salvador Dalí: The Early Years*. London: South Bank Centre.

Read, A. 1993. *Theatre and Everyday Life: An Ethics of Performance*. London: Routledge.

Ribeiro, R. J. 1988. *A Seduçcao e suas Máscaras*. São Paolo: Companhia das Letras.

Rieff, P. (ed.) 1963. *General Psychological Theory: Papers on Metapsychology*. New York: Macmillan/Collier Books.

Rivière, J. 1929. 'Womanliness as a Masquerade', *International Journal of Psychoanalysis* 10, 303–13 (reprinted in V. Burgin, J. Donald and C. Kaplan, *Formations of Fantasy*, pp. 35–44. London and New York: Routledge, 1986).

Rodríguez, A. and Lanning, R. 1995. 'Una olvidada fijación literaria del *trickster*: Pedro de Urdemals', *Bulletin of the Commediants* 47(1), 37–42.

Rorty, A. O. 1980. *Philosophy and the Mirror of Nature*. Oxford: Basil Blackwell.

Rostand, E. 1897. *Cyrano de Bergerac*. Paris: Charpentier (1903).

Rousseau, J-J. 1960. *Politics and the Arts: Letter to M. D'Alambert on the Theater*, trans. A. Bloom. Ithaca, NY: Cornell University Press.

Ruíz Portella, J. (ed.) 1995. *Federico García Lorca: Sonetos del amor oscuro. Poemas de amor y erotismo: Inéditos de madurez*. Barcelona: Altera.

Russell, R. and Barratt, A. 1990. *Russian Theatre in the Age of Modernism*. London: Macmillan.

Russo, M. 1986. 'Female Grotesques: Carnival and Theory', in T. De Lauretis (ed.), *Feminist Studies/Critical Studies*, pp. 213–29. Bloomington: Indiana University Press.

Sacher-Masoch, L. von 1971. *Venus in Furs*, trans. J. McNeil in G. Deleuze, *Masochism: An Interpretation of Coldness and Cruelty*, pp. 129–230. New York: Zone Books (1989).

Sagarra, J. de. 1986. 'El estreno de *El público*', *El País* (Madrid), 14 December.

Sartre, J-P. 1991. *La Nausée*, trans. R. Goldthorpe. London: Harper Collins.

Scarry, E. 1985. *The Body in Pain: The Making and Unmaking of the World*. New York and Oxford: Oxford University Press (1987).

Schumacher, C. 1981. 'Thomas Shadwell: The Libertine', *Obliques: Don Juan* 2, 67–74.

Sheppard, R. W. 1983. 'Tricksters, Carnival and the Magical Figure of Dada Poetry', *Forum for Modern Language Studies* XIX(3), 116–25.

Sinclair, A. 1990. 'Avant-garde Theatre and the Return to Dionysos', in P. Collier and J. Davies (eds), *Modernism and the European Unconscious*, pp. 246–64. Cambridge: Polity Press.

Smith, P. J. 1998a. 'A Long Way From Andalusia: Catalonia's Claims, and Newcastle's, on Lorca's Legacy', *Times Literary Supplement*, 7 August, No. 4975, 10–11.

—— 1998b. *The Theatre of García Lorca: Text, Performance, Psychoanalysis*. Cambridge: Cambridge University Press.

—— 1989. *The Body Hispanic: Gender and Sexuality in Spanish and Spanish-American Literature*. Oxford: Oxford University Press.

Smith-Rosenberg, C. 1985. *Disorderly Conduct*. Oxford: Oxford University Press.

Sobejano, G. 1967. *Nietzsche en España*. Madrid: Editorial Gredos.

Soria Olmedo, A. 1986. *Lecciones sobre Federico García Lorca*. Granada: Comisión Nacional del Cinquentenario.

—— (ed.) 1994. *Federico García Lorca: teatro inédito de juventud*. Madrid: Cátedra.

—— 1999. ' "Me lástima el corazón": Federico García Lorca', in J. Díez de

Revenga and M. de Paco, M. (eds) *Tres poetas, tres amigos: estudios sobre Vicente Aleixandre, Federico García Lorca y Dámaso Alonso*, pp. 205–24. Murcia: Caja Murcia.

Soufas, C.C. 1996. *Audience and Authority in the Modernist Theater of Federico García Lorca*. Tuscaloosa: University of Alabama Press.

Spinks, C.W. Jr. 1991. *Semiosis, Marginal Signs and Trickster: A Dagger of the Mind*. London: Macmillan.

Stallybrass, P and White, A. 1986. *The Politics and Poetics of Transgression*. Ithaca, NY: Cornell University Press.

Straub, K. 1991. 'The Guilty Pleasures of Female Theatrical Cross-Dressing and the Autobiography of Charlotte Charke', in J. Epstein and K. Straub (eds), *Body Guards: The Cultural Politics of Gender Ambiguity*, pp. 142–65. New York and London: Routledge.

Stubbes, P. 1583. *The Anatomie of Abuses*. Netherlands: Da Capo Press (1963).

Studlar, G. 1985. 'Masochism and the Perverse Pleasures of Cinema', in G. Mast, M. Cohen and L. Braudy (eds), *Film Theory and Criticism: Introductory Readings*, 4th edn, pp. 773–90. Oxford and New York: Oxford University Press (1992).

——— 1988. *In the Realm of Pleasure: Von Sternberg, Dietrich, and the Masochistic Aesthetic*. New York: Columbia University Press.

Suero, P. 1933. 'Crónica de un día de barco con Federico García Lorca', *Noticias Gráficas* (Buenos Aires), 14 October 1933, *OC* III, 539–53.

Suleiman, S. R. 1990. *Subversive Intent: Gender, Politics, and the Avant-garde*. Cambridge, Mass. and London: Harvard University Press.

Teit, J. 1898. *Traditions of the Thompson River Indians*. Boston, Mass.

Traister, B. 1984. *Heavenly Necromancers: The Magician in English Renaissance Drama*. Columbia, MO: University of Missouri Press.

Turner, V. 1969. *The Ritual Process: Structure and Anti-Structure*. London.

Ucelay, M. (ed.) 1990. *Amor de Don Perlimplín con Belisa en su jardín*, Federico García Lorca. Madrid: Cátedra.

——— (ed.) 1995. 'Introducción', *Así que pasen cinco años: leyenda del tiempo*, Federico García Lorca. Madrid: Cátedra.

Unamuno, M de. 1928. *El Otro/ El hermano Juan*. Madrid: Espasa Calpe (1946).

Unamuno, M de. 1982. *Niebla*. Madrid: Cátedra.

Urrutia, J. 1992. 'La inquietud fílmica', in D. Dougherty and M. F. Vilches de Frutos (eds) *El teatro en España: entre la tradición y la vanguardia 1918–1939*, pp. 45–52. Madrid: CSIC/ Fundación FGL/ Tabacalera.

Valente, J. A. 1976. 'Pez Luna', *Trece de Nieve: homenaje a Federico García Lorca*, 1–2, pp. 191–201. Madrid.

Van Gennep, A. 1908. *The Rites of Passage*, London.

——— 1960. *The Rites of Passage*, trans. M. B. Vizedon and G. L. Caffee. Chicago: Chicago University Press.

Vice, S. 1997. 'Bakhtin and Kristeva: Grotesque Body, Abject Self', in C. Adlam, R. Falconer, V. Maklin, and A. Renfrew, A. (eds) *Face to Face: Bakhtin in Russia and the West*, pp. 160–74. Sheffield: Sheffield Academic Press.

Vilches de Frutos, M. F., and Dougherty, D. 1992. *Los Estrenos Teatrales de Federico García Lorca 1920–1945*. Madrid: Tabapress.

Vitale, R. 1991. *El metateatro en la obra de Federico García Lorca*. Madrid: Editorial Pliegos.

Vizcaíno Casas, F. 1987. '*El público* de Federico García Lorca', *El Alcázar* (Madrid), 20 January.

Warner, M. 1985. *Monuments and Maidens: The Allegory of the Female Form*. London: Weidenfeld and Nicolson.

—— 1994. *From the Beast to the Blonde: On Fairy Tales and Their Tellers*. London: Chatto and Wyndus Ltd.

Weil, K. 1992. *Androgyny and the Denial of Difference*. Charlottesville and London: University Press of Virginia.

White, A. 1993. *Carnival, Hysteria, and Writing: Collected Essays and Autobiography*. Oxford: Clarendon Press.

Williams, P. 1979. *The Fool and the Trickster: Studies in Honour of Enid Welsford*. Cambridge: D. S. Brewer

Woods, G. 1998. *A History of Gay Literature: The Male Tradition*. New Haven and London: Yale University Press.

Woolf, V. 1941. *Between the Acts*. New York: Harcourt Brace.

Wright, L. B. 1927. 'Juggling Tricks and Conjury on the English Stage Before 1642', *Modern Philology* 24, 269–84.

Zolla, E. 1981. *The Androgyne: Fusion of the Sexes*. London: Thames & Hudson.

INDEX

Works by Federico García Lorca are printed in bold.